A Man of Intelligence

A Man of Intelligence

The Life of Captain Theodore Eric Nave
AUSTRALIAN CODEBREAKER
EXTRAORDINARY

Ian Pfennigwerth

ROSENBERG

First published in Australia in 2006
by Rosenberg Publishing Pty Ltd
PO Box 6125, Dural Delivery Centre NSW 2158
Phone: 61 2 9654 1502 Fax: 61 2 9654 1338
Email: rosenbergpub@smartchat.net.au
Web: www.rosenbergpub.com.au

National Library of Australia Cataloguing-in-Publication data:

Pfennigwerth, Ian.
A man of intelligence : the life of Captain Eric Nave,
Australian codebreaker extraordinary.

Bibliography.
Includes index.

1. Nave, Eric. 2. Australian Security Intelligence
Organization - Biography. 3. Cryptographers - Australia -
Biography. 4. Intelligence officers - Australia -
World War, 1939-1945 - Military intelligence - Pacific Area.
7. Military intelligence - Australia - History. I. Title.

940.548694

Cover design by Highway 51 Design Works

Set in 12 on 14 point Adobe Jenson Pro
Printed in China by Everbest Printing Co Limited

Contents

Illustrations

Acknowledgments

This book could not have been written without the assistance and support of many people. Foremost amongst these are the members of Eric Nave's family who have given me access to their father's records and correspondence and have shared with me reflections and reminiscences on their life with Eric. They have also directed my attention to many potential sources of information that I would not otherwise have uncovered.

The reading room staff at the National Archives of Australia in both Canberra and Melbourne have always provided excellent service in my search through the archives for traces of Eric Nave's career. The Research Centre at the Australian War Memorial has also been most helpful, particularly with regard to the manuscripts that Eric deposited there. The Defence Signals Directorate provided information and photographs.

A former ASIO officer was very helpful in reconstructing Eric's days at ASIO, and David McKnight generously provided me with notes of an interview he conducted with Eric in 1992. David Horner supplied not only encouragement but a copy of Eric's memoirs from which many of the quotations in the book are taken. He was also kind enough to review and correct the manuscript. David Sissons performed a similar task, at very short notice, and suggested a number of thoughtful improvements.

John Mack from the University of Sydney and Peter Donovan of the University of New South Wales were most generous in sharing the results of their quite extraordinary research project into World War II efforts to break into JN-25A and its successors. Their search in the US archives, in particular, has illuminated the contest of wills between Eric Nave and Rudolph Fabian in Melbourne in 1942.

I have been fortunate to have had the ready assistance of many members of the Central Bureau Intelligence Corps Association who shared with me their recollections of Eric Nave's work in Brisbane from 1942 to 1945.

Two friends from Navy days helped out. David Ruffin undertook a number of research tasks in Canberra, especially on Eric's days with ASIO and as national president of the Naval Association of Australia. Tony Howland in Sydney, whose keen eye has been responsible for spotting and correcting errors of grammar, syntax and writing convention, also helped with suggestions on getting the book to publication. My thanks to them both.

My wife Elizabeth, to whom this book is dedicated, has my appreciation for her support and patience, and for her many contributions to the finished product. Not least among these, it was she who suggested the title.

Ian Pfennigwerth
Port Stephens, November 2005

Glossary

This story is written for the layperson and the esoterica of codebreaking has been kept to a minimum. However, some of the jargon has entered the manuscript, especially through quotations, which I have rendered faithfully. A range of older terms are used in these so in place of the modern term for the breaking of codes and cyphers — 'cryptanalysis' — one encounters 'cryptography', which more properly applies to the construction of codes and cyphers.

I have maintained the distinction between codes and cyphers (sometimes spelt 'ciphers') throughout. Eric Nave worked mainly on codes as this was the stock-in-trade of the Imperial Japanese Navy. The only exception made is when I refer to the 'superencryption' stage of a book code when a 'reciphering' table or grid is employed.

I am only too aware that many books on military topics quickly adopt the use of abbreviations and acronyms that confuse the lay reader and detract from the pleasure of reading the story. I have strenuously tried to resist this and have limited myself to the use of only fifteen acronyms. The reader need only recognise the following:

ASIO	Australian Security Intelligence Organisation (after 1949)
DNI	Director of Naval Intelligence
FECB	Far East Combined Bureau (1935–42)
FRUMEL	Fleet Radio Unit Melbourne (1942–45)
GCCS	Government Code and Cypher School (1919–45)
HMAS	His Majesty's Australian Ship
HMS	His Majesty's Ship

IJA	Imperial Japanese Army
IJN	Imperial Japanese Navy
RAAF	Royal Australian Air Force
RAN	Royal Australian Navy
RN	Royal Navy
W	Signals intelligence derived from non-codebreaking analysis
WRANS	Women's Royal Australian Naval Service
Y	Signals intelligence derived from codebreaking

Where acronyms and abbreviations appear in quotations I have 'translated' them in square brackets where necessary, but readers will soon become familiar with the abbreviation 'W/T', which stands for 'Wireless Telegraphy'. Finally, foreign names are rendered in modern style in the text and these appear in square brackets after locations mentioned in quotations.

One further explanatory note seems necessary. In Chapter 8 there are several quotes which appear to be confused about Eric Nave's rank, but this is because the statements were made at different times. He was promoted Acting Captain on 12 October 1944.

Introduction

When Captain Theodore Eric Nave OBE, RN (Rtd) died in June 1993 at the age of ninety-four, his obituary in the Melbourne *Age* newspaper was led by the tasteless and inaccurate headline 'Code king warned of Jap bomb plan'. It is typical of the misinformation that surrounded much of his interesting life and varied work that he should be tagged at the end of it with credit for something that he patently did not do, and never claimed to have done — to warn of the December 1941 Japanese attack on Pearl Harbor. 'Code king' is another matter; that title he certainly could claim.

Eric Nave had the knack of being in the right place at the right time. His entry into the Royal Australian Navy owed a lot to good fortune, and his decision to study Japanese came during a brief interlude of Australian interest in having officers who could speak that language. In Tokyo, his examiner in Japanese later joined the British Government Code and Cypher School, taking with him the memory of an Australian called Nave with a natural affinity for the language, while the British naval attaché at the time became the wartime head of the Australia navy at a time when Eric really needed friends in high places. When asked to attempt to break into Japanese naval codes Nave displayed an unsuspected genius for the task. His loan service with the British navy coincided with intense diplomatic activity which demanded high quality Japanese translators. This led to accelerated promotion and his transfer to the Royal Navy — an historical first.

Sent to Australia in 1940 to recuperate from illness, he was 'hijacked' by the Australian navy and set up Australia's first central signals intelligence service. Ejected from this by the Americans in 1942, he found the Australian Army desperately seeking experienced codebreakers for General MacArthur's Central Bureau. At war's end he became the head codebreaker in Australia's new Defence Signals Bureau — still as an officer of the Royal Navy. And he never quite lost this knack even throughout his long and fruitful retirement. Not that his achievements have anything to do with luck — Eric was a hard working and intelligent man, his steely resolve softened by a great deal of charm and a sense of fun.

Yet few people know of the magnificent work done by this Australian. He receives brief passing mention in British accounts of the signals intelligence war; the US histories ignore him almost completely. A former Australian naval intelligence officer, I was unaware of Nave or his achievements until I commenced researching the historical application of operational intelligence by the RAN. Challenged by my ignorance, I resolved to find out more about the man. My research led me to the Eric Nave's family, to his unpublished autobiography — from which the unattributed quotes throughout this work are taken — and to official records in Australia, the UK and the USA. These clearly showed that Eric Nave deserves a book of his own in which his codebreaking career and its contribution to the defeat of Imperial Japan, as well as his post-war service to Australia, should be recorded and celebrated. This biography is my attempt to do that.

1 Early Days

This story has its beginning in the self-governing British colony of South Australia, which sits between the vast desert of the central Australian wilderness and the turbulent waters of the Great Australian Bight. Alone of the colonies set up by British settlers in Australia, South Australia had never resorted to taking British convicts as a cheap source of manpower to secure its future. Instead, under the British South Australia Act of 1834, the colony had been established and the government had sought to attract a new settlers and pioneers from a variety of European countries with the usual promises of cheap land and unlimited opportunities. To an extent, this advertising had been successful and the colony was a favoured destination not only for settlers of British stock but also for a substantial proportion from continental Europe.

Theodore Eric Nave's parents were the products of this diaspora. The union of a Hanoverian German father and a British mother produced Thomas Henry Theodore Nave, while the marriage of a Scottish mother with a Swedish father produced Ethyl Sophie Peterson. Thomas and Ethyl married young — both were twenty-one — in November 1897. They settled in the suburbs of the colony's capital, Adelaide, and had five children, of whom their eldest son and second child, Theodore Eric, was born on 18 March 1899.

This was an exciting time in the history of Australia. Queen Victoria was still on the throne in London and the external and defence affairs of each colony were largely the province of the Colonial Office of the

British Government. Despite deeply ingrained suspicions about the motives of each other, the six self-governing colonies had, after much bickering and discussion, agreed to form a federation, to establish a federal parliament in a greenfield location, to put in place a new federal constitution and to surrender certain of their prerogatives to a federal government to be elected nationally. For its part, the British Government had agreed that it would cede considerable authority to the new Australian Government on this transformation taking place, as it did when the Commonwealth of Australia Act entered into force on 1 January 1901.

While the new nation would continue to depend upon the British Foreign Office to represent its interests in foreign affairs for some time to come, in matters of defence the leaders and citizens of the new Australia were unequivocal on the need for their own defence forces. Prior to Federation, most of the colonies had maintained some form of military and naval force for their own defence, but the major shield against foreign aggression had been the power of the Royal Navy (RN). The colonies had agreed to support financially the Australia Squadron of cruisers maintained in their waters by the British, but this rent-a-navy arrangement did not seem appropriate to a sovereign independent nation, albeit one very conscious of its place within the protective arms of the British Empire. The term 'British' was more often used by the citizens of this new country to describe their nationality than 'Australian'.

While the British Government initially opposed the concept of a separate Australian navy, for the most part Australian governments were resolute in their determination to have their way. In the debates with the British, leadership was provided by Prime Minister Alfred Deakin, and Captain William Creswell was his technical advisor. Creswell was a Victorian, who had commanded the South Australian colony's gunboat *Protector* as part of the Australian contingent sent to the Boxer Uprising in China in 1900. At Federation he had been selected to take command of the new Commonwealth Naval Forces, which came into existence on 1 March 1901.

British reluctance to accede to the Australian plans for its own navy might have been sensibly based on the question of the ability of the new nation to afford and man such a force. At Federation the population of the whole country was a bare four million souls; the new state of South Australia had only 358,000 people, about half of whom lived in Adelaide. There was actually very little money in the new Federal Treasury to be spent on defence. Australians would have argued in response, again with justification, that it was all very well for the nation to be invited to place its faith in the Royal Navy, but said navy was rarely in evidence in Australian waters. However, with the rising power of Germany to concern it in Europe, the British eventually acceded to Australia's demand for its own navy, and in 1908 orders were placed on British yards by the Australian Government for the construction of a flotilla of destroyers for coastal defence. The first of these reached Australia in November 1910 to replace the odd assortment of obsolescent ships the Commonwealth Naval Forces had inherited from the former colonies.

In the following chapter the growth of Japanese naval prowess in the early years of the twentieth century will be traced but, while Eric was still in short pants, at the backs of the minds of Australian officials was a consciousness of the rise of a new naval power in the Pacific. The British welcomed the emergent Japan as an ally, one that could relieve them of a considerable naval burden in the Far East. For the RN, the force to be dealt with was that of Imperial Germany. Australians, perennially fearful of their vulnerability to an attack by the 'Yellow Peril' from the north, entertained other views.

Oddly, it was the German naval threat to the Empire that finally convinced the British of the benefits — perhaps even the necessity — of an Australian navy of some strength. Imperial Germany had established a number of strategic colonies across the Pacific and in the Far East, including bases in China, the Caroline and Marshall Islands, Samoa, New Guinea and the islands to the east of Papua. To protect and defend these interests Germany had established an East Asiatic Squadron of powerful modern cruisers in China waters, causing the British to create an equally powerful deterrent to German adventurism should war eventuate. From that point events moved very fast for Australian naval ambitions: one sign of this was that on 10 July 1911 the Commonwealth Naval Forces became, by royal decree, the Royal Australian Navy (RAN).

It is unlikely that the significance of these events had much impact on Eric Nave. His family was far removed from affairs of state and there were matters of more immediate concern. Thomas Henry's job was with the South Australian Railways, an important government utility in the colony and state. The railways provided the means by which the agricultural and mineral production was delivered to the state's ports and it linked South Australia with the eastern states. As well, a start had been made on a rail link with Darwin in the Northern Territory, a task that was not to be completed until 2004! At Federation, South Australia had nearly 3000 kilometres of rail track. However, South Australian Railways was not a generous employer and by the time Eric was five there were three more mouths for his parents to feed. While circumstances were straitened, his was an intelligent family, and Eric recalled:

> I liked school. I had great powers of concentration and an excellent memory and so, after the first year I was moved up two forms because I had done so well. Many years later these same powers of analysis and logic were to help me start breaking codes since there is, of course, no way of training a codebreaker. You either have that type of mind or not.

Studies presented little difficulty to Eric, who was normally top of his class. But there was one obstacle he had to overcome at school — his natural left-handedness. As was the practice in those days, this 'defect' had to be corrected and he was compelled to learn to write with his right hand, and he did so throughout his life thereafter.

Eric also began to display his interest in and success at sport, and cricket in particular, where left-handedness was no barrier. Until his forties he continued to play sport and, more often than not, it was on the cricket field that he enjoyed himself most. But as Eric applied himself to his studies and his games, attitudes in Europe slowly hardened towards conflict. Australians could feel both pride and relief when its new fleet, led by the battle cruiser *Australia*, sailed from the UK in July 1913 and on 4 October that year it made a ceremonial entry into its new base in Sydney. The Imperial Japanese Navy (IJN) excepted, this was at that stage the most powerful naval force in either the Pacific or Indian Oceans. Adelaide's main daily newspaper, *The Advertiser*, carried the story as follows:

> It was in serious and almost absolute silence that Sydney saw the little fleet come home in the early morning … The occasion was not one for noise and cheering. It was too big and too serious to translate into sound … It was the realisation of the responsibilities of Empire.[1]

The new fleet was to have little enough time to prepare itself for operations. A war warning was issued on 28 July 1914 and the fleet returned to port from exercises to store, fuel and ammunition. On 3 August the Australian Government placed the RAN under Admiralty control and the ships deployed to their war stations. Only eight days later an RAN squadron attacked Rabaul, the German colonial capital of New Guinea, as the initial operation of an active naval war that saw ships of the young RAN deployed all over the world. The most immediate result gained by the new Australian navy was the ejection of the Germans from all of their South Pacific possessions, largely by naval landing parties, and the deterrence of the German East Asiatic Squadron from attacks on the vital trade routes to Europe across the Indian Ocean. The first Australians to fall in World War I were sailors killed near Rabaul assaulting German positions and the first decoration of the war was won by an RAN officer in that action. The sinking of the German cruiser *Emden* by HMAS *Sydney* on 9 November 1914 off the Cocos Islands was the last action of the campaign.

The war now loomed very large for Eric Nave and his family. A stirring account of the attack on the German fortifications near Rabaul was carried in the Adelaide *Advertiser* on 11 November 1914, leading with the quote from one of the men wounded in the action: 'I don't wish to boast, sir, but really South Australia has reason to be proud of her boys.'[2] In an upsurge of patriotic fervour, and with the idea of foreign adventures having massive appeal for Australian youth, young men flocked to join the armed forces and especially to the Army, which needed to expand itself massively to

meet its expeditionary force commitments to the Empire. The age
of enlistment was set at eighteen but many younger than that were
able to convince the recruiters that they met this requirement. In the
meantime, Eric had completed secondary school.

> I had a strong feeling towards the law but the cost and length of training
> made it impossible for a family like ours. So, the law remained a dream and
> when I left school at 16 I sat the state Civil Service examination and joined
> my father at the South Australian Railways working in the office of the
> Comptroller of Accounts.

Eric enjoyed his employment with this prestigious government
corporation, travelling around the state with the paymaster and a bag
of money as the witnessing officer in the payment of the railway's
employees. It also introduced him to administrative duties, which
were to be the key to his future career, but the war cast its shadow
over all of this. After undergoing training in Egypt, the Australian
Imperial Force was committed to its first battles in the Allied assault
on the Dardanelles in April 1915 in an effort to capture Istanbul and
to force Turkey out of the war. It was the beginning of a long and
costly ground war for a country as sparsely populated as Australia.
Over the years 1914–18 nearly 420,000 Australian men enlisted in
the Army, almost one in seven of the male population over the age
of eighteen, and two-thirds of those were either killed or wounded
in the fighting in the Middle East, Belgium and France. Australians
commemorate their sacrifice on 25 April each year — Anzac Day.
Eric recorded:

> Although Australia was far away from the fighting and news took a long
> time to reach us the war made a great impression on me as it did most other
> teenagers. The casualty lists from Gallipoli, the returning wounded, the loss
> of distant relatives who had enlisted under age, all these events left a deep
> impression on me. Some of my friends were joining and I didn't want to be
> left out.

An opportunity for Eric to enlist before his eighteenth birthday
came from the expansion of the RAN to meet wartime demands.
This was nowhere as dramatic as for the Army — from sixteen to
thirty-seven ships and from 3800 to 5000 men. But the figures don't

tell the whole story. In 1914 the RAN was heavily dependent on officers on loan from the RN and on ex-RN sailors to man its ships. During the war the RAN enlisted many more than the 1200 men required to expand the fleet in a drive to 'Australianise' its ranks, and to return loan personnel to the RN. This was easier to achieve for sailors, whose training period was shorter than for officers, but the RAN College had opened its doors in 1913 to begin the slow process of 'growing' its own officers. Direct entry of officers to meet wartime needs was also pursued, and in mid-1916 the Navy advertised nationally for six midshipmen to perform administrative duties for the duration of hostilities. Eric had his excellent school results and railways experience to offer and, with his parents' approval, he applied and sat the requisite exam and then waited to hear the results. These were a long time coming, and an impatient Eric set off with his father for Melbourne to inquire why this should be so.

In these events we can begin to discern the run of good fortune that was to attend Eric Nave throughout his service career. He was of the right age and with the appropriate experience to apply for the positions offered. His family lived in Adelaide, relatively close to Melbourne (in Australian terms) and he and his father worked for the railways — the transport medium of choice in those days. While the Federal Constitution stipulated that the national capital must not be in either Sydney or Melbourne and the site of Canberra had already been chosen, in 1916 it remained a sheep grazing property. The new parliament building and the associated government offices would not be ready before 1927. In the interim the seat of the Federal Parliament and home of all major departments of state, including Navy Office — the headquarters of the RAN — was in Melbourne.

Eric's good fortune was to continue. On making inquiries at Navy Office, Thomas and Eric were told that Nave junior had failed the entrance exam in history. This seemed odd to them as Eric had always gained honours in history at school, but the Navy refused to allow the Naves to see the completed papers. Thomas, obviously a man of some determination, would not be deterred and assembled more firepower.

Instead, he contacted an old friend, Senator Sir John Newland, who only the day before had shown us over the Federal Parliament House, then in Melbourne. Later that day Sir John told my father we should pay another visit to Navy Office. This time we were told that I had passed and that there was a vacancy, which was offered to me. It was for a permanent commission in the RAN. A permanent naval career had never been in my thoughts but, as there was only a fortnight before I was to start my training, I had to make a decision on the spot. I accepted. It was an odd way to begin a naval career that was to change my entire life, but one I never regretted.

It was a remarkable chain of events — from reject one day to naval officer the next. The Naves had gone to Melbourne hoping to find that Eric had been offered a temporary commission to see out the war, but they returned to Adelaide with the son accepted into the permanent naval forces. In exchange for its offer of employment, the Navy had gained the services of Theodore Eric Nave, who had a number of very desirable qualities as a potential naval officer. First, he was a keen scholar, usually coming first or second in his class. Second, he was a keen sportsman, primarily a cricketer, but later showing his prowess at field hockey and skiing. Third, he was a fit young man of slim build and 178 cm in height who would adapt easily to the rigours of sea service. His first photos in naval uniform show a serious young man of attractive demeanour, but not his hazel eyes and brown hair: Eric was to cut quite a dash with the ladies. One other characteristic of Nave's is worth mentioning here: Eric was a gregarious fellow of great charm, and this was to stand him in good stead, not only in the Navy but throughout his life

Eric joined the RAN on 1 March 1917, on leave of absence from the South Australian Railways. The training that he and his five colleagues received at the Navy's training depot at Williamstown Naval Dockyard, located at the mouth of the Yarra River opposite Port Melbourne, was perfunctory in the extreme. At that time, specialist training for officers was generally conducted at RN training establishments in the UK, and it was to be some years before the training burden for most sailor ranks was assumed by the RAN. For 'Midshipmen borne for administrative duties', as Eric and his five colleagues were termed, training consisted of physical education and instruction at the only RAN specialist school then in existence — the Gunnery School. Here the midshipmen learned how to shoot small arms, to strip down a machine-gun, and the drill for a six-inch breech-loading gun. Eric remarked on this time, with some understatement, that 'the training program for young officers had not been worked out properly'. Proper or not, twenty-eight days after joining the Navy, Eric and his colleagues were posted to their first ships.

In this the Nave good fortune continued. By the end of 1916, with the main German threat removed from the Pacific and Indian Oceans, the Admiralty had asked for RAN fleet units to be deployed outside the Australia Station. The heavy cruiser *Australia* joined the Grand Fleet in UK waters and spent the rest of the war waiting for the German High Seas Fleet to emerge and engage it. She actually missed the principal naval engagement between the fleets — the Battle of Jutland — because she was undergoing repairs to damage caused in a collision with HMS *New Zealand*. The light cruisers were sent to various naval stations, including the Caribbean, but eventually they too found themselves in the North Sea. They had a slightly more exciting war than the flagship, including clashes with zeppelins, but a lot of their time was spent swinging around their anchors in British North Sea ports.[3]

It was to these ships that Nave's five colleagues were posted. Eric missed the opportunity of a trip to the UK but he got by far the best of the postings with an appointment to the cruiser *Encounter* based in Sydney. *Encounter* was older than the other RAN cruisers and was, in fact, on loan from the RN but manned by the RAN. Her duties were trade protection, a task that took her around most of the South Pacific and to South and South-East Asia. Eric joined her at sea in August 1917 from the destroyer *Yarra* and recorded that:

> For me the change in my lifestyle was remarkable. Only a month before I had been a clerk working in the SAR's accounts office and living at home. Now I was wearing the uniform of a Midshipman and at sea in one of His Majesty's ships. In truth I found it all a bit strange.

In keeping with Eric's former training routine, he was assigned an action station as part of the ship's gunnery team, but located halfway up the mainmast on the forward rangefinder. On this first cruise he experienced foul weather in the Great Australian Bight, and the comfort of sleeping in a hammock under those conditions, as the ship escorted troop transports from New Zealand to Fremantle. But soon their orders were changed and *Encounter* was despatched to the Pacific to find and destroy German merchant raiders suspected of operating in the area. The captain's plan was to deceive the Germans into thinking that the cruiser was an unescorted merchant ship by using a false callsign and originating radio traffic typical of the merchant marine. This deception plan did not succeed because two of the raiders were not, in fact, in the Pacific and the third had run aground. However, it did introduce Eric to that particular application of signals intelligence which was to play such an important part in his career.

The search for raiders took *Encounter* and Eric Nave to a great number of Pacific islands, including Tahiti. The ship also traversed and searched through the island chains to the east of New Guinea which were to be of such importance to the Allies in the dark days of 1942. Eric was visiting parts of that huge ocean which other ships rarely saw, while receiving valuable training in his primary duties — those of a paymaster. As the term suggests, paymasters were responsible for paying the ship's company, but they also fed and clothed them, kept their service records, advised on legal matters and performed secretarial duties. In many ships they had custody of the Secret and Confidential files and books, including codebooks.

In October 1918 Eric left *Encounter* and spent the next nine months in the seaman training ship *Tingira* moored in Sydney Harbour. It was while in that ship that he first conceived the idea of studying the Japanese language. To be promoted to the next higher rank of sub-lieutenant he had to pass a professional exam and to demonstrate competence in a foreign language. But which language should he choose? 'Looking through Kings's Regulations [the regulations governing the Navy] I noticed that extra pay of 6d per day was paid to those qualified in French or German, but those proficient in Japanese received 5/0d . This discovery set me thinking.'

Paymaster Clerk Nave not only thought about it but acted on

the information as well. In coming to his decision he might have been made aware that in July 1918 the Naval Board had decided that 'consideration will be given, on the termination of hostilities, to providing facilities for Junior Accountant Officers to be sent to Japan to study Japanese'. On 28 November 1918 he applied to his commanding officer advising of his decision to study Japanese, and asked whether the Naval Board was prepared to provide him with monetary assistance to engage a tutor.[4]

Official interest in having Australian service officers with Japanese skills had developed during the Great War, when Japan had been an ally. IJN ships had escorted Australian troop convoys and had patrolled the Indian Ocean to deter German raiders: for several months in 1917 a Japanese cruiser squadron had been active off the Australian east and west coasts. At first, it had been proposed that army officers under training at the Royal Military College Duntroon — one of the first Federal establishments built at the site of the new national capital — should study Japanese as part of their curriculum. This idea was modified when it became clear that not all cadets would have the aptitude, while those who did would require much more tuition than could be accommodated in their busy college timetable. A similar opinion came from the RAN College at Jervis Bay.[5] In the end it was decided that selected Duntroon cadets would be taught Japanese, and James Murdoch was appointed to a part-time lecturing position at the college in February 1917. The remainder of his time was to be spent at the University of Sydney. This arrangement proved unworkable and the solution adopted was that the Commonwealth should fund a chair of Japanese at that university, to which Murdoch was appointed in September 1918.[6]

The Naval Board asked how much it would cost them to support Eric's studies. He found this information and his investigations uncovered another officer, Lieutenant Commander Eric Kingsford Smith — brother of the famous aviator Charles — who was also interested in Japanese. Since the tutor, Mr Miyata, a language teacher at Fort Street Boys' High School, gave a discount for multiple students, this moved the Naval Board to approve Nave's study for a first, a second and finally a third term, each of ten weekly lessons. Anyone who has studied a language as complex as Japanese — and some of that complexity will be explored in the following chapter — will recognise that this was hardly the way to achieving competence, but it was a start. Eric Nave apparently believed that he could master the language to the required standard and applied himself to the task — a case, perhaps, of ignorance being bliss!

> When I nominated Japanese as my choice of foreign language there was quite a stir in higher circles. The Admiral decided that my [sub-lieutenant's] examination was to be deferred and I was told that I needed a total of 60% for a pass [in Japanese]. If I achieved a pass rate of 75% I got three months' accelerated promotion, and with 85% six months.
>
> Then I was told to present myself to Professor Murdoch at Sydney University for further examination. On arrival my spirits plummeted and all optimism flew out the window for there on the table was a Japanese newspaper. However, the professor quickly put my fears at rest. 'Don't be alarmed by the newspaper; I just want you to identify as many Japanese characters as you know and write down their English meanings. I want to find out what you know, not what you don't know.' Having done my best at this Murdoch then asked me to write down what I did in a typical day using as many Japanese characters as possible.

The results of the examinations for sub-lieutenant, including the foreign language component, were announced on 1 September 1919. Eric Nave had achieved 90 per cent — a first class pass — which shot him to the top of the seniority list of newly promoted officers. Remember that this result demonstrated not only Eric's professional competence but also his grasp of the difficult Japanese language. He had learned much and applied himself to his duties well since his entry into the Navy just two years previously. Just how well was shown by his next posting.

While engaged in his studies, in July 1919 Eric had been appointed to the staff of the Admiral Commanding the Australian Fleet, Rear Admiral John Saumarez Dumaresq RN in *Australia*. His responsibilities were the maintenance of the admiral's classified books and files, the personnel records and private files, a task of great trust to be given to a twenty-year-old. Admiral Dumaresq was

Australian, having been born in Sydney, but he had joined the RN in 1886. Dumaresq had earned a reputation for dash and gallantry during World War I and he was a noted innovator — it was under his command that HMAS *Sydney* became the first warship to fly off scouting aircraft in October 1917. He was also the inventor of the Dumaresq range predictor that Eric had used in *Encounter*. The task of the admiral and his staff was now to turn the collection of ships that comprised the Australian Squadron into a cohesive unit, after their return from the various stations they had been dispersed to during the war.

It was an interesting time for the flagship and for the admiral's staff. The Australian Fleet now stood at the pinnacle of its strength with a battle cruiser, three light cruisers, seven destroyers, six submarines and three sloops in commission — a considerable force for such a small nation. Ships and men had acquitted themselves well during the war, but now some of that experience was being lost as 'hostilities-only' men reached the end of their service. As well, there was no longer the harsh goad of active service to encourage the maintenance of standards of naval professionalism. Nevertheless, Admiral Dumaresq approached his task with enthusiasm and worked himself, his staff and his ships hard. Eric recorded that under the demanding standards set by his admiral he learned much, including teaching himself to be a competent touch-typist. But the main achievement was that, while carrying out these important duties, he had also made a great success of his Japanese instruction.

> I wrote and told my parents about my promotion and they were thrilled. So was I, not about the Japanese so much as the additional 5/0d a day which was additional to my Sub-Lieutenant's daily pay of 11 shillings. Japan at that time was a faraway country about which we knew little and cared less. In World War I they had been our allies but other than that I knew nothing about them.

Eric's insouciance about Japan was, fortunately, not shared by elements of the Australian Government and a scheme would shortly be introduced to send service officers to Japan to learn more about the country and to master the language.[7] There had been a tacit

agreement with the British Government before the Versailles Conference
that former German possessions in the Southern Hemisphere would
revert to Australian control after the end of the war. However, the British
had been unable to honour this agreement because certain islands were
firmly in the hands of Japan and the Japanese Government was entitled
to believe that these should remain under its control because of the
Japanese contribution to the Allied war effort. In any case, there was no
agency, and certainly not the RN, which was going to dispute Japanese
possession. For the Australian Government, the 'Yellow Peril' now had a
foothold at Truk, only 1000 miles from its shores.

British concern at Japanese strength, especially in the naval sphere,
was to lead to a decision to construct a naval base at Singapore and
to the Washington Naval Treaty of 1922, which attempted to fix the
ratios of naval strength between the principal maritime nations. Britain
and the USA were permitted the largest navies, with those of Japan,
France and Italy respectively at a lesser strength in the ratio 5:3:1.6.
The precursors to these negotiations were to have a direct impact
personally on Sub-Lieutenant Eric Nave with the announcement in
September 1919 that his ship *Australia* was to be decommissioned
and that the admiral's flag and his staff were to be transferred to the
light cruiser *Melbourne*. It was a rational decision, although a blow
to national pride. The battle cruiser, although only ten years old, had
been eclipsed by the advance of naval technology during the war, she
was expensive to run and was also in need of extensive structural,
engineering and weapons upgrading. The Australian Government,
looking for 'peace dividends', was not prepared to make the necessary
investment. *Australia* was to become a bargaining chip in the
international game of naval poker and she was eventually scuttled off
Sydney in April 1924.

Meanwhile, unknown to Eric, the Naval Board had followed up
on its July 1918 decision and was becoming very interested in having
an officer fluent in Japanese in RAN ranks. Professor Murdoch had
been most impressed by his performance and capacity to learn and,
in a letter of 13 September 1920 responding to a Navy Office request
for his views on Nave's capabilities, he remarked that:

I examined him in Japanese some months ago when I was most favourably impressed by the appearance he made. So far, of course, his work has been elementary merely; but I have little doubt that his linguistic coefficient of expansion is a big one, and that a student of his aptitude would profit from a course of Japanese in Japan even if sent there with such preliminary training as Mr Nave has had.

In October the Naval Board debated the issue and decided that Nave was to be the first Australian naval officer to train in Japan, and began to make the necessary arrangements through the Admiralty in London. It was not until early 1921 that Japan entered Sub-Lieutenant Nave's consciousness even more directly. Admiral Dumaresq was to attend a conference of Empire navies in Singapore with Nave attending as his secretary. The purpose of the meeting of flag officers was to find a means of controlling Japanese expansionist tendencies, as it was considered impracticable to maintain a comparable British naval presence.[8] A signal from Navy Office in Melbourne then advised that, following the conference, Nave was to proceed to Japan for two years' language training. As Australia had no diplomatic representation overseas at that stage except in London, Eric's studies were to be undertaken under the guidance of the British Embassy Tokyo. What a bombshell! Eric was excused from the Singapore trip and granted two weeks leave: then he was on his way.

> And so, because of a chance decision to learn Japanese taken only because it had seemed an interesting way of augmenting my pay, I found myself on 16 February 1921 on the quayside, my uniforms packed away for the next two years, about to board the 2000 ton passenger liner *Eastern* on route for Japan. Around my waist was tightly strapped the money belt in which I had secreted my advance of naval pay in the form of twenty-six gold sovereigns. Ahead lay the unknown. I had no idea what I would find when I reached Japan. Nor could I have realised that I was about to embark on an adventure that would lead me into the most secret world of intelligence and change not only my whole life but also the future of Britain, America and Japan.

At this juncture, a reader might well consider Eric's opinion of what was to follow somewhat exaggerated; if anything, it was an understatement.

Eric had an interesting voyage, with calls at several ports, including Hong Kong. He cleared Customs and Immigration at Kobe and finally disembarked at Yokohama. In an early example of an unfortunate RAN custom that prevails even today, Nave was not met on his arrival or given any instructions on what to do next. On his own initiative he struck out for the British Embassy in distant Tokyo, where he was welcomed by the Japanese Counsellor, Sir Harold Parlett, who will appear again later in the story. Parlett advised that two Australian Army officers, Captains Broadbent and Capes, had arrived six months previously and had taken up residence in a tea-growing area near Hakone, close to Mount Fuji, and that he would arrange for Nave to be sent to join them.

There was no prescribed language course; it was up to Eric to make the necessary arrangements and to sit the required exam at the Embassy at the end of each year. He set himself the task of studying morning and afternoon in a totally Japanese rural environment — accommodation, food and recreation, with weekly sessions with a bilingual teacher. This was a bold but correct decision as his results would show, and it involved Eric in a series of misadventures, both cultural and culinary, as he struggled to master the language. While he did engage a Japanese teacher for a few hours a week, most of his learning was conducted in conversation with Japanese in the course of their daily lives. It did have its compensations, such as a view of Mount Fuji from his study window. Eric climbed that mountain twice, once with two other language students and the second time with the family of the Dutch ambassador. After the second excursion he reflected on the appropriateness of the Japanese proverb: You're a fool if you haven't climbed Mount Fuji and a bigger one if you've climbed it twice.

The area around Hakone did have plenty of Western visitors escaping the summer heat of the Chinese east coast, however, so Eric was not entirely cut off. Through contacts with Western families he was able to stay abreast of events in the outside world, and to forge friendships that would endure and be useful to him during his time later in Europe. But the major part of his time was spent living in the company of Japanese, and through his immersion in rural Japanese society he soon developed an appreciation of Japanese social customs and of the history and activity of the region in which he lived. At the end of his first year he moved to the city of Zushi in preparation for his first examination, and there he shared accommodation with a British naval language student who was to become a significant figure in his later career — Lieutenant Commander Harry Shaw.

Eric was able to persuade his middle-aged cook/housekeeper to accompany him to Zushi but often his walks after an eight-hour day of study and swimming expeditions to the beach would have him returning to his quarters later than expected. 'Often arriving back late for dinner I apologised to my cook, who told me not to worry, "but if I was married to you I'd have a lot to say!" She was very good to me.'

While Eric was able to move about Japan without hindrance, he recognised that he was under surveillance, having more than one encounter with the Japanese Military Police, the *Kempeitai*. He was also aware of the growing Japanese trend towards secrecy and obfuscation about military matters, and he took care not to arouse any additional suspicions through his activities.

Eric became interested in the life of an early English seaman who had arrived in Japan in 1600 and had been engaged by the Shogun as a nautical expert.

> When he died he was buried on a hill overlooking Tokyo Bay in the vicinity of Yokosuka naval base. I decided to visit his grave and walked across the peninsula that forms the western arm of the bay. I took a snapshot of the grave of Bill Adams, a stone memorial now greatly worn by its age of 300 years. Being close to Yokosuka I was careful to photograph nothing else.

In September 1921, Eric's promotion to paymaster lieutenant was advised and then, at the end of his first year in Japan, he was summoned to the British Embassy in Tokyo for his examination along with the other service officers studying the language. The benefit of his immersion approach was demonstrated convincingly with a mark of over 90 per cent, the highest ever achieved by a service language officer. He celebrated with an excursion to Shanghai as a guest of an English family he had befriended in Japan, noting as his ship passed through the Inland Sea its suitability for naval construction in conditions of complete secrecy. Eric's return journey to Japan was by train via Beijing and Manchuria and thence to Korea, then a Japanese colony. It was, in fact, the first victim of a Japanese thrust for imperial domination over the rest of Asia.

Although Eric continued his studies in the countryside, a few months before his final exam he moved to Tokyo 'to get the atmosphere and to see many things not available elsewhere'. One such was an invitation to the autumn Chrysanthemum Party at the Imperial Palace for foreign diplomatic personnel, the card for which survives in Eric's papers. Of more impact on his future career, Eric became well known to the Japanese Counsellor at the British Embassy, Sir Harold Parlett, and co-author of an English-Japanese dictionary with a Mr Ernest Hobart-Hampden. Both were scholars of Japanese who could read, write and speak the language fluently. These skills were to draw them into the intelligence world in the near future, taking with them the recollection of a young Australian naval officer with very considerable language skills in his own right.

A developing Japanese sensitivity about the activities of foreigners manifested itself when Eric found himself the subject of a surveillance operation in the streets of Tokyo.

> I did not blame them for exercising some supervision over the movements of the naval officers as we were attached very loosely to the Embassy and had freedom to roam the country. They must have found any activities in my perambulations particularly unrewarding.

Eric was not the only one under surveillance and this sometimes took more direct forms. The British naval attache, Captain Ragnar Colvin — who was later to become the RAN's Chief of Naval Staff from 1937 to 1941 — reported that he found himself under persistent interrogation by a fellow 'passenger' on a train journey to Beijing. He escaped the interminable attention of his tormentor only after he responded in exasperation that he was 'going to Beijing to sell some secret information'. As well, Eric discovered that his private mail was being intercepted and read after a letter from his father was forwarded to him via the French, rather than the British, Embassy. The eavesdroppers had put the intercepted letter back in the wrong diplomatic bag.

It was during his stay in Tokyo that Eric became aware of the Japanese warrior code of *bushido* — 'the way of the knight' — through the story of the Forty-Seven Ronin, who in the early eighteenth century sacrificed their lives through ritual suicide after avenging the murder of their master. The story was well known in Japan, and the spirit of self-sacrifice that it celebrated was taught as the honourable course of action for any patriotic Japanese. Eric visited the temple at Sengakuji where the master and his forty-seven faithful knights were buried and remarked:

> I made my pilgrimage to ponder in the temple grounds the power and influence of *bushido* on the lives of these men, compelling them to obey the strict military code of those times. I could not help feeling that the spirit was still alive in Japan.

The timing of Eric's sojourn in Tokyo turned out to be very significant. In the summer and autumn of 1921 Japan and other maritime nations were preparing for the Washington Naval Conference, which was intended to prevent an arms race in the naval sphere by assigning every significant naval power a fixed ratio of warship strength. The Japanese sought parity with Britain and the USA; the British and Americans wanted to fix their respective ratios at 5:5:3, with the IJN at the lesser strength. Moreover, as will be explained in more detail in the next chapter, Britain had abrogated the Anglo-Japanese Treaty that had defined each country's mutual relationship and sphere of influence in East Asia for twenty years. As a result, the period was one of intense diplomatic activity of which even a supernumerary like Eric Nave became well aware.

Despite these intensely interesting developments, it was now time for Eric to leave the distractions of the capital and to return to the country to prepare for his final Japanese Interpreter exam. He re-engaged his old teacher who, when asked by Eric to teach him the polite forms of Japanese language suitable for use in official and diplomatic exchanges, recommended that he take a woman teacher for a month or so as it was women who used polite speech in contrast to the abbreviated slang used by men. Eric found a teacher from the local girls' high school willing to tutor him, and under her guidance he was persuaded at the end of his studies to deliver a lecture on the South Sea Islands — a region of great interest to the Japanese — to an assembly of several hundred female students. The lecture passed off well and had an amusing sequel. Captain Colvin paid a visit on Eric and found at the train station that he (apparently) commanded bows of the deepest respect from several groups of Japanese schoolgirls who happened to be in the area. It was only afterwards that Eric had to confess to Colvin that the bows were in honour of the Nave lecture.

While at Shizuoka Eric met an American naval officer who, like him, had been sent to Japan to study the language. American officers like these were to be significant in Nave's later career, but ironically, while the US Navy could spare its officers for four years, and the British Army for three, the Admiralty expected their officers to master the Japanese tongue in only two. In contrast, as a far from distinguished student of Asian languages, the author studied Chinese for nearly three and a half years before he could claim some familiarity with and fluency in that language.

However, two years seems to have been quite sufficient time for Eric Nave. In his final exam in April 1923 he scored a remarkable 92 percent, much to his own delight and that of his examiners. The British Ambassador not only warmly congratulated Eric but also wrote to the Admiralty and the Australian Government strongly recommending that his term of language studies be extended for another year. Disappointingly, the Australian Navy did not accept this recommendation and so Eric packed his bags and prepared to return to Australia. Reflecting on his time in Japan, Eric mused:

> It was a great experience for me to have had these two years for study in Japan at this particular time. Although a most daunting task to learn an oriental language with no school, qualified teachers or assistance of any kind, there were compensations for me … I was able to meet the simple people and I came to like them. An early personal inquiry was 'What nationality

are you?' When I answered 'British', Australia was virtually unknown then, their faces lit up at once. 'Allies!' they would exclaim. It was clear to me that the people generally attached great importance to be allied to a country with the world's premier Navy, and its largest Empire.

There is also no doubt that to understand and speak a people's language is the shortest road to understanding its people. So I had learnt not only a great deal of the language but much more of the people in this land of contrasts of the Samurai and the cherry blossom.

The reason for the refusal by the Australian Naval Board to extend Eric Nave's term in Japan was not solely due to the practical consideration that he was not actually rendering any effective service to the RAN while doing so. Rather surprisingly, in terms of historical developments but also in the light of activities to be examined in the next chapter, the Australian Government had made the decision that it no longer had any need for its service officers to study Japanese. It is difficult to establish just why this decision was taken, but budgetary influences played their part, as well as the general feeling in diplomatic and government circles that measures such as the Treaty of Versailles and the Washington Naval Treaty had created the necessary preconditions for a long period of peace between nations.[9] If the British Government could continue to advise its senior military professionals into the 1930s that they could plan on there being no war within the next ten years, it is hardly surprising that the Australian Government generally accepted this view. Whatever the reasons, from 1922 onwards only one RAN officer and one Defence civilian were sent to Japan for language training, a situation which would be bitterly regretted in 1941.[10]

For Eric Nave, this decision meant a return to his former naval world as a paymaster, after a period of foreign service leave to which his time in Japan entitled him. However, just a few weeks into this he was recalled to duty as the supply officer of the cruiser HMAS *Brisbane*, the current flagship, where the incumbent had fallen ill. Eric, who had never been trained in this role, abruptly found himself steaming off for an extended period of cruising and visiting Pacific Islands territories, including the Solomon Islands, with all the responsibilities of victualling and paying the ship's company. The compulsory count of the money in the ship's safe proved to be correct, but Eric could only hope that his predecessor had ordered the appropriate quantity of provisions. While this seemed to be the case, a new problem arose with the failure of the ship's refrigerators in which all the meat was stored. After dallying with traditional ways of disguising the fact that the meat was off — such as soaking it in vinegar — the onset of food poisoning in one mess compelled him to condemn the rest of the ship's supply of frozen meat, which went overboard. Now short of food for the ship's company, Eric resorted to traditional naval fishing using 'expanding bait' in the form of explosive charges detonated at around ten metres depth, which 'gave us all a few welcome meals'.

The cruise proceeded successfully, although the world of codes and ciphers intruded when it was discovered that the flagship's classified messages were being sent incorrectly coded. In his role as paymaster, Eric Nave was responsible for the custody of the codes, and he was therefore relieved to find that the code tables in question were indeed in the appropriate safe — but that was not where they were needed. The cruiser's Communications Department had failed to draw them, a situation which could have had serious consequences had an enemy been listening to the flagship's transmissions. This was a procedural error which, under normal circumstances, would not have come to the notice of a paymaster. It is interesting to speculate how much value this incident was in giving Paymaster Lieutenant Nave the background in communications procedure that was to stand him in good stead a few brief years later.

Eric's temporary and unexpected experience of eight months as supply officer of *Brisbane* demonstrated his ability to react to fast changing circumstances. He discovered later that the cruiser's commanding officer had requested that Eric stay on board as a permanent replacement for the supply officer, which speaks volumes about his ability despite his lack of former experience. But more senior officers were interested in having Nave work for them and Eric, after being allowed to complete his interrupted foreign service leave, found himself posted to the cruiser *Melbourne* as secretary to the Chief of Staff of the Squadron, who moved from cruiser to cruiser as circumstances dictated. In the paymaster world, Eric's star continued to rise.

> On 12 April 1924 I witnessed in HMAS *Brisbane* a sad and very unfortunate event, the sinking of HMAS *Australia*. She was towed out of Sydney Heads into deep water where various charges were detonated and very reluctantly she rolled over and disappeared. She had to be scrapped under the Washington Naval Agreement for limitation.

That intense diplomatic activity that Eric Nave had witnessed during his time attached to the British Embassy in Tokyo had produced this very visible and concrete result. At one stroke the strategic weapon that the battle cruiser represented had been destroyed, leaving Australia totally dependent upon someone else's navy to counter the might of the IJN.

However, Eric Nave was about to have a much closer and more personal encounter with the IJN with his appointment for six weeks as the escort officer to Vice Admiral Saito Shichigoro, the commander of the Japanese Training Squadron, during its cruise to Australia and New Zealand between December 1923 and February 1924. It was the first visit to these waters by the IJN since the war, and the three heavy cruisers *Asama*, *Yakumo* and *Iwate*, all of which had fought in the Russo-Japanese campaign, had a top-flight echelon of officers embarked. Admiral Saito had fought at the famous Battle of Tsushima in 1905. He and several of his officers had been awarded British honours for their part in World War I. The commanding officer of *Yakumo* was a Captain Yonai Mitsumasa who, in later life, occupied the positions of Commander-in-Chief Combined Fleet, Minister of the Navy in 1937 and finally Prime Minister of Japan for a brief period in 1940.[11] The young Lieutenant Nave was not only exposed to potential greatness on the Japanese side. The Governor-General of New Zealand at the time was Lord Jellicoe of Jutland fame, for whom Admiral Saito had enormous admiration. At one point in the tour, Eric acted as the interpreter between the two admirals as they re-fought and discussed the two great strategic naval battles of their age.

Immensely exciting though this was, the value to Eric Nave from the attachment came in his opportunity to serve on board a Japanese flagship, a very rare honour in a time of deteriorating trust between Japan and the West. He had a first-hand opportunity to study and observe the officers and men at work and play, the state of their ships and weapons, and their performance during various drills. Given that the ships' companies may have been individually selected for the cruise, Eric came away very impressed by the quality of the IJN and especially of its officers. Watching an exhibition of *Gekken* — fighting with wooden staves — Nave remarked to the commander of the ship that one of the petty officers seemed very good at it.

> This prompted an instant reply, 'Him good?' in an incredulous voice. He stopped the bout, took off his uniform coat and challenged my nominated champion. The unfortunate petty officer received quite a battering, whereupon the Commander returned to our group with a broad grin.

More than this display of fighting prowess, it was the skill and professionalism of the IJN that impressed itself on Eric. The officers quizzed him extensively on Australia and its place in the world, and were very willing to share with him the sources of their own professional and patriotic attitudes. On farewelling Admiral Saito he recorded:

> I left this ship full of admiration for the excellence and dedication of the ships' companies. They were so similar to our own ships. They could be most valuable allies or alternatively formidable adversaries for any enemy. The officers united in their loyalty to their Admiral, through him to the Navy and finally to the Emperor. I had truly been sailing with the Samurai.

On completing his duties with the Japanese squadron Eric Nave returned to the more familiar world of a paymaster in the Australian Navy. As he noted, whereas he had been on the staff of the Rear Admiral Commanding the Australian Fleet before leaving for his language studies, he was now on the staff of the Commodore Commanding the Australian Squadron. The difference was more than a change in terminology. The RAN squadron now comprised three cruisers, four destroyers and a jumble of smaller craft. A number of officers had been compulsorily retired as surplus to requirements. In order to maintain a modicum of operational expertise the Australian Navy had agreed to send one of its cruisers in rotation to serve on another British naval station, where the larger numbers of ships permitted a higher tempo of exercises and activities.

This work is not intended as a critique of *Betrayal at Pearl Harbor*, but there are some allegations made in that book which need to be cleared up as the Eric Nave story progresses. James Rusbridger, the principal author, persistently maintained that the Australian Naval Board remained in ignorance of what it was Paymaster Lieutenant Nave was doing in the China Fleet and later on in his attachment to the Admiralty in London. The truth is otherwise. Not to get too far ahead of the story, in 1921 RAN ships were issued with copies of the Japanese Naval Telegraphic Code, a *kana* code used in signalling, and directed to start intercepting Japanese naval messages. When he arrived with his itinerant Chief of Staff in HMAS *Sydney* in September 1924, Eric applied himself to the task not only of training telegraphists in reading *kana* but also in attempting some code recoveries. As he wrote to his commodore:

> I would suggest that all ships in the Fleet be instructed to intercept as many messages in Japanese as possible … Telegraphic messages in Japanese are more difficult than in English, as the Japanese ideographs are not easily abbreviated. After reading plain language messages, I propose attempting to decode ordinary Japanese economic code messages, with a view to later breaking down the ciphers.[12]

It is not clear what put the idea of codebreaking into Eric's head, but this letter conclusively dispels any suggestion that the RAN was unaware of what he was attempting. Furthermore, the Naval Board accepted his suggestion, regretted that a 'rating with the required knowledge of Japanese Morse is not at present available', and directed the Commodore to make arrangements to have one so trained.[13] Young Lieutenant Nave was making an impression on his superiors as his Officer's Report of April 1924 makes clear. His commanding officer thought him, 'a thoroughly loyal and conscientious officer, whose example could not fail to be of considerable value to his fellows.

Equitable and cheerful temperament and good social qualities.'[14]

However, for Eric the pace of his regular work had not diminished and his fate was again to be touched by developments in the international arena. The British Admiralty convened a third conference on the security situation in the Far East in March 1925 and Nave's ship was selected to be the flagship for the First Naval Member, the leader of the Australian delegation to Singapore. He described the situation as follows:

> The Washington Disarmament Conference of 1922 had had its effect on Australian defence policy, and it was important that some combined and agreed plans be made for the defence of the Far East region. Singapore, because of its geographical position, had a part to play: a floating dock for capital ships was discussed and the provision of oil fuel storage.

This conference and its predecessor marked the origin of the concept of Singapore as the major British base in the Far East, as it was acknowledged that the 1921 idea of controlling Japan was not feasible. The British Government had decided to develop a base at Singapore in July 1921 but the 'floating dock and oil storage' idea was to become the substantial Singapore Naval Base, a major British defence investment and the cornerstone of the 'main fleet to Singapore' policy. In time, this was also to become Australia's main line of naval defence, and Singapore exerted an almost hypnotic influence on the defence policies and military plans of three countries — Britain, Australia and Japan.[15] It was not until the Japanese launched their attack on Singapore through Malaya in 1941 that the first two of these countries found that they had been victims of sustained wishful thinking. The third, although initially successful in its military operations, had started a war that it could not win especially in the face of the industrial and technological power of the United States, a decision that would lead to its total defeat three and a half years later.

Eric Nave was to play an important role in all of this, and his call to action arrived a lot earlier than for most – just a few months after the conference. In May 1925, while he was happily serving as Secretary to the Chief of Staff of the Australian Squadron, a signal arrived from Navy Office advising that the Admiralty had asked for Nave by name and that he was off to serve as an interpreter on the staff of the China Fleet. Although he was lukewarm to the idea, the Admiralty would not take no for an answer, and by 26 June Eric found himself embarked in a Japanese steamer bound for Hong Kong to take up his new position.

2 First Breaks, 1925–27

Eric Nave's summons by the Admiralty was one small part of a strategic drama in which he would find himself playing an important role. As his comment on Japan being 'a faraway country about which we knew little' indicates, he was probably unaware of the background to the relationship between Britain and Japan although he did know that the Japanese had been allies. Possibly he did learn why the British were prepared to abrogate the alliance in 1921 during his time attached to the British Embassy. However, a brief description of the circumstances and the historical events which were to turn Britain and Japan from allies to enemies in the space of twenty-five years is warranted.

In September 1894, five years before Eric Nave was born, a most significant naval battle took place off the Shandong Peninsula in the Yellow Sea between the Chinese mainland and Korea. The antagonists were the Chinese North Seas Fleet and the Imperial Japanese Navy's Combined Fleet, and the result was crushing defeat for the Chinese. The battle was the first fought by modern armoured vessels and both sides were using Western technology (mainly British). Moreover, the opposing fleets had had the benefit of Royal Navy assistance in training their forces. The result clearly showed the superiority of the Japanese in absorbing Western military technology and training, and using it effectively.[1]

British involvement on both sides was not just a cynical exercise in commercial exploitation. With growing political and economic stakes in China, the British Government was keen to do what it could to prevent the steady disintegration of the Chinese State as the Qing Dynasty atrophied and its control over its population diminished. Other powers were making their claims on Chinese territory, and military defence measures were required to attempt to keep the foreigners at bay or, at least, under control. One of the countries nibbling away at Chinese interests was the nascent power of Meiji Japan. Another was Tsarist Russia. A strong and well-trained Chinese navy, under British tutelage, could exercise a moderating role on the ambitions of these two nations.

The British role in the development of Japanese naval power was somewhat different. Prompted by commercial contacts resulting from the opening of Japan to the West and the restoration of the Emperor, Japan had sought the assistance of what was the most powerful and technologically advanced navy in the world to assist in the development of its own fleet. The RN obliged with instructors and doctrine, followed by technology. The Japanese modelled their navy on the British, down to and including the ranks and uniforms. Japanese naval officers were trained in the UK while Japanese naval architects and shipbuilders studied in British institutions and shipyards. The IJN purchased it ships from the British. Relations between pupil and master were cordial and even warm: there was much admiration by the Japanese for the RN's operational success and, in particular, for its aggressive spirit. Lord Nelson had said, 'No captain can do wrong who lays his ship alongside that of an enemy', and this spirit imbued the fledgling IJN.

That the Battle of the Yellow Sea was fought was beyond British control, but the outcome had a clear impact on British relations with Japan. Japan was obviously a rising star in the region. A strong and assertive Japan would check Russian ambitions in Manchuria and North China while simultaneously resolving the continual political disturbances to which the region was prey. With the northern borders secured by the Japanese and the IJN acting as its warden, British efforts could be concentrated on ensuring that when the Qing Dynasty imploded the ensuing power struggle in China could be managed. In short, the British threw in their lot with Japan.

In practical terms the British had no other option. By the end of the nineteenth century the RN was outgunned in the Far East, while the naval ambitions of a rising German Empire gave great cause for concern at home. The focus of the coming naval arms race would be in Europe, and Britain needed an alliance to ensure that its interests in China were protected. This could not be with one of its European rivals, so Japan was the obvious choice. In 1902, when Eric Nave was just three, the first Anglo-Japanese Treaty was signed. The two navies agreed on signals codes and tactical formations, and even discussed command arrangements. If not 'as close as lips and teeth', as the Chinese expression goes, the alliance was almost as close in terms of naval operations. Under the terms of a second alliance, signed in 1909, the British agreed that the RN would put its ships under the command of a Japanese admiral as necessary.[2] However, cooperation was not total. The British were aware of the potential threat that a powerful IJN posed, while the growing indigenous capacity for warship design and production in Japan seemed likely to reduce RN influence over that navy. For the Japanese, there were limits to their support for British interests in Asia: they did not feel any responsibility for India, for example.

In Australia, undergoing the latest in a series of 'Yellow Peril' scares, the alliance was not wholly welcomed. Australians were concerned about the growth in Japanese naval power, particularly after the defeat by the IJN's Admiral Togo of a Russian fleet sent around the world to reinforce Russian defences in the Far East at the strategically important Battle of Tsushima in 1905. The Russians lost every ship but one, the Japanese fleet suffered only moderate damage. A certain Cadet Yamamoto, later to become a Commander-in-Chief Combined Fleet and a victim of Allied codebreaking, was wounded in the battle.

This was one of the factors that influenced politicians and naval figures in the newly federated Australia to reject a concept advanced by the British of an Imperial fleet to which Australia would contribute men and money, but which would remain under Admiralty control.

They struggled instead to establish an Australian fleet, funded by Australia and under Australian control, but part of an Imperial Navy, and they succeeded. The main force of the new navy steamed through Sydney Heads on 4 October 1913 led by the battle cruiser *Australia*. Eric Nave was fourteen and was probably caught up at the wave of national pride that swept the country at this significant expression of Australian-ness.

On the outbreak of World War I, British and Japanese fleets cooperated to eject the Germans from their Chinese possessions and to force the German Squadron out of the Far East altogether. The British were able to withdraw their battleships from the Far East for service in home waters and the IJN responded to other British requests, one of which was the expulsion of Germany from its territories in the Marianas and Caroline Islands. Once there the IJN stayed, much to the consternation of Australia, which had been operating under the impression that the British Government would underwrite its own occupation of all former German possessions south of the Equator. However, with the Japanese in undisputed possession, there was no regional force with the power to eject them. At the Versailles Treaty discussions Britain backed Japan in recompense for naval services rendered in the Pacific and other theatres, which had extended well beyond the letter and spirit of the alliance.

These services are generally not recognised or have been forgotten in the West. For example, during World War I British and Canadian warships operated under Japanese control in patrolling the west coast of Canada. The IJN provided escorts for the ANZAC convoys from Australia to the Middle East, and the heavy cruiser *Ibuki* was part of the escort from which HMAS *Sydney* was detached to engage and sink *Emden* in November 1914. Contrary to popular belief, on reaching Colombo, the Australia cruisers were despatched on other tasks and it was *Ibuki* and a British cruiser that escorted the troopships to Aden. Japanese cruisers and destroyers patrolled the Indian Ocean searching for German merchant raiders, and a squadron of Japanese destroyers was despatched to the Mediterranean at British request. For brief periods IJN cruisers patrolled off the Australian east and west coasts

The IJN even found itself being asked to sell some of its battle cruisers to the RN, which was a nice reversal of the student-teacher relationship. The Japanese Government rejected British requests for their ships to be sent further afield, although it did promise to send the fleet if Britain itself was invaded. The RN had no complaints about the professional way in which the IJN had conducted itself.[3] The Commander-in-Chief Malta commented that Japanese destroyers under his command were superior to the French and the Italians and, as has been mentioned previously in connection with the visit to Australia by *Asama*, *Yakumo* and *Iwate*, Japanese naval officers were awarded high British honours for their part in the war. But the strategists were worried. Concern began to grow about the depth of Japanese commitment to the alliance, and measures were put in place to limit the degree of technological cooperation and the exchange of Secret information with Japan.

In Australia there seemed to be acceptance, however grudging, that Japan was now a Pacific naval power and that *realpolitik* demanded it be taken seriously. It was these considerations that spurred discussions about the inclusion of Japanese in the curriculum at the Royal Military College Duntroon and caused the establishment of the Department of Japanese at the University of Sydney in 1917 under the aegis of the Federal Government.

Towards the end of World War I, the British evaluated the Japanese performance as allies. The considerable assistance given in matters naval, as well as economic and financial support, was noted approvingly. The negatives accumulated over Japan's ambivalent attitude towards German *agents provocateurs*, who had operated in Japan to foment feeling against British rule over India and the Anglo-Japanese Alliance itself, and because of the Japanese Government's apparent support for Indian nationalists.[4] The British also believed that Japan had taken advantage of British preoccupation with events in Europe to progress its own interests in China at the expense of those of its ally. It was not an analysis conducive to the continuation of the alliance, given British sensitivities over India, and some elements of racial discrimination had also begun to taint the discussions.

Australian perceptions of Japan as a potential aggressor were fuelled by the visit in 1919 of Lord Jellicoe, who came to discuss post-war security arrangements. Jellicoe's distrust of and scorn for Japan found fertile ground in Australia and New Zealand.

For British naval strategists the alliance had served its purpose. Britain, weakened by the war and facing grave economic stringency, could no longer match the IJN in the Far East in either quality or quantity of ships, and would thus be unable to bring any effective military or political pressure to bear on Japanese actions. The purpose of the alliance had thus been overtaken by events. In its place, the planners thought that an international naval agreement limiting the relative sizes and numbers of ships in the fleets of the world's powers offered a more effective option, and this was the path adopted by their government. The Anglo-Japanese Alliance was dissolved in December 1921 and the Washington Naval Treaty entered into force the following year. The effect on the Japanese of this 'betrayal' was alarming. A British military attache in Tokyo recalled that 'In Japan there was a dull glow of resentment, which every now and again showed signs of bursting into flames.'[5]

Under the surface of this diplomatic and strategic activity there was matching activity in the world of intelligence. Japanese sympathy for Indian nationalists and for German efforts to stir up trouble there became clear through the breaking of German codes and from human intelligence. Signals intelligence also played its part. In 1916 the Japanese had asked for permission to use a British-owned landline from Yunnan in China to send diplomatic traffic to Tokyo. The British agreed, but sent copies of the Japanese telegrams to India for translation. They revealed Japanese interference in Chinese domestic affairs. The British might have been able to monitor Japanese government and commercial traffic on the British-controlled cables out of Hong Kong to Singapore and India, but evidence of codebreaking on this traffic is not persuasive. An effort to decrypt traffic sent to the Japanese Embassy in London was led by the British Army, and there is some evidence to show that progress was made in breaking this code by 1918.[6]

However, there was no organised RN effort to intercept Japanese naval radio traffic until 1921. Lacking a Far East wireless interception and direction-finding network, and having to rely on the relatively low-capability shipboard transmitters and receivers then available, gathering Japanese naval traffic was not an easy task for the RN. Even when IJN traffic was intercepted, the British had no way of understanding what these intercepted messages were about, first because if sent in plain-language few could understand Japanese and second because no IJN codes had yet been broken. This is an appropriate point at which to introduce the reader to the art and science of codes and their breaking.

This book is not a treatise on cryptanalysis; there are a number of excellent works on codebreaking listed in the Bibliography. But to appreciate the role Eric Nave played in the drama of the war against Japan, readers should have some understanding of what it is he actually did. The starting point is some broad definitions of the systems by which letters, numbers or symbols are substituted for the plain-language elements of a message to provide security for the contents. The two major subjects of the science of both creating these systems (cryptography) and breaking them (cryptanalysis) are codes and ciphers, sometimes spelt cyphers. In general, codes are based on codebooks, in which a word, number or phrase is converted into the appropriate code group chosen from the codebook in use by the originator of a message. The result is string of letters or numerals, which is reconverted using the same codebook at the receiving end into the original plain-language text. In a cipher the individual letters, numbers or symbols are changed into different letters, numbers or symbols in accordance with a predetermined rule or system. This is called 'transposition'. Eric Nave dealt with both codes and ciphers.

To illustrate the code process, here is a hypothetical example based on the Australian Squadron of the RAN in which Eric served before he was lent to the Commander-in-Chief China. The commodore commanding the squadron (signals abbreviation CCAS) sitting in his flagship, the cruiser *Sydney*, wants to send two of his cruisers, *Brisbane* and *Melbourne*, on a trade surveillance task to which his staff have assigned the codeword 'Operation PENGUIN'. Orders for PENGUIN have already been distributed to the ships and other authorities concerned, and it is now time to set the operation in motion. The two cruisers are exercising off the Australian east coast at present and the commodore wants the ships to be fully stored, to have full bunkers of coal, to have their magazines topped up with ammunition, their crews embarked and all minor maintenance completed beforehand. He wants *Brisbane* to take charge of both cruisers and to proceed as directed in the orders for PENGUIN at 8.00 am Sydney time on 17 February 1922.

The commodore's staff prepares the necessary message using a standardised jargon used by the Navy, sometimes referred to as 'signalese'. In essence this is also a form of code, designed to ensure that instructions are clear and unequivocal, and readily understood by those who have to carry them out. Here is how the message might appear when presented to the commodore for his approval prior to its despatch:

FROM: CCAS

TO: BRISBANE

INFO: MELBOURNE

SECRET. BEING IN ALL RESPECTS READY FOR SEA TAKE MELBOURNE AND PROCEED AT 162200Z FEB TO EXECUTE OPERATION PENGUIN.

Note that all the preparations required to be made by the ships have been encapsulated in the opening phrase, thus saving a lot of signalling. The time for the ships to sail is rendered as Greenwich Mean Time (single letter suffix 'Z'), Sydney being 10 hours ahead of Greenwich.

The message is approved by the commodore and it arrives in the ship's Signals Office at 11.15 am on 9 February 1922. It is given the date/time group of 090115Z, and this will be its reference for the rest of time. The Secret classification on the message indicates that it must be coded and so it goes to the coding room. Here the coder on duty opens up his copy of the current edition of the Naval General

Codebook, a big ledger-size volume with cloth covers into which lead sheets have been bound. If there is ever any possibility of the book being captured by an enemy, it will be ditched over the side and sink to the bottom.

There are 10,000 code groups in the book and these have been assigned to words and phrases, places and ships' names arranged alphabetically. In the second half of the book is a list of all code groups in numerical order, starting with 0000 and ending with 9999, with their assigned meanings. This is used in the decoding process. So the coder turns first to the 'S' pages in the first half and finds 'Secret', for which there are five alternative groups. He has been trained to vary the code groups and to avoid always selecting the first alternative, so he picks the third group and writes it down on a message form — '7623'. The phrase 'Being in all respects ready for sea' is a standard on many naval messages, so the designers of the codebook have included a number of alternative groups (known in the trade as values) on the 'B' page for it. Out of the ten available, the coder chooses the seventh and writes it down on the message form — '0231'.

As he works through the commodore's message, the coder repeats the process. He finds there are code groups for all the words and phrases except for 'PENGUIN'. This needs to be spelt out and the code maker has provided values for the phrases 'commence spelling' and 'end spelling' as well as for all the letters in the alphabet, and every numeral as well. Understandably, this section consumes a number of pages of the book. But at last (and the process may have only taken a few minutes in the hands of an experienced coder) the commodore's message is ready for transmission. Before it is sent, one further security measure is applied. The commodore and the recipients all have signal callsigns, and these are also transformed by use of a different code that changes weekly. For this week the commodore is 6JQ8, *Brisbane* is G5L4 and *Melbourne* is V62F.

The coder hands the message form to the Wireless Office for transmission and it is placed in the stack of messages to be transmitted in Morse code over the flagship's radio. What the telegraphist sees are the following code groups:

G5L4 V62F de [this is] 6JQ8. 090115Z.

7623   0231   8926   5538

['Secret''Being in all respects ready for sea''take …and' *'Melbourne'*]

6073 0045 8993   9979 3345   5874   8851
['proceed''at' '16''2200Z''execute''operation''Commence spelling']

8914 8862 8901 8870 9013 8891 8904 9996

['P' 'E' 'N' 'G' 'U' 'I' 'N' 'end spelling']

Leading Telegraphist 'Scrubby' Forrest is on watch in the Wireless Office and he gets to send the commodore's message. An accomplished and fast Morse operator, Scrubby is proud of his skill and the way in which he slightly abbreviates the regulation length of Morse dot and dash symbols to get through the transmission quicker. And as he ends the transmission with the regulation 'BTAR' he gives it his own special flourish.

At the receiving end, the telegraphists on duty in the two cruisers copy down the message that Scrubby is sending and pass it through the hatch into their coding rooms. The duty coders quickly break down the address groups and then decode the message using the current edition of the Naval General Codebook. The decodes are then passed to the Signals Office for typing up and delivery to their commanding officers. The commodore's instructions have been sent and received — swift, clear, unequivocal — and secure? Not entirely.

Although the example used has been in English using RAN procedures and the Morse code, it will serve to illustrate a few points before moving to the rather more complex case of the Japanese language. To an enemy codebreaker the 'secure' message, even though unbroken, still has something to tell him, especially if he has been collecting and reviewing RAN messages for some time. First the addresses. 6JQ8 is issuing instructions to two other units: deduction — this is the callsign of a superior authority. In fact, Leading Telegraphist Forrest has told the codebreaker who 6JQ8 is because of his special Morse characteristics and the flourish at the end of the transmission. Scrubby has sent lots of messages, both coded and uncoded, and his distinctive style (or 'fist', as it is known in the trade) has been firmly associated with the flagship. So, our codebreaker has his first break — it is a message from CCAS. This is an example of what is known as traffic analysis.

The message has been coded, hence its contents are most likely classified. He also knows that coded values in RAN messages vary from between 0000 and 9999 — the Naval General Codebook system, to which he has assigned the name 'Kangaroo B', thus has 10,000 values all told. From interceptions of unclassified traffic, the codebreaker knows that the classification always appears as the first word of the text in RAN signals. So, the message is either Confidential or Secret, but the value used — 7623 — coming from the latter half of the codebook, suggests 'Secret', and that fits in with experience from previous coded messages. The long string of values towards the end of the message, all from the tail-end pages of the codebook, suggest that letters are being used to spell out a word. If this judgment is correct then in the Kangaroo B system, 8851 and 9996 are probably 'commence spelling' and 'end spelling'.

There are two groups in very close proximity — 8901 and 8904 — which suggests a repeated letter. Since the letter 'e' is the most commonly used in the English language, and the codebreaker has plenty of coded messages to work on, he can assign 8862 the value of 'E' with a high degree of confidence. As codebooks are designed to cover most eventualities, the need to spell a word suggests something unusual — a word or name not included in the normal codebook values. So the commodore is ordering two addressees to do something or go somewhere unusual. Interesting!

At the end, the enemy codebreaker opens up a ledger marked 'Kangaroo B', a skeleton codebook in which he has been collecting and noting groups from messages sent using the RAN Naval General Codebook, and enters his 'recoveries' from the commodore's message — the values of 'E', 'Secret' and 'commence spelling' and 'end spelling'. And he alerts the Intelligence staff that CCAS is using the callsign '6JQ8' and that the Australian Squadron is up to something, possibly involving two ships. A little more grist has been added to the intelligence mill.

Now, the example moves from the hypothetical to the actual by changing sides, dates and locations. It is now August 1925 and the action is taking place in the RN cruiser *Hawkins*, flagship of the Commander-in-Chief China Station — Admiral Sir Edwin Sinclair Alexander-Sinclair — which is anchored in Shanghai Roads in China. *Hawkins* is a handsome vessel, displacing nearly 10,000 tonnes with twin funnels and raked masts fore and aft. She is heavily armed and has a good turn of speed, but in her 172 metre length and 18 metre beam she has to accommodate 774 personnel. In 1925 she is only seven years old. In his cabin, which doubles as his office, Lieutenant Eric Nave, in his first month of secondment from the RAN at the express request of the Admiralty, is sitting, in his shirtsleeves, hunched over a pile of red-printed message forms and sweating profusely. Eric thought he was being attached to the Admiral's staff as a Japanese interpreter — which is what the message from Navy Office to the Commodore Commanding the Australian Squadron said he was going to do. But when he reported for duty his new commander had informed him of the true nature of his duties. Eric's own words sum up his feelings about his situation:

> In summary, the Admiral was to arrange for the interception of Japanese Naval wireless traffic for examination by me and to send this to London with my remarks. What an assignment; sent to another service where I knew nobody, not a wireless officer, but to examine foreign Japanese wireless traffic for no stated purpose, because they had no idea what instructions to give. All I could do was to see if I could produce something of value to somebody.
>
> I was given a Telegraphist named Valentine, one of the neatest and most beautiful writers I have ever seen. When we started we could not even read Japanese Morse, so I bought some [phonograph] records to study messages at leisure.[7]

Something rings not quite true in this statement. It seems unlikely in the extreme that the same Paymaster Lieutenant Eric Nave of HMAS *Sydney*, who had led the charge in getting the RAN interception of IJN messages on a firm footing, would have lost his grasp of *kana* Morse by the time he reached *Hawkins*. Similarly, in *Sydney* Eric had announced his intention to attempt to break IJN codes, so it could not have been true that he conceived of the Admiralty task as 'for no stated purpose'. This is not the only inconsistency that occurs in the memoirs, but it should be remembered that they were written when he was in his eighties.

However, this is the point at which the story cannot sensibly proceed without a rudimentary introduction to the Japanese language and to Eric's Morse difficulties. The following explanation will perhaps not satisfy speakers of Japanese, but it will suffice for the general reader. The language is not alphabetic — where words are built up from an arrangement of twenty-six vowels and consonants as in English. It is phonetic. Arrangements of phonemes, or sounds, tied together grammatically, make words and sentences. There is a finite number of sounds that can be used, so that homophones — the same sound but with different meanings — are inevitable and frequent. In spoken Japanese the meanings of homophones are distinguished largely by context. In written Japanese they are distinguished by the use of three separate systems of rendering the sounds of Japanese, or syllabaries — *kanji*, the ideographs derived from Chinese; *hirigana*, Japanese symbols used to make words not found in Chinese; and *katakana*, the symbols devised to 'spell' foreign names and words in Japanese. Since even *kanji* can have more than one meaning, resolving which meaning is intended can sometimes cause ambiguities and difficulties, although context is again a good guide.

Japanese sentences are generally constructed so that the main verb appears at the end and adjectives and adverbs precede the nouns and verbs they qualify. Japanese words have no gender, nor do they have plural forms; auxiliaries are used to signify number. In short, the Japanese language is quite different from English and its transmission by telegraph or radio must also be done differently.

The problem of transmitting Chinese characters by Morse code had been solved by the development of the Chinese Telegraph Code, where ideographs were assigned values in a four-figure code. Thus, a Chinese telegraphist confronted with the task of sending the correct one of the ninety-odd meanings represented by the phoneme *shi* would simply select the value that represented the appropriate ideograph. A Japanese operator could use the same system with any of the *kanji* symbols in a message, but that method did not extend to *hirigana* or *katakana*: a different system was needed. First, Japanese words were rendered into a literal system based on the Roman alphabet known as *romaji*, and second, they were transliterated into the *kana* system of transmitted symbols — forty-six in all — which could represent any of the syllabaries used in a written message. To record and read a Japanese message, one first had to learn to recognise and write out *kana*. To add spice to this considerable task, the Japanese also inserted English Morse code symbols in their messages where appropriate.

To disguise what was going on from those not authorised to know about it, the RN gave the cover name of 'Procedure Y' to interception of foreign naval message traffic. The Admiralty had been encouraging telegraphists of the Imperial navies to become proficient in reading *kana* since 1921. However, there was little by way of financial incentive to do this, and some official objection to operators being diverted away from their principal roles of sending and receiving their own naval traffic. So the idea only caught on amongst those telegraphists with an interest in mastering a new skill and who were prepared to spend their own time off watch doing so. They recorded intercepted IJN messages, coded or not, on message forms printed in red to distinguish them from the normal black lettered naval messages. While in *Sydney*, Eric Nave had done his best to stimulate interest in Procedure Y in the Australian Squadron and by 1925 there had been some interceptions, but not nearly enough to make a firm start on the process of recovering Japanese naval codes.

Increased emphasis on making a start on this task had led to the Admiralty request for the services of Nave. His excellent Japanese language results had come to Admiralty attention through his association in the British Embassy in Tokyo with Captain Colvin, Sir Harold Parlett and Mr Ernest Hobart-Hampden. Hobart-Hampden was now a member of a highly secret signals intelligence organisation with the cover name of Government Code and Cypher

School (GCCS). However, GCCS was unable to issue Eric with much by way of instruction on how to do his job because the task had never been attempted before — nobody really knew how a coded Japanese naval message might be constructed. But it was clear that anybody attempting to solve the problem would need more material to work with, and hence the formerly voluntary task of recording *kana* messages was now made compulsory for ships of the China Fleet. As Eric put it:

> I had excellent co-operation from wireless operators, particularly those in gunboats in isolated ports. The Flag Lieutenant [aide to the admiral] and Fleet Wireless Officer were a great help … With Telegraphist Valentine working full time for me, instructions could be issued to all ships on the China Station to intercept Japanese naval traffic and forward the messages to the flagship.

But where to start with unravelling Japanese naval codes? The Japanese language itself provided a clue. The British intercepted a message that was repeated several times. It was prefixed by the word *en*, which Eric surmised was an abbreviation of the Japanese word *enshu* meaning 'exercise'. The message comprised the Roman alphabet A to Z interspersed with the forty-six symbols of the *kana* syllabary. So now Eric had confirmation of the basic building blocks of the Japanese naval signalling system. Next came the callsigns. The fleet's intercept operators discovered that Japanese naval traffic was sent from Tokyo Radio, which changed its callsign from the commercial callsign 'JJC' to the naval 'AB' at hourly intervals. By intercepting these naval transmissions it was possible to identify the signal addresses for all the main shore bases used by the IJN.

> This immediately led to identifying the main naval bases of Yokosuka, Kure and Sasebo and to the lesser bases under their umbrella. Yokosuka repeated signals at times for Chichijima, Kure for Maizuru, Sasebo for Bako, etc. The addresses were spelled out at the beginning with a break between those for action and those for information.

Eric then discovered that the callsigns for operational authorities were abbreviations of their full titles. For example, the IJN used

'DA' — an abbreviation of *daijin* — for the Minister of the Navy. The Commander-in-Chief (*shireichokan*) used the abbreviation 'SHICHI'. Ship formations were identified by the Roman numerals of their squadron plus an abbreviated form of their type — 'KUTA' for destroyer squadron (*kuchikutai*). Thus '12KUTA' was the address group for the 12th Destroyer Squadron. Individual ship names were also abbreviated, but these were easily recoverable. In an early exercise in traffic analysis, Eric was able to derive from this study of callsigns 'a great deal of the naval organisation, the extent of authority of the main naval bases and that destroyer and submarine squadrons 1 to 10 were homebased on Yokosuka and 11 to 20 on Sasebo'.

The message formats also had interesting features and aids to cryptanalysis. The IJN did not use date/time groups as did the RN, but identified each message with a sequential number plus a date and time. As in Western practice, long IJN messages were broken up into parts for coding and transmission. This was indicated at the beginning of each message so that the group '42715' meant that this was the 427th message of the day and that it was the first part of a five-part message.

A rather more upbeat Lieutenant Nave reported to the Naval Board in September 1925 on his work in *Hawkins* and the progress being made:

> My job is to supervise the interception of Japanese W/T messages, correct intercepted messages, and issue 'Hints to Operators', thus training them to the work. Also collection of call signs, wave lengths etc. Unless the volume of interception increases it will not keep me fully employed.[8]

While Eric was able to translate messages sent in plain-language Japanese 'which at times provided useful intelligence', coded messages remained opaque until a breakthrough suggested by the wireless operator of a British gunboat located at a port on the Yangtse River. The operator recorded the transmission from a Japanese ship in the port and then wrote on the message form: 'This message probably reports the sailing up river of the French gunboat X'. This was, as Nave wrote, 'a reasonable assumption'. It is standard naval practice to report the arrival and departure of all warships and on the premise that IJN messages used standardised reporting formats, just as British messages did, he made his first attack on the coded message. In the code groups recorded would be the words for 'French', 'gunboat', 'sailed' (or departed), 'upriver', and a time and probably the name of the port of departure as well. It was a start, and a fruitful one. Eric was now ready to begin compiling his own ledger of recoveries.

Code groups are teased out by comparing similar messages intercepted over a period of time. Values tentatively assigned become confirmed by frequent use and by reference to observed activity. Another opportunity occurs in the transmission of plain-language and encoded texts from the same unit, a practice that compromises callsigns and identities and is of great assistance of the codebreaker. Codebreaking is normally neither an easy nor a rapid process but, if sufficient intercepts are made and their circumstances noted, and if the cryptanalyst is dogged and intuitive enough, then the code will eventually yield its secrets.

Eric Nave revealed an unexpected aptitude for this kind of work and 'before long was able to decode all Japanese Naval Reporting Code traffic towards the end of my first year'. Note that this was one code, the *tasogare* basic Naval Reporting Code, and a relatively minor one at that, but a start had been made. There were other gains: 'The secret callsigns of all naval bases, major commands, battleships, cruiser and destroyer flotillas had already been collected and forwarded to London'.

Many a British naval officer has incurred the displeasure of Their Lordships of the Admiralty over some mistake or misdemeanor, a judgment that is added to the officer's service record and stays with it for the rest of his time in the Navy. Eric's little codebreaking coup warranted a relatively unusual message from the Admiralty to C-in-C China. The import was conveyed in a letter dated 16 June 1926 from the Admiralty to Navy Office in Melbourne:

> Their Lordships are of the opinion that the very great difficulties which are inherent in this problem [W/T Procedure Y] could only have been overcome by great zeal and ability on the part of those concerned. In this connection the Commander-in-Chief, China has been instructed to convey

to Paymaster Lieutenant T.E. Nave, RAN an expression of Their Lordships' appreciation for his part in this matter.[9]

That seems a fair judgment: Eric was now working up to seven days a week on his task, adding to his recovered values in his ledger replica of the *tasogare* codebook and to the list of recovered secret callsigns. Importantly, he had also completed the identification of the abbreviated organisational callsigns, address prefixes such as 'Naval Officer Commanding', which needed only the location to show what might be being planned for a particular area of Japanese naval activity.

It is also appropriate to consider the conditions under which Eric worked. The cruiser *Hawkins* had been designed and built for service in European waters, yet here she was operating in the quite different conditions of the Far East. In summer the heat was intense, even though awnings would be spread to shield the upper deck from the direct rays of the sun. Eric said of a trip the cruiser made up the Yangtse to Nanjing [Nanking]:

> In the summer with the relentless sun beating on the ship's side it became so hot that you could not bear your hand on it inside the cabin. At night the choice lay between sleeping on deck with the insects or having to sweat all night in the cabin.

There was no air-conditioning, and air would either be circulated by a ceiling fan or by a wind scoop projecting from the ship's side through the scuttle (porthole) of Eric's working space and directing the breeze into it, provided it was one that opened. Eric mentions that he had a scuttle, as he had to draw curtains over it after returning from an all-night session in a Shanghai nightclub, but he doesn't say whether it could be opened. He states only that he was 'cooped up in my small cabin'. In fact, at the height of summer the Commander-in-Chief would normally take those ships of the China Fleet that could be spared from patrol work on a cruise to more temperate parts of the station than Hong Kong or Shanghai. Wei Hai Wei, an island at the eastern tip of the Shandong Peninsula, and the former base of that North Seas Fleet so comprehensively defeated by Japan in 1894, was a favourite spot.

Despite the presence of Chinese galley staff on board *Hawkins*, the Royal Navy's traditional diet continued to be served. 'Our menu could be told by the day of the week: Sunday — roast pork, apple pie and custard: Monday — roast beef: Tuesday — roast mutton: Wednesday — cottage pie'. Port visits and trips to places like the French Club in Shanghai broke the monotony, and there was more exotic fare closer at hand: in Hong Kong a meal at the Army Garrison Officers' Club introduced Eric to that Sino-British delicacy, 'Cheesy Hammy Eggie Topside'.[10]

Keeping fit was a matter of getting enough exercise, and as a keen sportsman Eric played for the ship's cricket and tennis teams. The sporting facilities at Hong Kong were excellent, while in Shanghai ships' officers were made honorary members of the clubs in the International Settlement. Contacts he had made with English families while he was in Japan were useful in getting him off the ship, and he made some good friends amongst the officers of *Hawkins* and the admiral's staff.

> I was now in another Navy on a foreign station to be cooped up for about two years with about 30 officers, none of whom were previously known to me. We wore the same uniform but there were differences, superficial maybe but real nevertheless. Mess conversation was initially of unfamiliar places, subjects and people. However, after a few months I merged and found new friends.

This appears to be understatement on the part of Nave. At that time a considerable proportion of British naval officers came from upper middle-class families, and there was a sizable contingent of the aristocracy amongst their ranks. Eric had thus to overcome three significant barriers before being accepted by the wardroom officers of the flagship as one of their own. First, he needed to demonstrate competency in his duties; second, the perceived social embarrassment of his humble origins had to be disproved; and third, his inferior status as a 'colonial' had to be overcome. As one who has faced similar barriers — albeit in more modern times — the author appreciates Eric's success in dealing with all three issues. He could not discuss his secret work, but the Commander-in-Chief's high regard for him trickled down to the wardroom. Tact, discretion and his reputation for forthrightness when called for took care of the 'humble origins' discrimination. The third, and most difficult, was dealt with by Eric's charm, energy and willingness to play the British at their own game — and win. In *Hawkins* he made several friendships which were to continue throughout his life, a considerable achievement.

One of the British officers who seems to have attached himself to Eric was Prince George, fourth son of King George V and later the Duke of Kent. The Prince had been compelled by his father to pursue a naval career — something he hated — and had been further ordered to serve in the one of the far-flung corners of the Empire so that he would be removed from the distracting influences of the Court. A very lonely young man, interested neither in the Navy nor in participating in sport, he often sought Eric's company and this imposed on Nave an unlooked-for responsibility as the Prince's 'minder'. Condemned by his heritage to perform official duties in the Far East, a task which he found painful, the Prince was eventually sent back to Britain to end his period of purgatory. In later life, however, this link was useful to Eric.

Life on the China Station in the 1920s was by no means unpleasant, although sometimes dangerous when local warlords chose to present some opposition to the passage of a British warship up or down the rivers, or to threaten British interests. At one point the Commander-in-Chief was compelled to issue instructions that any attacks on RN ships by Chinese armed bands were to be responded to by the ships' main armament. This measure seems to have been quickly effective. However, the continued disturbances around Shanghai compelled the ship to land armed parties on many occasions to keep the peace. It was the time of the Northern Expedition by the armies of the Cantonese warlord Chiang Kai Shek to capture Shanghai on behalf of the Nationalist Guomindang (KMT) cause, so it was a lively time for the China Fleet in its role of protecting British property and lives.

A few months after joining *Hawkins*, Eric persuaded the Commander-in-Chief to forward to London a proposal that the modest collection effort on Japanese naval messages be augmented by the establishment of a Far East interception and direction-finding network of shore radio stations. This was eventually to be done, but in 1926 the Admiralty had other concerns and did not agree.

> Owing to the necessity of economy, it is not possible to provide any special organisation for this purpose on the China Station. The material must, therefore, be provided by H.M. Ships under your command. To enable this to be done, ships should be specially detailed for the duty when opportunities arise, less important W/T communications being sacrificed if necessary ...
>
> [I]t is hoped that favourable opportunities of sending H.M. Ships to the vicinity of Japanese ships, more especially those engaged in exercises or manoeuvres, will be utilised.[11]

The Commander-in-Chief clearly took the Admiralty's advice to heart, and more intercepted material began to arrive in Eric's cabin from the fleet. His was slow and painstaking work and virtually a full-time job for a single codebreaker. Eric thus enjoyed the distractions of his visits to Hong Kong and Shanghai and a cruise the flagship made to Singapore, Malaya and the Netherlands East Indies, but the grind of the intercept and decoding work never stopped. However, the additional coverage of Japanese naval communications by ships of the China Fleet yielded another dividend.

> With the widening of the interception coverage I found a number of messages which had all the appearance of plain language, as the count of *kana* signs was normal, but they made no sense. This traffic was from naval intelligence officers in shore appointments in Nanking [Nanjing], Shanghai, Tientsin [Tianjin] etc. Then I found that by exchanging the even numbered signs with the identical sign in the line below I got a clear text. So, in my second year, I could claim to have solved two codes even though at this time they were fairly simple.

This break provided a very useful intelligence source, as the Japanese messages demonstrated clearly how far the IJN had infiltrated Chinese military and political circles. Furthermore, the discovery identified a means used by Japanese code makers to disrupt the work of enemy codebreakers, knowledge that was to be useful in attacking higher level Japanese naval codes in the future.

In the autumn of 1926 the Commander-in-Chief paid a visit to

Yokohama and Eric found himself in the familiar role of interpreter again. Prince George, on whom the Japanese penchant for extreme forms of politeness was quite lost, declared 'They are all mad!', but the visit was a success. Eric had the opportunity of renewing acquaintances with officers from the Training Squadron, including Admiral Saito, and had the unusual duty of playing ice breaker at a formal reception on board the flagship. The British midshipmen were reluctant to dance with the attractive young Japanese women guests, daughters of high officials, who had been included in the official party, so it fell to Eric to do some 'volunteering' of partners. One of the ladies present, and mother of one of the Japanese belles, was a Countess Watanabe, whose husband had been a diplomat, and who spoke excellent English. 'She told me that she was a Christian, and in reply to my inquiry as to why she had accepted Christianity, she said "So that I should not meet my husband in the next world".'

Eric must have been a considerable asset to the wardroom of *Hawkins* but, social occasions like these aside, he had to work solidly at his codebreaking task. From what was effectively a standing start in July 1925, within two years in HMS *Hawkins* he had discovered a great deal about the structure and 'grammar' of IJN messages, recovered a plethora of secret callsigns, had sketched the command structure of the Japanese Navy, and had broken two codes to boot. What he could not solve had been sent back to the Admiralty, from where it was passed to the Japanese Section of GCCS. This was a very comprehensive effort and one that won him enormous respect in naval and codebreaking circles. His 'first' — the breaking of a Japanese naval code — could not be widely proclaimed at the time, and it may look relatively unimportant when compared with what was to come, but it was an illustration of the principle that from tiny acorns mighty oak trees grow.

In contrast to his views on joining the China Fleet, in reflecting on these achievements Eric recorded:

> This period of duty in HMS *Hawkins* 1925–27 was, I can recall, the happiest and most fulfilling time of my life. When I look back, the reasons are basic and obvious. Firstly, I had been given an original task, entrusted with the

organisation of interception of Japanese wireless traffic. The Admiralty instructions were noteworthy for the complete lack of information and directions, purely because they had no knowledge on which to base their orders. I had to organise this interception myself, success or failure depended on me alone.

His superiors also thought that Eric's time in *Hawkins* had been valuable. In August 1927, the Chief of Staff wrote in his personal report on Eric:

> This officer has been employed entirely on Procedure Y, and has carried out the work with exceptional keenness and ability He has considerable tact, a pleasant and cheerful personality, is keen on games and sport. Social qualities good.

The Commander-in Chief added in his own hand: 'I concur. Mr Nave has carried out his special duties with marked success and great zeal'. [12] As personal reports on naval officers go, this one was excellent.

James Rusbridger's claims about Australian naval ignorance of Nave's work can now be put under further scrutiny. In the National Archives of Australia there is a record dated June 1926 containing 'Notes on Japanese Wireless Telegraphy Procedure' and a copy of the *tasogare* codebook compiled by 'Paymaster Lieutenant T.E. Nave RAN'.[13] Furthermore, Their Lordships of the Admiralty saw fit to suggest to the Naval Board that 'a favourable notation' be made in Eric's service record, and they explicitly explained the reason:

> Their Lordships are extremely gratified at the progress being made on the [China] Station in spite of the difficulties added by the Japanese morse signs, procedure and language, and consider that the results reflect great credit on the China Squadron in general and the officers directly concerned in particular.[14]

The Australian Naval Board had entertained the idea that, when Eric had finished his time in *Hawkins*, he would be sent to Tokyo for a year of refresher training in Japanese. At first the British agreed but then asked that he be allowed to stay in the ship for a full two years. The British were being coy. The Australian Naval Representative in

London reported in November 1925 that:

> the Director of Naval Intelligence has expressed a hope to me that this
> Officer [Nave], who is engaged on most important work, may be allowed
> to complete two years' service in the appointment. The D.N.I. points out
> that the work on which this Officer is engaged is considered to some extent
> a refresher course in itself, although the Admiralty admit the opportunities
> for colloquial work are limited.[15]

As his two-year exchange posting with the RN drew to a close,
Eric was told that the Admiralty was not finished with him yet. It
had asked for a further loan of Paymaster Lieutenant Nave's services
for two years, this time in the Admiralty itself, and had made the
offer more attractive to the RAN by offering to pay all the expenses
involved. Interestingly, Eric had not been consulted about this
proposal, but the Australian Naval Board consented, and all parties
agreed that he should report for duty in London after spending
his foreign service leave in Australia. On 16 August 1926 he left
Hawkins in Shanghai, where he had joined her two years earlier, and
commenced his journey home.

3 Government Code and Cypher School

One can easily imagine that Eric Nave had a lot on his mind as his steamer SS *Changte* made her way south from Hong Kong towards Australia. Since joining the Navy in 1917, he had spent four years overseas and was facing the prospect of another two, at least. In between these periods of overseas service he had either been serving in seagoing billets or attached to a senior officer's staff and moving from flagship to flagship. Apart from his time as a language student, what shore time he had enjoyed was brief and unrelated to his paymaster professional duties.

That was another issue. While learning Japanese and breaking Japanese naval codes had been most interesting and were enterprises in which he had excelled, they had very little bearing on his professional career. If there was to be any hope of promotion to lieutenant commander and beyond then Eric must, before too much more time had elapsed, arrange to be posted to a billet where his paymaster skills could be displayed and reported upon by RAN senior officers. In accepting the Admiralty's offer the Australian Naval Board had apparently overlooked this most necessary step in the selection process. Did this mean that he was not considered suitable for promotion? After all, in some Service circles intelligence work was regarded as 'not gentlemanly' and inferior to that of other branches. The RAN itself had dropped Intelligence as a separate staff division in 1924.

Then again there was the question of his family and personal life. His parents, Thomas and Ethyl, were now in their fifties. While Eric was not very close to his mother, he had a firm bond with Thomas, in whom he confided his thoughts and to whom he turned for advice on more than one occasion. Once in the UK, there was almost no chance that he would see them before his tour of duty at the Admiralty was completed, and the same consideration applied to his brother and sisters, who were now in their twenties or late teens. As for his personal life, he was now twenty-seven and had had few opportunities to meet and form relationships with any girl whom he might consider marriage material. Eric's memoirs leave little doubt that he had an eye for the ladies and he enjoyed a full social life but at this stage, in his shuttling around the ports of the Pacific and the Far East, he had not met the girl he would want to marry.

Fortunate the biographer who is able to access a collection of his subject's letters. In fact, none of Eric's correspondence from his early years has been unearthed, but there is an interesting collection of letters written to him by his father in the period 1920 to around 1932. By studying these paternal responses it is possible to deduce the issues that Eric raised with his father during this time. One revelation is that he formed an early fascination with the workings of the stock market, and father and son exchanged views on the composition of Eric's portfolio and on trading in shares. During Eric's frequent absences, Thomas kept the portfolio in order and regularly reported the state of Eric's finances. But on the girlfriend front, there was little activity in Australia. Many of his former shipmates in the Australian Squadron had married, and during Eric's foreign service leave in Australia he was invited to stay with several of these couples, underlining his lack of progress in forming personal relationships.

Set against these rather discouraging aspects of his present position, Nave could reflect with some pride on the esteem in which the Admiralty held his codebreaking work and the fact that he had been asked for by name — this was not simply an exchange position he was destined for. As well, he had the satisfaction of knowing that he still had his naval commission. The Australian Government had been zealous in cutting its Defence budget after the war, which generated both a rapid reduction in the size of the RAN and savage cuts in its personnel strength. Many young officers, including the mainstream graduates of the RAN College, had had their commissions abruptly terminated, but Eric had been spared this humiliation.

Finally, he must have been somewhat excited about his next posting. For many Australians of the day — and for some time after that — the UK was 'home' and London was the centre of the universe. Comparatively few had the opportunity to travel so far to actually see it, but from school instruction, the media and books, all were familiar with its sights and wonders. The chance of getting to England had been a powerful motivation for so many young men to join the armed forces during the Great War. Now Eric would be making the journey in far more comfortable conditions than those of a troopship, and he had the prospect of interesting and safe employment at journey's end. Many, including his family, would have seen the posting to London as the chance of a lifetime.

The Admiralty was, of course, the supreme professional naval organisation in the British Empire. A tour of duty in an Admiralty staff division was highly prized by RAN officers and was a comparatively rare privilege. As he had been selected to undertake such a duty, Eric could well believe that his professional star was in the ascendancy and that his prospects for further naval service were indeed rosy. On balance then, personal prospects aside, his future was far from bleak, and he embarked with considerable relish upon his voyage to the UK on 27 November 1927 as a guest of the Orient Line in SS *Ormonde*:

> I enjoyed a number of these passages from Australia to England. What a glorious experience they were. Congenial company could always be found; there was a swimming pool and a variety of games to pass the time, deck tennis for the energetic, and others for the less energetic. After the afternoon shower the men dressed for dinner and the ladies made themselves glamorous, so it was indeed pleasant to join your own group for a pre-dinner drink. The menus provided in those days gave the greatest variety of foods so you could reckon on a superb dinner and when complemented by some good Australian wine we had a feeling of repleteness and peace with the world

On the six-week voyage, affable and gregarious Eric, now with a stock of stories of the China Fleet to add to his repertoire, made a number of contacts with British businessmen returning home and Australians on posting to the United Kingdom. These were to stand him in good stead during his time in the UK and beyond. As well, he developed an appreciation for fine Australia wine. To pass the time on board he began to learn Italian, and had his first opportunity of trying his skills during the ship's stopover in Naples. Like so many with an affinity for languages, Eric was not satisfied with having just one qualification under his belt.

Neither the Britain towards which Eric was cruising nor the Royal Navy he was to be attached to were what they had once been. The war had impoverished the Empire and Britain had run up huge debts, particularly to the US. Around three-quarters of a million Britons had been killed and more than twice that number wounded in the fighting. When the huge industrial energy built up to prosecute the war had wound down with the Armistice, and the first rush of post-war demand for consumer durables had abated, British industry found itself at somewhat of a disadvantage in competition with other nations. Prosperity did not return and industrial disputation grew. The Great Depression in 1929 simply worsened an already unhappy economic situation. This had its inevitable effects on the Navy. Post-war British governments made massive cuts in defence expenditure, at first seeking what we now call a 'peace dividend', and then motivated by the belief that there would be no war within ten years. The successful negotiation of the Washington Naval Treaty in 1922 ushered in what was referred to by politicians as a 'naval holiday'.[1]

Some commentators have pointed out that the Washington Treaty was a grave setback for the Royal Navy, no longer the supreme international naval force and now destined to share 'first place' with the US Navy. The difference was that the RN had a widely dispersed Empire to defend while the US Navy did not, so that the apparent parity of the 5:5:3 agreement with the Americans and the Japanese amounted, in fact, to an inferiority compared with the US. However, others point to the fact that the Americans never attempted to build a navy to the levels allowed by the treaty while the British certainly did. In 1929 the RN was unquestionably the largest navy in the world, but this was shortly to change. The Admiralty succeeded in persuading successive British governments to keep the naval estimates healthy, which facilitated the modernisation of older capital ships and the construction of new classes of cruisers, destroyers and submarines. But this golden age in naval construction unfolded against a backdrop of worsening economic conditions and by the end of the decade the naval vote was too large for the nation to sustain sensibly.

Commenting on the RN as it was in 1929, Eric Nave presented a rosy view of the situation when he wrote:

> It was a time of the peak of British world-wide supremacy and influence, the Navy having docking and fuelling facilities at convenient locations throughout the world. They had a degree of control over the world-wide communications of nations as we knew from the copies our office received daily ... The ships were magnificently manned and many of the men of the ship's companies had long traditions of service with the ships and dockyards, having pride in the performance and appearance of their ships. I remember querying Phillip Mack [a friend from *Hawkins* days] once on the value of all this 'spit and polish'. He explained, as he himself had been buying enamel [paint] for the superstructure out of his own pocket, that they could go ashore, look back on their ship and say 'Doesn't she look beautiful'. That's when you win the Regatta and the guns hit the target constantly.

However, in truth all was not well with the Navy, or its personnel. The noted historian of the British Navy, Corelli Barnett, gave his markedly different view of the state of the RN two years afterwards. The provisions of the Washington Naval Treaty had stifled its force structure and technological development, while government financial cutbacks and a decade of peace had blunted its readiness for war. The RN could still put on an impressive show of strength but it had reverted to being 'a kind of fashionable yacht club' rather than a competent fighting service.[2]

Nevertheless, for Eric Nave, his time with the Admiralty promised much. In distinct contrast to the circumstances of his arrival in Japan in 1921, when Nave's ship arrived at Tilbury outside London he was welcomed by a British shipmate from *Hawkins*, Commander Phillip Mack. Not only was he instructed in the correct procedure for taking up his posting at the Admiralty, but his friend invited him to await his instructions in the Mack country home in Norfolk. It was a very good introduction to the RN way of doing things and a testament to Eric's gift for making firm friends.

Shortly, his instructions arrived and in January 1928 Eric reported to the Director of Naval Intelligence (DNI) at the Admiralty. In fact, he had a gift for the admiral. When his leave had been completed and before his ship sailed for the United Kingdom, Eric had reported to the DNI in Navy Office. There he had contributed his knowledge of the situation in the Far East, and he had assisted the Directorate in the task of assessing records of Japanese radio activity in the mandated islands. These had been collected by *Franklin*, the steam yacht of the Administrator of Papua New Guinea, which the RAN had pressed into service as an early example of a seaborne intelligence collector. He took these with him to London, as well as the intercepts made by an ex-RAN Procedure Y telegraphist, now the radio officer on the island of Nauru.[3]

Once at the Admiralty, however, the Nave bubble of expectation was pricked. He learned that his real destination was the Government Code and Cypher School (GCCS), which was classified as a posting 'outside Admiralty'. Eric indicates in his memoirs that he had never previously heard of this organisation, and perhaps he is correct. While serving in *Hawkins* he had been very much a part of the RN; he reported to an admiral and the results of his codebreaking endeavours, as well as material he was not able to decode, were sent — so far as he or anybody else knew — to the Admiralty. He was not to know that the Admiralty transferred the coded material to the oddly named GCCS, an agency of unusual provenance and equally unusual relationships with its major 'customers'.

However, either Eric had not been listening or Navy Office had forgotten to tell him that GCCS was his destination in London. The Admiralty had made this clear in a letter to the Australian Naval Board in August 1927:

I am commanded by My Lord Commissioners of the Admiralty to inform
you that they desire this officer [Nave] should join the Government Code
and Cypher School, about December next, after he has completed his
foreign service leave in Australia.[4]

There might have been some uncertainty in Australian naval circles
about what this organisation did and what Nave's posting might
entail. Eric's disappointment on finding the answer to both questions
is recorded later, but he should have known about GCCS.

When Nave joined it, GCCS was nominally and financially the
responsibility of the British Foreign Office. The agency had been
formed at the end of World War I as a compromise designed to
defuse disagreement between the War Office, Admiralty and the
Foreign Office about the control and coordination of 'military' signals
intelligence. Explained very briefly, each of these organisations had
engaged in codebreaking during the war, the most famous example
of which was the decoding by the Admiralty's Room 40 of the
Zimmerman telegram, which revealed German plans to launch a
submarine assault on neutral shipping servicing the Allies. This
intercept is credited with bringing the Unites States into the war
on the Allied side, which swung the balance of forces against the
Germans.[5] Here was a case of the interception of a diplomatic signal
by a Service agency, a responsibility the Foreign Office thought ought
to be its own. In fact, the two armed services intercepted and decoded
messages of any kind and controlled almost all the intercept stations
and the codebreaking staffs as well. The Foreign Office wanted
this to cease, and to establish its own signals intelligence service to
undertake the interception and decoding of diplomatic traffic. The
Army and Navy strenuously resisted this takeover attempt. In 1919
the British Cabinet established GCCS 'to study the methods of
cypher communication used by foreign powers and to advise on the
security of British codes and cyphers.'[6]

After remaining under the overall control of the Admiralty after
the Armistice, the responsibility for the coordination of military and
diplomatic codebreaking activities was given to the Foreign Office in
1922, following a Cabinet review of the arrangements for intelligence.

This decision was based, in part, on the fact that the vast majority of the codes being broken by GCCS were diplomatic rather than military. In reality, however, the Foreign Office had little interest in its new acquisition and its director remained a former naval education officer, Commander Alistair Denniston, who had been responsible for the codebreaking activities in Room 40. The naval connection was reinforced by the fact that the person to whom Denniston reported was Admiral Hugh 'Quex' Sinclair, in his position as the newly created Chief of the Secret Service. It was Sinclair, a former Director of Naval Intelligence, who kept the new agency afloat in the face of Foreign Office neglect, reputedly by employing ex-servicemen and retired public servants who were all drawing a pension, their salaries being topped up to normal rates out of his own pocket. It was also Sinclair who, in 1938, purchased a manor estate outside London called Bletchley Park, of which much more will be heard in this story.[7]

GCCS was divided into sections, each department of state being responsible for staffing the relevant section. Head of the Naval Section, formed in 1921, was another former Room 40 codebreaker — Commander William 'Nobby' Clarke. With hostilities at an end and no identified enemy service whose codes and cyphers should be attacked, the concentration within the Naval Section was on diplomatic traffic, and the big diplomatic interest at the time was the Washington Naval Treaty. The British were able to read Japanese diplomatic cables sent to their negotiating team at the talks, thus strengthening their bargaining hand at the expense of the Japanese — and the Americans.[8] GCCS was only able to translate these messages because it had obtained the services of Ernest Hobart-Hampden, who had now retired from the Foreign Service. In 1926 Sir Harold Parlett also joined GCCS.

Following renewed Admiralty interest in IJN codes, the increase in intercepts of Japanese naval traffic now arriving at GCCS made it necessary for the section to organise a Japanese Navy cell. This was formed in 1924 by Paymaster Commander E.P. Jones, whose Japanese language credentials are not made clear in the archives. In 1925 Jones was to be relieved by Lieutenant Commander Harry

Shaw, the language student who had shared accommodation with
Eric Nave in Japan. However, there were no other RN Japanese
interpreters available to staff the intercept end of the cell. Conferring
with Hobart-Hampden, Nobby Clarke became aware of the
achievements of Eric Nave and he lost no time in setting the wheels
in motion within Admiralty to ask for Eric's services in the China
Fleet. Thus it was Nobby Clarke who set Eric Nave's feet firmly on
the codebreaking ladder and who was to engineer the request for his
services in London at the end of his time in *Hawkins*.

When Nave declined an extension to his exchange in the China
Fleet, it became Harry Shaw's turn to go to the Far East to relieve
him. No other British naval interpreter had shown the aptitude for
the task that the Australian had. In fact, Shaw had complained that
the volume of IJN intercept material now arriving in GCCS from
the China Fleet demanded the attention of at least two Japanese
interpreters, but there were none to be found. The record shows
that between 1917 and 1939 the RN succeeded in graduating only
seventeen Japanese-language officers, far too few for the scale of the
work they were to be called upon to undertake.[9]

Nave made only three mentions of Clarke in his memoirs: he may
not have known of Clarke's role in this chain of events, or he may have
been reluctant to share the credit for his codebreaking. Very possibly,
he may not have been overly delighted to find that his exciting and
interesting posting in Admiralty was nothing of the sort, and was
thus not of a mind to give acknowledgment to the person responsible
for this apparent change in his prospects. As his remarks in a letter
written to James Rusbridger on 3 March 1989 show, Eric obviously
did not get on with his head of section. He described Clarke thus:

> He was clearly pleased to be head of the Naval Section and I took him my
> list of new groups I had solved for the Naval code book which he would
> forward to the Admiralty for transmission to the China Station. He was
> only a P.O. [post office] which I found unsatisfactory as I had no contact
> with anyone else. Clarke had no apparent organising ability other than
> to arrange a 'cuppa' and a few beers after the office, both of which I soon
> abandoned as a waste of time.

So much then for his direct superior at GCCS, but Eric also recorded his disappointment at finding out how the Admiralty was to employ him:

> Having crossed the Horse Guards Parade, we walked to my new office, where I met the staff and commenced my new duties, to found a Japanese Naval Section. My main task was to decipher and translate the telegrams to and from Admiralty Tokyo to Japanese Naval Attachés in Europe. These cables passed through British hands somewhere and I had copies of them on my desk every day.
>
> There I was again chained to a desk in a room by myself starting another entirely new task for which I was quite untrained. The office hours were 10.00 to 1.00pm and 2.30 to 5.30 which felt luxurious at first but later on when the codes became more difficult, I found it quite enough.

As outlined above, Nave's claim to be the founder of the Japanese Naval Section is not substantiated by official records. Shaw was at GCCS when Nave arrived and he did not depart for his tour of duty in the China Fleet until a few months later. It is also odd that Eric regarded himself as 'quite untrained' for his codebreaking duties. One account of the first meeting between Nave and Commander Denniston has the latter telling Nave that, partly as a result of his codebreaking achievements in *Hawkins*, 'Whitehall was beginning to take the Far East situation more seriously'.[10] Whether he realised it or not, Nave was the only experienced breaker of Japanese naval codes the British had. There was certainly nobody else who could train him in the task.

Important though the naval attache cables were, Nave also worked on the new four-*kana* Naval Operational Code. It was by using this code that the IJN sought to give protection to its sensitive operational information, not just the movement of its ships — which direction finding and traffic analysis might also provide — but details of what they were to do when they arrived at their destinations, operations orders and reports on the results of those operations. By the end of 1928, Clarke was able to report that over 800 values had been recovered, largely through the efforts of Eric Nave, and that a degree of intelligibility of messages encoded in this system had been achieved.[11]

In attacking both these codes Nave made use of peculiarities in IJN signalese. Japanese naval messages from a commanding officer to his superior traditionally began with the introductory phrase 'I have the honour to report to Your Excellency that ... ' which provided a useful crib. If sufficient messages were intercepted and compared, then it would be possible for a cryptanalyst to determine values for this phrase or for its component parts. As well, just as in the reference to Operation PENGUIN in the message sent by the Australian commodore to his two cruisers in the last chapter, the need for a Japanese coder to shift to *romaji* to spell out a foreign word or place name provided a codebreaker with a clearly distinguishable feature at which to attack the message.

Other aids to codebreaking were the orthographic rules — the conventions of the Japanese language. These are not dissimilar to those of any language. In English the most common letters in descending order of frequency of use are E, T, A, O and N. On top of this, there are conventions on the order in which letters may be used — 'I before E, except after C' and so on. The letters T and H are frequently closely associated in words like 'the', 'that', 'this', 'through' and the like. In Japanese the letter Y is almost always followed by A and almost never by E or I. Double vowels are prevalent and they appear also in a descending frequency of use. Nave noted that the combinations YUU and YOO frequently occurred preceded by a consonant. Most Japanese words end in a vowel, and so on. Further peculiarities of Japanese provided other points of codebreaking leverage.

> The formidable task was to build the [code] book of 97,336 groups although fortunately for this the earliest book I had to tackle had the groups in alphabetical sequence. It was still a massive undertaking but I had already learned a good deal of Japanese naval signal construction, and this was a help.
>
> I decided to analyse all groups in a skeleton book and discovered two which outstripped the rest in frequency. These had to be the Japanese prepositions (or, more properly, postpositions, as they follow the words they govern) *no* = of and *ni* = to. This was confirmed in that the group for *no* followed *ni* in my alphabetical codebook, whereas in the messages themselves the reverse was more common. From this analysis I could now

place the group for *wa*, commonly used to indicate the subject matter and thus commonly occurring early in the message.

This laborious, time-consuming work of indexing was now showing results but only those who have undertaken research work can appreciate the hours of toil with no tangible result. The daily decipherment and translation of the Naval Attachés' messages had priority for this was real intelligence.

Some explanation of what Eric Nave was getting at is appropriate. In Japanese, suffixes (or 'postpositions') are used to indicate the possessive and to indicate the subject of a sentence. To illustrate this simply, consider the sentence 'This is Mr Smith', which becomes *Kochira-wa Sumisu-san desu*. The suffix *wa* indicates that 'This' — *kochira* — is the subject of the sentence. Then, in offering his business card (*meishi*) Mr Smith would say 'Here is my business card' (*Watashi-no meishi desu*), where the *no* suffix indicates that the business card is his. The English word 'to' indicating in the direction of is, in Japanese, the suffix *ni*. Thus 'I am going to Japan' is *Watashi-wa Nihon-ni i-kimasu*, the subject of the sentence being 'I' (*watashi*) and Japan (*Nihon*) being the destination. These suffixes are most useful in revealing to a codebreaker the general structure and content of a sentence, and were well exploited by Eric.

A skeleton codebook is developed by inspired guesswork, such as was demonstrated by the enemy codebreaker in Chapter 2 working on the commodore's message, or by luck when the same text is sent in code and in plain language. For example, in attacking the naval attache code Eric discovered that the Japanese attache in London was cabling Tokyo leading articles from significant British newspapers. This provided Nave with an excellent crib from which to make assumptions about which group represented which English word. The cryptanalyst's task could be greatly complicated when cryptographers produced a codebook in which the values were not in alphabetical order, but in practice this also made life difficult for the coders as well.

One other thing needs to be explained before the story proceeds, and that is how the attache's cables found their way onto Nave's desk every morning. The answer is very simple: the British Government simply used its powers under the Official Secrets Act of 1920 to compel cable companies operating out of British territory to supply it with all their customers' traffic within ten days of receipt. Sacks of messages were delivered to GCCS every day, where a team of sorters would review them and copy those whose origins suggested they would be of interest to the government, before returning all messages to the cable companies. This action created a prime source of information for the codebreakers to work on and the rule was also applied to other parts of the Empire. The Cable & Wireless Company's repeater station on Malta handled all traffic between Europe and the Far East, and gave GCCS access to messages passing between Japan and its European embassies.[12] The Japanese apparently never suspected that their cables were being intercepted in this way.

Nave's reference to the decryptions and translations of the naval attaches' cables as 'real intelligence' contains an important observation which was later to cause problems for the British and the Americans alike. There are three phases in the sequence of converting an intercepted message into intelligence. The first is clearly interception — one has to know what frequency a target is using and to have a receiver tuned to it to capture the message for cryptanalysis. This problem was neatly solved for GCCS in the case of the Japanese naval attaches' cables, where the Japanese gave the cables to the cable company and the company delivered them to the British Government. However, as explained in Chapter 2, while Eric served in HMS *Hawkins* interception of IJN messages was a matter for the China Fleet's receivers and telegraphists. The second phase of the process is the decryption and translation of the intercept, the rendering of the target message into a form intelligible to intelligence and other staffs. The third — and most would argue the most important —phase is the melding of the intercepted and decrypted/translated information with other intelligence to produce a balanced picture of what is occurring.

Intelligence staffs are not different from other mortals, and they bring their preconceived notions to their work. A poorly translated intercept, or one in which missed or unreadable groups cause ambiguity, can be interpreted as supporting conventional wisdom even when, in fact, the message ought to indicate a change of enemy plan. Not all intelligence will mutually support a developing opinion of what the target is up to: judgments have to be made, and they are sometimes wrong. Cryptanalysts see only one form of this intelligence and their inclination is to believe that the products of their work are the most accurate indication of target plans and activities. In doing so they are inclined to forget that not all messages can be intercepted, and that radio is not the only means of transmitting orders and instructions. Frequently, especially at times of high activity, there are simply not the means to decrypt and translate all the intercepts, and important messages can be and are missed when the selection of those for decryption is made.

These issues were not a consideration when Eric Nave was decrypting and translating the cables to and from Japanese naval attaches. The context was clear and there was little ambiguity. Prepared for distribution in blue folders – hence their name 'blue jackets' or 'BJs' — the GCCS product, based on the interception of Japanese diplomatic traffic, went to intelligence staffs in the three Service ministries and to the Far Eastern Department of the Foreign Office. The latter, in particular, had few other sources of intelligence available and thus staffs tended to accept the BJs at face value as 'real' intelligence.[13] In today's parlance the BJs would be referred to as 'unevaluated' intelligence and possibly not acted upon without independent confirmation.

Nave explained what his decryptions revealed:

> In the office the daily intake of messages kept me busy and I made it a practice to translate and hand in every message that was readable. We learned of the various purchases the Naval Attachés made in Europe. At this time the Japanese Navy would buy one or two items of equipment in Europe and then take it back to Japan for research and experiment to produce a better article for themselves. This practice paid off, as we were to learn in the last war that their binoculars were better than the Zeiss pattern and their aeroplanes and torpedoes were often superior products. When the manufacturers became aware of the Japanese practice the price was adjusted and the buyers found it disproportionately more expensive to buy one or two items.

So, interesting and important as his work was, Eric found life at GCCS strenuous. His room, described by one commentator as 'small and shabby', contained a desk, two chairs and a secure cabinet. Eric himself noted that the agency had probably no more than forty staff, all of whom, including the director, worked on intercepts. He observed that 'I was to miss the camaraderie of ship life'. Living accommodation was the first priority on taking up his posting and Eric found it in Ravenscourt Park near Hammersmith in the west of London, in a suite of rooms he shared with two Australian civilians working in the city. Although quite close to his workplace, it did have the disadvantage of being close to a London Underground line, which at that part of the network runs above ground. The noise of trains every five minutes was something he grew accustomed to. The housekeeper, a widow, was a character who was wont to announce, 'I'll have to get married again; I can't stand these cold winter nights alone in bed', but she kept a good house and provided a bed and meals for Nave for two years. The flat was on the fourth floor, which held a certain challenge for Eric.

> I have a strong memory of a number of times I came home, changed in a hurry into dress clothes and left behind my flat keys. Returning late at night with the others asleep, I would take off my coat, shoes and hat, get out a window in the stair well, reach for the downpipe and edge my toes along a narrow projection until I reached my room. Years later I looked at the drop — four floors to a spiked iron fence, marvelling at my stupidity.

Having no friends in London, Eric sought to overcome his isolation from company of his own age. He joined forces with four or five other young men he had met through his naval contacts to form the Tuesday Lunchers, who met each week in a pub not far from the Admiralty. His former shipmates from *Hawkins* were also extremely kind in inviting Eric to their country homes for weekends, in the course of which he made a number of useful and congenial acquaintances. It was a very new experience for a young man from Adelaide to spend weekends in stately homes on lands that had been gifted to the families from Tudor times. He gained some insight into the rather feudal arrangements at work on these estates, as well as being introduced to the sports of the landed gentry.

> I count myself very fortunate to have been sent to a position in London at this time when England was still in the Victorian era. World Wars cause many dislocations and the 1914–18 War had resulted in the disappearance of many of the monarchies of Europe. There were also social changes and these were fast emerging, but to see the old order, enjoy and be part of it was a great experience. Observing the England of this time and mixing with people became very important to me socially and on the sporting field and made up for the complete lack of any company in my one-man office.

As in the China Fleet, Eric showed an interest in sport in London, both as a means of keeping fit and for the social value. One of his *Hawkins* shipmates introduced him to field hockey, which Eric had not previously played. His natural talent soon advanced him from the sixths to the fourths, and was to have other advantages. The director of GCCS was also a hockey player and arranged for Eric to join his club. During a tour of France at Easter 1929 with the club's thirds, Eric was called upon to fill a gap in the firsts, where he had the disconcerting experience of playing alongside English and Irish internationals. Regrettably, he did not record the result of the game or his role in it, but it must have been an exciting time for the young Australian.

A businessman friend made in Shanghai during his time in the China Fleet invited Eric to spend his first leave in Scotland. They toured the country in a temperamental Fiat open roadster, playing golf and catching salmon. Through another friend Eric was also introduced to soccer and attended FA Cup matches during the season. The same friend proposed Eric as a member of the Surrey Cricket Club, which enabled him to watch the Australian touring side play Surrey and the England team at The Oval. But to play cricket, Eric joined the West Kent Club, the oldest in England. Eric became a mid-order batsman and a spin bowler. As he commented, 'The office worker now had a satisfactory exercise programme'.

That first summer Eric attended his first Royal Levee, where Service officers and others presented themselves to their monarch. This was expected of him as he had been appointed to a position in

Admiralty. The occasion required full dress uniform of which, Eric observed, 'The cost was ruinous'. Fully set up in cocked hats, gold epaulettes, gold-laced frock coats and trousers, and carrying swords, Eric and his friend Phillip Mack set off down Pall Mall for St James's Palace, where the ceremony was to be held.

> It was one thing to parade oneself on the Quarterdeck of HM Ships or naval establishments but it was a new experience for me to walk along the street among those engaged in their normal daily tasks. It seemed this part of London belonged to the establishment for we excited little interest.

The two officers reached the palace and joined others attending the levee. In due course, Eric paid homage to King George V by approaching the throne, bowing and retiring. Amongst the royal entourage he noticed his *Hawkins* shipmate, Prince George, in his naval lieutenant's uniform and looking miserable. Eric recalled feeling sorry for the Prince, compelled to undertake this kind of official duty in which he had no interest and from which he gained little pleasure.

Eric Nave himself gained little pleasure from an unwelcome event of a different kind shortly afterwards, when he received a letter from the British Inland Revenue containing a demand for a substantial amount of income tax. Eric protested, until he discovered that the Admiralty's offer to the Australian Naval Board to meet all the expenses of having him in London had not been specific on an unpleasant fact. Had Eric been on exchange service with the RN he would have been paid by the RAN, and would therefore have paid no Australian tax on his earnings while overseas — the government was clearly more generous in those days! However, as Eric's salary and allowances were paid by the Admiralty, this left him liable to British tax, and the British Government was far less generous in taxation matters. 'The standard rate was much higher than any I had paid in Australia' but he had no option but to comply with the Inland Revenue demand.

Meanwhile, the cables between Tokyo and its embassies continued to flow onto Eric's desk. The British Government had announced that it would convene a second round of negotiations on naval disarmament in London from January to April 1930. This changed the nature of many of the attaches' cables, and also the importance which was attached by the British to the information contained in the GCCS BJs. In his role as a codebreaker Eric continued to chip away at the naval attache code, but his other role as interpreter put him under some pressure to ensure that translations of the notoriously difficult Japanese text would accurately reflect the sense and tone of the originals. In a later chapter this issue will be explored more fully, but Eric recorded:

> Building a codebook in a foreign language made a good knowledge of the foreign 'telegraphese' essential and this I had acquired during my work in *Hawkins*. However, reading the daily London messages meant they must be handed in, translated promptly to Intelligence since, should it take too long their value diminished greatly and inclined to become history. It was fortunate for me that I had available in the next room two eminent Japanese scholars, Hobart-Hampden and Sir Harold Parlett who were always willing to come to my assistance when needed.

As Eric observed, the small staff of GCCS was almost all actively engaged in the codebreaking and BJ production tasks, with an administrative cell comprising only a handful of personnel. 'It was probably the most valuable intelligence output per person ever seen', and neither GCCS later nor any of the other Allied agencies that were to emerge during World War II could match this performance. One should add, however, that the volume of traffic and the cryptographic complexities later organisations had to deal with were vastly greater. Commander Denniston also took the 'School' part of the agency's title seriously to ensure that his personnel remained abreast of developments in codes and cyphers.

> During one winter a programme of research and education was conducted. We were taken through the various forms of code and shown how to work each system, starting with Playfair [a famous digraphic transposition cipher] and progressing through more difficult systems. Although of no practical application to my work I found it quite interesting and a real change for me, having been sent to Japan to learn Japanese with no school and no teacher and then appointed to the China Station to organise interception of foreign

radio traffic with no prior training. Looking back, so much depended on the individual, whether he was conscientious and able.

Paymaster Lieutenant Eric Nave was clearly regarded by his masters as 'conscientious and able'. Although only a junior member of the GCCS staff, he was invited to join in the party celebrating the birthday of the head of GCCS, Admiral Sinclair — a considerable honour. More practical evidence of the esteem in which his efforts were held came in a letter from the Director of Naval Intelligence telling him that Their Lordships had decided that his work 'was deserving of higher rank'. With the concurrence of the Australian Naval Board he was promoted to the rank of lieutenant commander with the seniority of 1 September 1929, but with effect from the date of taking up his appointment at GCCS. This meant well over a year's back pay at the higher rate. 'I inquired as to whether this was but a way of paying my tax bill, but was told this was not so.'

So Eric had progressed from paymaster clerk (probationary) in March 1917 to paymaster lieutenant commander in twelve and a half years — a phenomenally rapid rise. To put that into some kind of context, the leading members of the first entry into the RAN College in 1913 took fourteen years to achieve that rank. It is true that Nave was operating in a special environment in which he did not compete for promotion with other officers of his age or specialisation. By the same token, there was thus no reason at all why he should not have remained a lieutenant. This accelerated promotion marked Eric Nave out as a significant talent, which was shortly to be recognised by the British in a very different way.

At the end of 1929 Eric took leave and joined a mixed party on a skiing holiday in Switzerland. During his absence, his place at GCCS was taken by an RN language officer, Lieutenant Commander Chichester, who had commenced his studies in Japan in 1921, the same year as Eric. However, as the Disarmament Conference approached the tide of messages between Tokyo and the Japanese naval attache in London increased to the point where it completely overwhelmed poor Chichester.

Chichester clearly could not cope with the necessary book building to make decipherment possible, and so I had to tackle this immense pile of messages. Many were so lengthy they were sent in several parts. I was able to discard those containing newspaper comments on the disarmament problem, sometimes supplemented by the Naval Attaché's talks with knowledgeable people in London. However, I came upon one prize, a long telegram in many parts explaining to the Naval Attaché and the Conference delegates why Japan was satisfied with the ratio of 3 against 5 for the United States, but must insist on maintaining that balance.

The IJN also revealed why this apparently inferior ratio was acceptable. In military terms, in any clash with the US Pacific Fleet the IJN would be operating on internal lines of support. Its enemy, on the other hand, must make a long voyage across the wide Pacific to get to grips with the Japanese, and during this transit it would be attacked by IJN submarines and harassed by aircraft from Japan's island bases — the 'unsinkable aircraft carriers'. On meeting the Japanese Combined Fleet the Americans would be short of fuel and supplies, battle weary and, if the submarine force had played its part, at depleted strength. What Nave had discovered was the essence of what was to become known by the Japanese as their theory of 'decisive battle'. On these principles the IJN designed and equipped its ships and aircraft, trained its men, developed its weapons and tactics, exercised constantly and ultimately deployed its forces. The discovery of this theory was a significant intelligence coup for the British: the strategic basis for a potential enemy's war fighting plans does not fall into one's hands every day. Had it been effectively applied in RN preparations for battle with the IJN, it might well have proved a decisive element in British favour.

> The message created quite a sensation as well it might and I received many congratulations. I might add that it took days of sustained research and help from my colleagues Hobart-Hampden and Parlett, and there were many new groups added to my new Japanese Naval Attaché's codebook as well.

A possible reason why this information was not applied to British preparations for a potential conflict with Japan is revealed in Eric's observations on the other deductions that could be made from the intelligence he had gained. 'Firstly,' he wrote, 'there was no indication of any plans for war with Britain.' The second deduction to be made was that the Japanese had clearly assessed that the greatest threat to their plans for territorial expansion in Asia would come from the Americans. Although they might wish to avoid war with the US, it was an eventuality for which they had commenced serious planning. Eric also noted that a certain newly promoted Rear Admiral Yamamoto Isoroku was a member of the Japanese delegation to the disarmament conference.

Well before this time the US Navy itself had begun to prepare its own set of war plans. Potential enemies included Britain (Plan BLUE) and Japan (Plan ORANGE). The isolationist policies pursued by successive US administrations before and after World War I had bred a belief in high strategic circles that America might be attacked from almost any quarter. Looked at from today's perspective this may seem an odd approach to strategic planning, but even in the midst of World War II important and influential American military and political figures kept a suspicious eye cocked on their British allies. As will be revealed, there was even reluctance in some US quarters to share intelligence on Japan with the British. In 1930, when the 'special relationship' between Britain and the USA had not yet been given expression in the fight against common foes in Europe and Asia, there was little or no contact at a strategic level between the two navies. There were certainly no avenues for the exchange of intelligence of the kind that Eric Nave had uncovered. Whether the American codebreakers had independently discovered this information will be considered in a later chapter.

The Admiralty was impressed by this most timely demonstration of the value of signals intelligence, and the significant contribution that Nave had personally made in the field did not escape their attention either. Their Lordships were keen to keep the services of Paymaster Lieutenant Commander Eric Nave, but they had their hand forced when the RAN inquired as to when it might expect the same officer back in Australia. He had been selected for a key position in his branch as secretary to the commander of the Australian Squadron. The RAN had also responded to a letter which Eric had sent asking

about the RAN policy for promotion of officers of the Paymaster
Branch to the rank of commander. The policy was for promotion
after eight years at the lower rank but 'for bright ones, Foley and
Nave', to be promoted after six years. In summary, Eric was about to
take up the most senior seagoing posting his branch could offer and
had a reasonable certainty of achieving the rank of commander by
1936. It seemed that his immersion in Intelligence had not damaged
his career options and that his future in the RAN would be bright.

Then the Admiralty weighed in with its own offer.

> The Admiralty reacted quickly. I was sent for and informed that the
> Intelligence Division was anxious to secure my services on a permanent basis
> as I was the only experienced officer in this new and important field. The
> Admiralty realised that this continued borrowing would seriously interfere
> with my career in the Royal Australian Navy and now wished to offer me a
> transfer to the Royal Navy

This was a dazzling and unprecedented offer. Close though the
two navies were, with the majority of specialist training for Australian
officers taking place in British schools, and with many RAN officers
serving in or alongside RN ships, there had never been a case where
the Admiralty asked for an Australian officer to become a part of
the RN. Their Lordships also sweetened the pot with the added
inducement of granting Eric the qualification for a full RN pension
on his retirement, backdated to the date that he had joined the RAN.
This was particularly attractive, as the RAN at that time did not have
a pension scheme; instead it had a system called 'deferred pay'. This
was only a proportion of an officer's salary paid as a lump sum on
the termination of his service, a much inferior option to a pension.
When Eric did transfer to the RN, his deferred pay for thirteen years
of service was only worth £739 Australian. Eric was also verbally
informed that his promotion at least to the rank of commander RN
was guaranteed.

If Eric had had some thinking to do about his career in 1928
on the way back to Australia from China, he was now faced with
a decision of far more fundamental importance. If accepted, the
Admiralty offer involved the cutting of many ties with friends and

family in Australia of whom, admittedly, he had seen very little over the past five years. His brilliant advance up the ranks of his branch in the RAN would come to an end, never to be resumed. His career in the RN would most likely be a succession of desks to which he would be more or less chained, often working alone and denied the camaraderie of mess life in a ship. It meant that he would have to make his way in an organisation in which he could only ever be a 'colonial' and a latecomer, no matter how successful his work, and to live in a country he did not know well, but for which he was forming a warm affection.

Nave sought the advice of senior paymaster officers in Australia House, the Australian High Commission establishment in London, and from senior British officers who had served with the RAN. These mentors were patient in talking through the issues with Eric but unanimous in their advice that he should accept the Admiralty offer. Still, it was one thing to offer advice but quite another to give up a whole way of life. It was a time when employees tended to stay with an organisation for the extent of their working life, and cutting the painter to take up a position in a different organisation not at all common. It cannot be said that Nave made the decision to transfer to the RN lightly or quickly, but in the end he accepted, with two conditions. He was to be allowed to return to Australia to settle his affairs there, and the verbal guarantee of promotion was to be put in writing. The Admiralty agreed to both conditions, and Eric's transfer to the RN was recorded in no less august fashion than being announced on the front page of the *London Gazette* of 2 December 1930.

This weighty decision taken, Eric made use of his friends and contacts to ensure that he learned more of Britain and British society. While never wanting to relinquish his identity as an Australian, and proud of it, he felt it important to become fully engaged in his adopted country's activities. He continued to participate in a range of sports — his cricket team attempted to persuade him to impersonate the famous Australian batsman Don Bradman to get past an obstreperous doorman at one nightclub — but he also set out

The London Gazette.

Published by Authority.

The Gazette is registered at the General Post Office for transmission by Inland Post as a newspaper. The postage rate to places within the United Kingdom, for each copy, is one penny for the first 6 ozs., and an additional half-penny for each subsequent 6 ozs. or part thereof. For places abroad the rate is a half-penny for every 2 ozs., except in the case of Canada, to which the Canadian Magazine Postage rate applies.

** *For Table of Contents, see last page.*

TUESDAY, 2 DECEMBER, 1930.

At the Court at *Buckingham Palace,* the 27th day of *November,* 1930.

PRESENT,

The KING's Most Excellent Majesty in Council.

WHEREAS there was this day read at the Board a Memorial from the Right Honourable the Lords Commissioners of the Admiralty, dated the 15th day of November, 1930 (C.W. 7745/30) in the words following, viz. :—

"Whereas by Section 3 of the Naval and Marine Pay and Pensions Act, 1865, it is enacted, *inter alia,* that all pay, pensions, or other allowances in the nature thereof payable in respect of services in Your Majesty's Naval or Marine Force to a person being or having been an Officer, Seaman or Marine therein, shall be paid in such manner and subject to such restrictions, conditions and provisions as are from time to time directed by Order in Council:

"And whereas, in view of his exceptional qualifications and experience in certain specialist duties, we consider that it would be of the greatest value to Your Majesty's Naval service to secure the continuous employment in the Royal Navy of Paymaster Lieutenant-Commander Theodore Eric Nave, Royal Australian Navy:

"We beg leave to recommend that Your Majesty may be graciously pleased, by Your Order in Council, to sanction his transfer to the list of Accountant Officers, R.N., on the following terms, with effect from the 30th August last:—

(*a*) The Officer to be included as a Paymaster Lieutenant-Commander with his existing seniority in the establishment of, and subject to the regulations affecting Accountant Officers, R.N.

(*b*) All claims by him to defered pay which may have accrued under R.A.N. Regulations to be relinquished and the amount thereof to be transferred to R.N. Funds as a contribution towards his R.N. retired pay, subject to which all previous service as an Officer, R.A.N., to count as though it had been service in the Royal Navy for purposes of retired pay, widow's pension, etc.

(*c*) To be allowed to proceed to Australia on transfer and on arrival there to be granted 91 days' leave. During passage to Australia and until the expiration of this leave to be granted full pay at R.N. rates.

"The Naval Board of the Commonwealth of Australia and the Lords Commissioners of Your Majesty's Treasury have signified their concurrence in these proposals."

His Majesty, having taken the said Memorial into consideration, was pleased, by and with the advice of His Privy Council, to approve of what is therein proposed.

And the Right Honourable the Lords Commissioners of the Admiralty are to give the necessary directions herein accordingly.

Colin Smith.

to learn more of the cultural heritage of Britain. The ancient roots and sources of many customs and traditions impressed him, as he described in this recollection of a visit to Oxford.

> The atmosphere of Oxford was serene and the architecture tended to draw one back into a past age. I always returned to London feeling better for the visit, feeling that I had absorbed something of the glories of those earlier years and age, of a period which had done so much to form and develop the British way of life and character.

However, his Australian past intruded now and again. On two occasions Eric was approached by officers of the IJN for assistance in their endeavours in Britain. One request was from Captain Yonemura of the cruiser *Asama* during its 1924 cruise to Australia, now a rear admiral and Hydrographer of the Navy. The other approach was from a Japanese officer who was compiling a Japanese/English dictionary of naval terminology. Both requests embarrassed Eric. He could not, of course, meet these Japanese in his office because of the work he was engaged upon, but he also felt a kind of obligation to respond. 'Most of all I felt a sense of guilt as I really liked these people and enjoyed their company and now I was virtually spying on them. So to avoid the predicament I did nothing.' This was a wise course of action to adopt. As Eric was to discover, the Japanese were remarkably successful in convincing Westerners who had lived and worked in Japan to help them to collect information, and these renewed relationships were frequently converted into obligations verging on committing espionage.

At his desk in GCCS Eric pursued the four-*kana* Naval Operational Code and also tackled a new nine-letter code dubbed '43', but only in the time left after dealing with the attache cables and preparing translations for the BJs. With only one codebreaker available for the task, progress on recovering the codebook values was not spectacular but steady, which is the usual pace of cryptanalytical success. Nevertheless, it was now possible for him to reconstruct many messages and his recoveries were passed via Nobby Clarke to the Admiralty and thence to the China Fleet flagship. Eric's comment was that 'There were hours of work involved in this task which can only be fully appreciated by one who has done similar research'.

There were now two more Japanese naval codes broken for which Eric could claim a significant part of the credit. In his eighteen months at GCCS he had greatly increased that organisation's ability to recover information from the naval attache's code, evidenced by the skill shown in decoding the cables in the period leading up to the London Naval Disarmament Conference in 1930. His work on the Naval Operations Code was also significant, especially when one realises that his research could be undertaken only in the gaps left by the higher priority task. These achievements had confirmed his mastery of the art of codebreaking and had led not only to his accelerated promotion, but also to the unprecedented offer made by the Admiralty to retain his skills within their intelligence organisation.

Then in June 1930 he was relieved at GCCS and made his return voyage to Australia to settle his affairs before returning to transfer to the RN.

4 China Station, 1931–33

As the cost of a round-the-world steamer and train ticket was the same whether one travelled via Canada or Suez, Eric elected to go home via Canada. Crossing the Atlantic took a few days only, but Eric managed to make friends with one attractive young lady, unfortunately already engaged to be married, who was seated at his table. After partnering her in a game of deck tennis and inviting her to sit in on a game of bridge, Eric was embarrassed to realise that he knew only her first name and could not introduce her to his partners. To solve his problem, he employed a standard tactic: 'By the way, how do you spell your name?' 'S-M-I-T-H' was her response, to the amusement of all but Eric. Miss Smith bore no grudge, however, and arranged to meet Eric in Montreal, where she took him on a tour of the countryside and held a dinner in his honour.

On reaching Vancouver to join the steamer *Arorangi* for the voyage across the Pacific, Eric encountered the Australian lawn bowls team. Being a man short for a friendly match with a Vancouver side, they pressed Eric into service. 'Consequently, I played my first game of bowls for Australia, it being also my last.' Eric surfed in Hawaii and enjoyed a prosperous day at the Auckland racetrack, but then he was home again.

At Navy Office in Melbourne, the Secretary of the Board explained that the RAN had never had an officer transfer to the Royal Navy before and that the only way this could be accomplished was for Eric to resign his RAN commission. It seems this had not been explained to him before, and his letter of resignation was written in Navy Office and is dated 16 October 1930, that is, after he had been awarded his RN commission. It seemed a technicality, but Eric's Australian commission was signed by the Governor-General of Australia, whose authority to grant such did not extend to Britain. Thus, the termination of the appointment of Theodore Eric Nave in the RAN was backdated to 29 August 1930, the day before he had transferred to the Royal Navy. Then it was home to Adelaide, six months earlier than his posting to the Admiralty had suggested, but with the possibly of another visit somewhat remote.

Eric makes scant mention of his farewell from his family when he sailed from Adelaide to take up his new life as an RN officer. In contrast to the previous departure, he knew exactly where he was going and the nature of his work, but he also knew that the opportunities of seeing his mother and father again were now much less. Eric's memoirs are filled with the details of the interesting and important people who voyaged with him but the passing mention only of his family suggests that the parting was not without pain. Eric maintained that his father, in particular, always supported his career decisions, but it must have cost Thomas Nave a great deal to farewell his eldest son in December 1930.

Back in the UK Eric was required to take a specialist Supply administration course in Portsmouth commencing in February 1931. To be promoted, Eric required a pass in this course although it had nothing to do with codebreaking, and he must have wondered why he was doing the study. He found the law subjects — international, criminal and courts-martial — of most interest, although finding fault with some of his instructors. The course does not appear to have been particularly onerous and Eric enjoyed his weekends in London or at the homes of friends and classmates. On its completion, he reported to the Admiralty where his head of branch congratulated him. 'You have come top of the course. Now we are appointing you to HMS *Kent*.'

> I was disappointed, I'd had enough of China, so I ventured 'Not China again, Sir'. 'Yes, it's a flagship, I've been keeping it for you.' So there it was,

have my stint of leave and prepare for overseas … I was disappointed to be sent back to China Station again where I found the climate did not entirely suit me. But there was no denying that as a Japanese interpreter it was the obvious place for me.

Before his departure for the Far East, Eric set off with naval friends for a holiday on the Italian Riviera. In the course of his leave he received two letters, one from the Admiralty advising that he was about to receive an invitation to a ball at Buckingham Palace and that he 'should make it convenient to return in time for the occasion'. The other was the command from the Palace that he should attend. Cutting short his leave, he and a friend drove back to London where he again donned the Royal Levee full dress uniform and presented himself, this time at Buckingham Palace. At the ball, he encountered Prince George again who, after supper, invited Nave to 'come and meet the family'. The King and Queen were engaged with the royal guests in whose honour the ball had been arranged but Eric did meet 'David' (later King Edward VIII), 'Bertie' (later King George VI) and 'Henry'. The two future kings of England seemed to share Prince George's disdain for formal occasions.

Throughout his memoirs, Eric Nave mentioned many women as friends, acquaintances or wives of same, but he was almost entirely discreet about any closer relationships he might have formed. In this he was simply displaying gentlemanly good taste but it is a dimension of his life that is somewhat frustrating for a biographer. It is interesting to note, however, that for this Royal Ball Eric was unable to take up the opportunity to be the escort of the daughter of an admiral serving in the Royal Household, because 'I was already committed'. This suggests a more serious relationship, but we are not told the lady's name.

The letters from his father paint a rather more illuminating picture of Eric's *amours*. At this point in his life, Eric was giving serious consideration to proposing marriage to a Miss Margery Berry. Not having Eric's own letters, it is not clear how the couple met, but Thomas was very much opposed to the union. His concerns were probably not much different to those any father might hold about a young lady whom he had never met as a match for his son, but Thomas displayed a curious preoccupation over whether Margery was well enough brought up and whether her dowry would be satisfactory. In any event Eric did not proceed with his proposal, although continuing to see the lady. The day before *Kent* sailed for the Far East the wardroom held a farewell party. 'To my joy and surprise Margery Berry came down. We had enjoyed some good times together and this was the last time I was to see her. Not long after I had a letter saying that she was to be married. It was obviously a farewell visit.'

Nave had joined HMS *Kent* at Chatham Dockyard in July 1931. The ship was a heavy cruiser built under the Washington Treaty limitation of 10,000 Tonnes. At 180 metres in length and 21 metres beam, she was bigger than *Hawkins* and, even when acting as a flagship, her complement was 75 fewer, so conditions on board were more comfortable. Completed in 1926, she mounted eight eight-inch guns in four turrets as her main armament and was equipped with numerous anti-aircraft and anti-submarine weapons as well. In short, *Kent* was a formidable command. If she had a drawback it was that her high freeboard, flush upper deck and three tall thin funnels made *Kent* and her class — which included the Australian ships *Australia* and *Canberra* — some of the most unattractive cruisers afloat.

Eric found that he was not to join the Commander-in-Chief China Fleet's staff as he had feared, but was to be the ship's deputy supply officer. His only previous experience of this type of duty had been his brief period as supply officer of the light cruiser HMAS *Brisbane* in 1923, so his first posting in the RN presented quite a challenge, but his instincts served him well. From his earliest days on board he set out to 'identify the individuals who held the power; a matter of great importance'. These were not so much the commissioned officers who had the formal responsibility but the senior chief petty officers and warrant officers who had established their own bases of authority within the ship and his department. He was also assigned to one of the divisions into which the 900 men of the ship's company had been carved up, for whose welfare and administration he would be

responsible. 'This rather pleased me as I would be involved with the
ship's company and not papers in a secret room'. This, as he was to
discover, was a premature statement.

Kent was under the command of Captain J.H. Godfrey, later to
become Director of Naval Intelligence at the Admiralty during the
first half of World War II, and hence one of Eric's 'customers'. Eric
liked his new captain and he found the other officers a pleasant lot
as well. As the future flagship of the China Fleet, the soundness of
these inter-relationships would be important in *Kent* while under the
constant gaze of the Fleet Commander during the two and a half
years of her commission in the Far East.

After stopping in Portsmouth to embark her spotter aircraft and its
spares, *Kent* sailed via Gibraltar, Malta, Suez, Aden and Colombo to
Hong Kong. While on passage, the captain received the startling news
that the British Government had decided to dock one shilling per day
from every serviceman's pay in order to make money available for social
welfare programs made essential by the continuing Depression.

> It was impossible to think of anything more unfair or more stupid. An
> Admiral would scarcely notice the loss of a shilling a day but for an Able
> Seaman on five shillings and tenpence it was a terrific slug. In our case it was
> particularly bad for the ship's married men who had made allotments to
> their wives whilst away for two years ... each man was obliged to retain for
> himself a basic sum for his own maintenance and thus the shortfall meant
> reducing the wife's allotment.

This ill-judged policy decision by the Government caused the
Invergordon Mutiny in the British Home Fleet, in which the many
men refused to obey the orders of their officers. The mutiny was
suppressed, the ringleaders jailed and junior sailors involved dispersed
amongst other ships of the Navy, but it caused huge embarrassment
and led to the curtailment of the careers of many officers of that fleet.
Captain Godfrey must have thanked his lucky stars that his ship was
sailing alone when the news was announced and that he had time
to put in place measures to deal with the inevitable disappointment
and disgruntlement. Godfrey's plan was simple; those for whom the
new pay scale would cause special hardship were given unofficial

employment on board so that they could earn their shilling a day back. 'I had no complaints in my division. The captain deserved the greatest credit for his thoughtful handling of this potentially dangerous situation.'

In Hong Kong, the ship worked up to battle proficiency and then prepared to embark their Commander-in-Chief, Vice Admiral Sir Howard Kelly, and to become his flagship. A taciturn man but not without a sense of humour, Kelly was well regarded by his officers and men as decisive. He showed this quality almost immediately by replacing Captain Godfrey as flag captain with an officer he already knew, and appointing a Commodore Geoffrey Layton to be his Chief of Staff. Layton was also soon to be another 'customer' of Eric Nave, this time in his role as Commander-in-Chief Eastern Fleet in 1940.

As Admiral Kelly settled on board his new flagship, he would have been very well aware that British fortunes in the Far East were at a critical juncture. There were two principal causes of this. First, the continuing financial crisis in Britain together with the effects of the worldwide Depression had devalued the power of British military and commercial interests, especially in China. In China the previous melange of competing warlord fiefdoms had largely been replaced by powerful national movements, on one side the Guomindang or Nationalists, and on the other the Chinese Communist Party. Both claimed to be the government of China, and neither accepted the presence of foreign concessions on Chinese soil willingly. However, for the present they were more intent on fighting each other, so British interests were more or less safe from Chinese attack.

The second reason was the expansionist policies of Japan. Since its naval victory in 1896, and its defeat of the Russians in 1905, Japan had steadily encroached on her neighbours' territory on the Asian mainland. She had occupied the island of Taiwan in 1895, claimed the Liaoning Peninsula in north China in 1896, been forced out the following year but had regained it in 1905. In 1910, after tussles with the Russians, Japan had annexed the Korean Peninsula. 1914 had seen the Japanese seizure of the German-held Pacific islands north of the Equator, an occupation confirmed by mandate at the Versailles Peace

Conference. Her Kwantung Army had since carried out low-level operations in the disputed territory in the southern part of Manchuria between China and Korea, forming a series of shifting relationships with the foremost warlord, Zhang Solin. By 1928, Zhang had become superfluous to the Kwantung Army's requirements; he was assassinated and a staged attack on Japanese Army facilities became the excuse for an all-out assault on Manchuria. In September 1931 the Kwantung Army established the puppet regime of Manchukuo under the reign of Aisin Gioru Pu Yi — the 'Last Emperor'.

Some analysts have postulated that in the 1920s, with Germany no longer a naval threat, the Admiralty had worked hard to invent an aggressive Japan to support its efforts to retain a sizable fleet in the Far East. There is a deal of truth in this claim but, in the end, the Admiralty strategy did not succeed in protecting the RN from severe budgetary cuts from 1929 onwards.[1] By the 1930s, however, there was no need to invent any Japanese threat to British interests, as this was transparent to all. The role of the China Fleet and its composition had changed accordingly. From a few cruisers and destroyers showing the flag and protecting British lives and property, which Eric Nave was involved in during his time in *Hawkins*, the fleet had grown to nearly one hundred vessels and was expected to be in readiness for operations. With its heavy and light cruisers, destroyers and submarines and shoals of smaller vessels for riverine operations, the China Fleet was still no match for any force the Imperial Japanese Navy might wish to deploy. However, it did display British determination to defend British interests and the fleet was a powerful medium for moderation in Japanese stratagems.

The great naval base that was intended to support the British exercise of military power in the Far East and to deter any Japanese designs on extending their empire into South-East Asia – Singapore – was far from ready. Approved in principle by the British Cabinet in June 1921 with the view to having the base operational by 1925, work commenced slowly but in 1924 it had been stopped and then resumed. In 1926 a sub-committee of the Committee of Imperial Defence recommended that work on the main defences of the base should be postponed and in 1928 the Cabinet agreed that work should proceed slowly as a consequence of the economic difficulties in which the British Government found itself. In fact, work was stopped again in 1929.[2] Until it was completed, British battleships could not sensibly be deployed to the China Station as there were insufficient support facilities for them in Hong Kong, and no dock large enough to accommodate them. The display of British naval power represented by the China Fleet was more bluff than substance. If Admiral Kelly realised this he gave no hint of his uncomfortable dilemma to his staff, and certainly not to the officers of his flagship.

Having their admiral embarked was a mixed blessing for the men of the flagship. They were involved in a great deal more ceremonial than other ships and had to maintain extremely high standards of cleanliness and appearance. Where other ships of the fleet would be given thirty-six hours' notice of a readiness inspection by the admiral, for his flagship that was reduced to twenty-four. As the admiral's staff did not include a supply officer it was left to Eric Nave to meet the admiral's requests for services, such as laundry, provisions and entertainment. The admiral liked to give dinner parties for important guests, culminating in a film show. It was up to Eric to have ready a selection of movies for this purpose, which worked to the advantage of the ship's company because they all had to be the most recent releases. However, one cannot please admirals all the time. After one dinner party Eric was astounded to be informed, with a grin, by Admiral Kelly that he had seen that night's film 'at my prep school!'

There was one other personal drawback for Eric Nave in being honoured with the admiral's presence on board, and this was to create some difficulties later in the commission. The admiral enjoyed playing bridge when the ship was at sea and, soon after the staff had joined *Kent*, Eric was invited to play one evening as the admiral's partner. 'So for the next two years I had a nightly commitment for Bridge at sea and we remained partners. He must have been satisfied, for we never cut for partners again.' This commitment virtually ruled out any relaxation time for Nave and became a burden when he found himself engaged, once again, in codebreaking.

As for life on the China Station, it was 'more of the same'. As Eric remarked, 'Shanghai was always an interesting place to visit; being an international city all forms of entertainment, exercise and vice flourished'. Sailors are rarely out of place in that sort of environment and Eric found himself at one point experiencing a run on British currency postal notes, which were being taken ashore and exchanged at a very profitable rate of exchange into the local currency. The flagship was also used by the unofficial Chinese embarked as messmen, cooks, laundrymen, tailors and bootmakers as their mode of smuggling copper and silver coins between Hong Kong and Shanghai for a similar purpose. *Kent* was fortunate; the Commodore Hong Kong was embarrassed to find that he had been personally involved in a racket smuggling opium through the Naval dockyard, where his personal rickshaw was used to transfer the drugs landed from sampans through the dockyard gates. This vehicle was never checked by security. Instead the guards always opened the gates, stood to attention and saluted smartly as the commodore was whisked by — with the opium secreted by his rickshaw man under the seat.

Corelli Barnett, characteristically and somewhat caustically, portrayed life in the China Fleet as one of pure pleasure, a round of sports, shore excursions and parties, with the most important event of the naval calendar the Fleet Regatta. The economic disparity between the British and the Chinese meant that it was possible to employ unofficial Chinese labour to perform the menial tasks on board ship, something even the lower deck resorted to.[3] All these observations were true to a point but they screened a rather more active fleet than Barnett depicts, especially on the basis of intelligence on IJN capabilities and activities that Eric was helping to provide. Admiral Kelly was no fool and, as events were to prove, he had the measure of the IJN as well.

Nave played tennis and hockey for *Kent* and was also sought out as a partner for deck tennis with the admiral, who regarded exercise as important and his example spread. The retreat to Wei Hai Wei in summer was always the occasion for a highly competitive sports program between ships of the fleet. One wonders what the ghosts of Admiral Ding, Commander of the Chinese North Sea Fleet and loser to the Japanese in 1895, and his staff thought of the activities of these new barbarians.

Nave's despatch to the China Fleet, although not at first as a direct replacement for Harry Shaw, nevertheless saw Shaw taking up duties in the Japanese Naval section of GCCS. The shortage of Japanese linguists continued to bedevil the Director of Naval Intelligence and Shaw's place in the China Fleet could not immediately be filled. In due course, a Japanese interpreter joined *Kent* for signals intelligence duties. He was Lieutenant Guy Windeyer, another Australian and son of a famous Sydney barrister. Windeyer had joined the RN and had completed his language training in 1928: his posting to the China Fleet was to test his cryptanalytic capabilities.

> Guy was a good rugger player, and did his best to cope with the work I had founded, but he was clearly not cut out for it. One day the Fleet Intelligence Officer came to my cabin with some sheets of paper and asked what they were. The list contained the callsigns of all the battleships, heavy cruisers and other Japanese naval vessels. They had been picked up in the sea, having been thrown into the sea by Guy's marine steward with the contents of his wastepaper basket.

This was a particularly serious security lapse. The information was Top Secret, and had the Japanese come to know that the British had succeeded in penetrating their callsign system's security it could have caused a far-reaching change of codes and ciphers. Nor was this a remote possibility. The ship was anchored off Wei Hai Wei and the base employed a Japanese barber, who might easily have found the documents washed ashore or landed in fishing nets on the island. By coincidence, there was another Japanese barber employed at the dockyard in Hong Kong. British officers preferred to patronise these gentlemen because their premises were cleaner than those operated by Chinese barbers. The deduction could only be that Japanese Naval intelligence had created good cover for two of their agents in important places and that great care had to be exercised in limiting their access to official or classified information by any means.[4]

By this stage, for reasons unknown, the IJN had introduced a new code to replace the Naval Operation Code that Eric had worked on at GCCS. US Navy cryptanalysts called this the 'Blue' code and the codebook contained over 85,000 values. It had an extra level of complexity because it was a 'superencrypted' by the addition of a string of randomly generated figures taken from an additive book or additive table current at the time. When a coder had completed the transformation of the plain-language message into code groups, he then selected a line and column in the additive book at which he chose to begin and then added the code groups to the figures that followed, using Fibonacci arithmetic, in which tens are not carried to the next column.

To illustrate this process, take the message 'Sail for Nagasaki at economical speed'. The coder opens the codebook and selects appropriate groups, with the resultant signal 15263 (sail) 78772 (for) 67406 (Nagasaki) 51609 (at economical speed). Then, selecting at random the twenty-sixth row and the tenth column of the third page in the additive table book, and indicating this in the message with the group '32610', he begins the additive process by writing the additive numerals below the coded groups thus:

Groups	15263	78772	67406	51609	
Additive	29875	74207	69142	30869	
Transmitted	34038	42979	26548	81488	32610

The transmitted values bear no relation to the groups in the codebook and each time a group is used its transmitted value will be altered through use of the additive table. At the receiving end, the coder finds the correct start point in the additive book and strips the additive values from the groups by Fibonacci subtraction to reveal their true values.

Received	34038	42979	26548	81488	32610
Additive	29875	74207	69142	51609	
Groups	15263	78772	67406	51609	

As a cryptographic stratagem this was not new, but it did severely complicate the task of cryptanalysts. To attack the additive tables a codebreaker needed patience, a copious supply of messages in the new code, and some luck. He had to look for repetitions or correlations between messages. If the context made the contents of the message reasonably obvious, then it was a matter of comparing the transmitted groups with those in similar messages. The process was one which lent itself to mechanical solution and in time the use of calculating machines and punched card readers greatly simplified and accelerated the stripping process.[5] Eric Nave and Guy Windeyer had pads of paper and pencils to do their work, and it was tedious. Nevertheless, breaks began to come and progress was made, but this was done in the time that Nave had to spare from his other duties.

> This proved to be a great strain and I would have been wise to avoid it as I found out later. However, when I commenced to get good results from starting to build up the new Japanese Naval Code Book there was no turning back, but I was fed up when he [Windeyer] went ashore, leaving me to struggle with his job.

The situation worsened when Windeyer was transferred to another ship in the fleet for ship duties and Nave was instructed to take over his codebreaking task.[6]

> However, I still had my own divisional ship duties and other semi-official jobs, Cinema Officer and Mess Secretary, which I steadily found very onerous, and my evening Bridge sessions as the Admiral's partner I found no longer enjoyable but very trying. In truth I had far too much to do in this humid climate. I was always in a heavy sweat playing the many ship and Navy games and it started to take its toll. We knew nothing of salt tablets at this time which is probably what I needed together with early relief from my ship duties.

These were probably the first symptoms of a health problem that was to have a major impact on the course of Eric's career in codebreaking. Those who have experienced a summer in eastern China will appreciate how enervating conditions can be.

One of the perquisites to set against the disadvantages of flagship life was that *Kent* made all the desirable trips around the China Station. The ship visited Kobe in Japan, where Eric led a small party of officers on a hike though the countryside with an overnight stay in a Japanese inn. A visit to the former German colony, Qingdao, where the centre of the city had, incongruously, been constructed as a Germanic town, he found very interesting. This had been the base from which Admiral von Spee's squadron set out in World War I, deterred from the more lucrative commerce-raiding westerly passage to home waters by the presence of the Australian Squadron. *Kent* also visited Qinghuangdao, the port where the Great Wall meets the sea. This enabled some personnel to spend three days in the ancient former capital Beijing — Nanjing having that honour at the time. Eric's sightseeing included the former British Embassy, where he found the bullet-pocked outer wall a sobering reminder of the Boxer Rebellion of 1899–1900.

Throughout all these activities and distractions, Eric's codebreaking continued to yield benefits. He decoded a message instructing the Kwantung Army in Manchuria that its operations were not to extend south of the Great Wall. The Kwantung Army had shown itself to be of an independent mind from its political masters in Tokyo in deciding that it would occupy Manchuria, and the order was a belated attempt to bring this force under Japanese Government control. An information copy of the order had been sent to the Japanese naval commander for China in the naval code and this was an important piece of strategic intelligence. Incidentally, that it could be decoded at all gives a good indication of the progress that had been made on breaking the new code, both in GCCS and in *Kent*. Eric handed the information to the Fleet Intelligence Officer and it was not long before he was summoned to see the Chief of Staff, Commodore Layton. The admiral had read Eric's decode and had ordered it signalled to the Admiralty, War Office and Foreign Office. The commodore asked Nave:

> 'He can't send this off by W/T can he?' 'No sir' from me. 'Will you go and tell him so,' I was instructed. Not exactly an attractive assignment for a Lieutenant Commander to tell an officer of full Admiral's rank that we can't send a message he had just initiated. When I knocked at his day cabin door I had a friendly 'Come in Nave'. I showed his signal signed for despatch, his face coloured a bit, and when I said 'I think sir …' 'And who asked you to think!' A bit shaken I replied 'I thought you expected me to sir'. So I

suggested that the message must go by landline as it could be disastrous for this to be intercepted and decoded by the Japanese. He readily agreed, much to my relief. I did think the Commodore might have done this himself, but I suppose he reckoned it was my job and I could best explain why his signal could not be sent as ordered.

It is worth noting that the attack on Manchuria by the Japanese provoked a massive increase in the normal levels of Japanese military radio traffic. This created huge opportunities for intercept stations and codebreakers, and the haul of red signal forms for local handling or despatch to GCCS provided much grist for the cryptanalytic mill. The British Army had established an intercept station in Shanghai and this considerably boosted the intercept take from Japanese operations.[7]

Intercepts also revealed a little more about the depth of Japanese espionage in China. Eric decoded a message informing the Japanese naval commander that a person named 'Shinkawa' had arrived in Shanghai. On reporting this to GCCS, who suspected this to be the cover name for an Englishman who had agreed to spy for the Japanese, he was instructed that all further intercepts that mentioned this individual were to be sent directly to the Director of Naval Intelligence. Eric's discovery did alert the Shanghai authorities and allowed them to keep Shinkawa under surveillance.

During a visit by the flagship to the Netherlands East Indies in January 1932, where Eric resumed his acquaintance with the family of the ambassador he had met during language studies in Japan, the news arrived of a Japanese military attack on Chinese positions in and around Shanghai. The Japanese were apparently responding to provocations by the Chinese who, incensed at the Kwantung Army's actions in Manchuria, had undertaken a campaign of boycotts of Japanese goods, and attacks on Japanese business and individuals around the International Settlement in Shanghai. The operation was a classic case of using a sledgehammer to crack a nut, as the IJN had committed a marine amphibious force backed up with air support from two aircraft carriers. *Kent* steamed at maximum speed back to Shanghai via Manila Bay, where she fuelled. The vibration in the ship was so severe it was difficult, or even impossible, to write other than with a constantly shaky hand.' Nave was still awaiting a replacement to take over his ship duties, and he bore the brunt of the interpreting task during the intense diplomatic activities that were to occur over the next few days.

Admiral Kelly was indisputably the Senior Naval Officer present in Shanghai and naval protocol required the commanders of all navies represented there to come to his flagship to pay their respects. On the arrival of *Kent*, the IJN rear admiral in command of the forces attacking Shanghai instead sent a more junior officer to tender his apologies as he was very busy at the moment — which was patently true. Admiral Kelly, however, was having none of that. Nave, acting as interpreter, was instructed: 'Tell this officer that I have important matters to discuss with the Japanese admiral and I wish to see him now'. Surprisingly, this imperious command was obeyed, and the Japanese commander, Rear Admiral Horie Teikichi, came on board *Kent* at around 1 am the following morning. The 'important matters' were the cessation of hostilities, and Admiral Kelly convened a conference later that day of all senior foreign officers on board his flagship.

> The Japanese were told that their military operation so close to an International Settlement constituted a serious threat to life and property. They argued that their only object was to protect life and property, whereupon they were informed that if the Chinese withdrew beyond the limits of the area there would be no need for their [Japanese] presence, to which they had to agree. The Commander-in-Chief then extracted an undertaking that when the Chinese withdrew beyond a specified kilometre limit they would withdraw their troops from the Shanghai area. This was a significant achievement.

Although the fighting continued for several days, the Chinese eventually withdrew their forces the required distance from the International Settlement. Nave was then despatched to the Japanese flagship to remind Admiral Horie of his commitment to withdraw his own forces, and he was instructed to obtain a copy of the message ordering the Japanese withdrawal.

> I was not to return without it. After some delay I was given a carbon copy of

the order on flimsy rice paper. I returned in triumph and handed the message to the Commander-in-Chief who said, as he was at lunch, 'Translate it'. Back I went to my cabin and grappled with this indistinct piece of paper, finding translation difficult, but I handed my effort in and commenced a late, cold lunch. Having only started, the Admiral's marine orderly summoned me back again. 'Nave, put this into understandable English.' The fact is I was beginning to feel the strain of doing two jobs.

The incident demonstrated the moral force of the British Commander-in-Chief at a time when he was not in a position to extract an agreement of this kind from the IJN commander through the threat of superior military power. It should be borne in mind also that Admiral Horie was not a member of the 'war' school of naval officers and was, in fact, criticised by his peers for 'lacking aggression' in his handling of the incident.[8] However, the whole episode showed that Japan did have aggressive designs against China proper, and that it was prepared to use its armed forces to pursue its goals, regardless of any threat posed to other nations. Three other elements emerged for British intelligence from the incident. There had been no warning of the Japanese attack from signals intelligence or other sources. The IJN had manoeuvred its fleet into position and, as well as the marines, had landed three divisions of the Japanese Army without any apparent disruption to normal activity patterns that would have alerted analysts. This revealed a Japanese competence in amphibious landing operations hitherto unsuspected, as well as the ability to enforce a high degree of security over its military operations in peacetime. These were disturbing revelations and led to a shake-up in British intelligence arrangements for the Far East in which Eric Nave would be involved.

The second element of intelligence was to prove fatal to British preparations for a potential war against Japan in South-East Asia. The fact was that the Japanese forces had not performed well against the supposedly inferior Chinese. The attempt by the IJN fleet to reduce the Chinese defences at the mouth of the Woosung River leading to Shanghai had been unsuccessful. The Chinese Nineteenth Route Army defending Shanghai had proved very adept in blunting and containing Japanese attacks. They had not given up their positions because of Japanese military pressure, but as a requirement of the ceasefire brokered by Admiral Kelly. This was noted by British observers, including Captain Godfrey, and it influenced their future views on Japanese military prowess. They tended to deny, or at least to downplay, evidence that the Japanese too had learned from Shanghai and taken remedial action.[9]

The third element was that the speed with which these events had taken place completely undermined long-held strategic theories, which had suggested that a build-up to any hostilities would be slow. This would leave time for Britain to assemble in the Far East the material support, like food, ammunition, fuel and spares that it would require for a war. The suddenness of the Japanese assault on Shanghai showed that these theories were of questionable relevance, and one result was the development of the concept of a 'period before relief', during which the forces and resources on hand should be prepared to resist any Japanese aggression. [10]

There was no let-up in Japanese radio traffic now that the Shanghai Incident, as this incursion was called, had been concluded, and Eric was kept very busy. Still without a relief for his deputy supply officer duties, the pace was beginning to tell on him. One afternoon the admiral's flag lieutenant arrived in Eric's cabin with the news that he was expected to join the Admiral for a bridge party ashore the same evening. Much to the surprise of all, and the disappointment of the admiral, he declined. 'This shook him a bit, but I just felt I could not cope with it.'

Work on the new IJN code was Eric's principal task and one day he had a suspected value confirmed in the most satisfying way.

> I now decoded a message advising the Japanese Admiral that a convoy would be arriving off the Bell Buoy [at the mouth of the Yangtse River] at 0800. I gave this to the Fleet Intelligence Officer saying that I could not be certain of the group for 'convoy', it was this new book. Next morning the convoy arrived on time.

Admiral Kelly's term as Commander-in-Chief was now coming to an end and the flagship sailed to Hong Kong where the transfer to his successor, Vice Admiral Sir Frederick Dreyer, was to take place. There was news for Lieutenant Commander Nave too. He was able to greet his long-awaited relief in *Kent*, but the Admiralty had decided that at the end of his two years he would be detached from the flagship for a three-month task to investigate radio traffic from the Japanese Mandated Islands of the Pacific. He was to transfer to the submarine depot ship HMS *Medway* for this task, taking with him only one petty officer telegraphist experienced in intercepting *kana*. It was a bitter disappointment for Eric.

It was with some regret that the fleet farewelled Admiral Kelly, whose reputation over the handling of the Shanghai Incident had increased the esteem in which he was held. Nave refers to him as 'a truly great Admiral, dignified at all times, a diplomat, a strong character and a great leader'. However, their new Commander-in-Chief was a man to be respected as well. The reason Admiral Dreyer is most remembered today is that he was the first to articulate the results of his studies of Japanese military and political developments, which led him to accurately predict the nature of the coming war and how the Japanese would fight it. His views were not taken as seriously as they should have been, the conventional wisdom in the West holding that the Japanese had neither the means nor the will to undertake a campaign of such breathtaking scope and precision. Dreyer's was not quite a voice crying in the wilderness, but one that was heard but not believed. Nave described one of the early efforts by Admiral Dryer to expound his views, shortly after taking up his position:

> This dynamic Admiral now summoned a conference in Shanghai which turned out to be one of the most important I ever attended. It also revealed the farsighted, penetrating nature of his mind. The whole emphasis was on Far Eastern Intelligence and the future intentions of Japan. The key speaker was the head of the Secret Service in the Far East, Mr B … The Admiral questioned him closely on the build up of Japanese oil fuel reserves … What was the purpose of these massive oil reserves, were they the amount needed for an intensified campaign in China for several further years? Analysis revealed clearly that they would only be justified by a war against a major world power lasting quite some years!
>
> The conclusion he reached, a brilliant deduction in 1933, was that

war with the United States and probably Britain was inevitable and she was preparing for it, a logical and sobering thought. Admiral Dreyer then instructed me, 'Now when you get to London you will tell Their Lordships what we are thinking here.'

Before leaving *Kent* to take up his work on the Japanese mandates traffic, Eric was summoned to the admiral's presence and sat down while Dreyer read to him 'The letter I am sending to the Admiralty about you. It was handed to me by Admiral Kelly and I would say I am in complete agreement.' The admiral's report on Eric Nave was extremely flattering and showed how his work had been appreciated by Kelly, and was being appreciated by Admiral Dreyer. It was a fine end to a good commission in which Eric had taken over the work of the codebreaker and made significant inroads into the new IJN Operational Code, superencrypted though it had become. His role during the Shanghai Incident was also not neglected.

However, the final three months of Nave's time in the China Fleet were to be anti-climatic. There were suspicions by most Western powers with an interest in the Pacific that Japan was fortifying the island possessions it had seized from Germany. If true, this would not only be in breach of the conditions on which she was given the League of Nations Mandate over the islands and the terms of the Washington and London Naval Disarmament Treaties, but would also represent a serious strategic threat and an escalation in war preparations. The surmise was that a study of radio traffic emanating from the islands would reveal developing military capabilities. The fact that the Japanese did little to fortify their island possessions until very late in the piece meant that Eric's mandates task was fruitless. His search was part of a program initiated by the Admiralty in conjunction with GCCS to improve the collection of Japanese traffic in the Far East, which commenced in June 1933. While the mandates yielded nothing of interest, there was a greater volume of consular traffic intercepted as well as Japanese Army traffic, mainly from Manchuria.[11] The overall success of this operation was to lead to the establishment of British intercept and cryptanalytical facilities in Hong Kong, a tradition which, apart from the period of Japanese occupation 1941–45, continued up until the return of the colony to China in 1997.

Disappointed at not being returned to London at the end of his *Kent* time, Eric was also frustrated by the lack of any meaningful intercepts from the mandates. 'The three months of work was a complete waste of time and I hadn't even the stimulus of some success for encouragement. Any military activity in those islands was clearly not carried on service W/T channels.' To put a further dismal cap on this episode of his career, Eric fell ill, and his treatment involving 'a strong tonic with arsenic'. It was time for him to leave. There was, however, one significant consolation: he was permitted to make his own way back to the UK and took the opportunity to book his passage via Adelaide. This provided an unexpected and very welcome respite, and chance to see his family.

5 The Drift to War, 1933–37

Writing of his leave in Australia after HMS *Kent*, Eric said: 'Since my loan to the RN in 1925 my life had all been away from Australia so the visit was purely to keep in touch with the family. My leave in Adelaide was both enjoyable and physically beneficial.'

Enjoyable though his reunion with his family was, and how much his health benefited from the change of climate, there were plenty of reminders for Eric that his decision to transfer to the RN had been a significant influence on his whole career and lifestyle. He discovered that all of his friends in Australia were now married, leaving him the odd man out, and he mused on his 'long nautical taxi ride' back to Southampton on the changes in his life since 1925. He reflected on the severing of the majority of his ties with Australia and on the role that superior authority had played in his choices. 'Personal choice no longer exists, such as is available to the civilian.' These were not happy thoughts and it appears that he was a very lonely man at this point in his life.

It's worth making the point here that Eric, a friendly man who loved to tell stories, was trapped in a web not of his own making when it came to talking about his work. It was highly classified and accessible only to a select few. Innocuous questions about his line of business from friends and acquaintances outside these ranks might have caused acute embarrassment to him when he was obliged to provide evasive answers. He could not even confide in his family. It should come as no surprise if Eric Nave the codebreaker appears to readers to be stand-offish and even elitist. It was only after his retirement, with his codebreaking and security work behind him, that he could indulge his passion for wholehearted contact with others, and his friends of that period speak of the warm human being who, for most of his working life, was prevented from engaging in normal social contact.

However, Eric's duty in the RN called and he reported back to GCCS in October 1933 to find that some changes had been made. As explained in Chapter 4, the Shanghai Incident in which Nave had played his part had caused considerable concern in British intelligence circles. Various remedial measures were proposed, including the establishment of more intercept stations in the Far East and an increase in the numbers of Japanese linguists. Essentially for financial reasons, neither of these proposals could be acted upon immediately, but steps were taken to improve the RN's collection capability on the Japanese fleet. In 1934, a British cruiser shadowed the IJN Combined Fleet during its manoeuvres off the Shandong Peninsula, with impressive intercept results.[1] In addition, efforts were made by GCCS to increase its take from the diplomatic cables it was receiving.

Eric's friend and linguist colleague, Harry Shaw, had been sent to the China Fleet to replace Eric, and in his former office in London Eric found Lieutenant Commander Dick Thatcher, also a paymaster, who had completed his language course in Japan in 1932 and had been posted to the Naval Section to assist Nave. Help had arrived at last. But this was not to last for long. In due course, Thatcher too was sent to the Far East.

> There had been quite a change in the Naval Attaché code with a monthly key change. The system had been broken and he was asked to work out the changes each month. He had replied 'We will do it when Nave arrives'. I had a talk with Hugh Foss [a civilian member of the Naval Section], who had done the research and was able to solve the system. I found that the break came from the letters F, V and J; letters not used in Japanese. 'F' is used in 'FU' but this is really the romanising of 'HU'. The letters had special uses such as a final 'N', long vowels etc.

ak ew ノ類	ew	fo	ge	gu	hy	if	in
ak	相成	内話	的薄	ツイデ	チェック スロヴァキア	ゼン	二十日
av	立場	相成タ(シ)	内紛	轉電	積リ	本年	獨逸
ba	ツガ	立至(ル)	相成候我等	内密	本月	ツウ	ゼンケン
ce	在…大使	我方	直ニ	明カ	乍ラ	テツ	通知
di	二月	在…代理大使	本日	タダシ	アン	十九日	會談
eg	來訪	本國政府	在…公使	カレ	對案	豫メ	ナイ
em	本國	ラン	然ルベ(ク)在…代理公使		會議	態度	アラヴ(ル)
ew	ベク	豫テ	レイ	會計	在…總領事	ヤク	タキ
fo	ガン	ベン	者(フ)	レン	十八日	在…總領事代理(事務代理)	ハツ
ge	承認	難(ク)	四月	カレ	聯合	ヘイ	在…領事
gu	會見	三月	ガワ	ベンボウ	發表	聯盟	然ルニ
hy	メン	極(メ)	主張	ゲキ	ベシ	カタ	八月
if	希臘	面談	ヘン	十七日	ゲン	ベツ	電信
in	移民	平和	面會	心得	クン	傳達	別定(第…號)
ix	返電	イン	佛國	訓電	電送	主義	原因
mu	總理大臣	ノ如(ク)	否ヤ	ドク	見計(ヒ)	七月	シュク
no	例ヘバ	訓示	十六日	一方	ジツ	見込	試(ミ)
pi	訓令	同盟	總領事	情報	一般	英國	ミン
od	エイ	不取敢	條件	總督	ノミ	一般的	假令
oy	申添(フ)	條項	取扱(ヒ)	五月	ツツ	述ベ	委細
re	, comma	十五日	専ラ	取計(ヒ)	波蘭	國民	ニ依ル
sa	故	一　横線	波斯	モシ	國際	西比利亞	ステートメント
uc	從來	行懸	…點線	コン	六月	取極(メ)	露國
uz	何分	ヅン	コンミット	/ 斜線	太平洋	若ハ	取消(シ)
wu	十四日	困難	ゼンゴ	行懸(ミ)	パーセント	増加	求(ノ)
xy	根本	前段	ナン	ゾウ	ユウ	?疑問點	歐米

Japanese Diplomatic Codebook

This page from a Japanese diplomatic codebook of the early 1930s illustrates the use of *kanji*, *katakana*, *romaji*, and even English words in its construction, The code maker has distributed the vocabulary across the values to impede the codebreaker so that, for example, neither months nor days of the month are arranged sequentially, There are no prepositions on this page except for 'at' contained within a phrase, so example sentence construction is difficult, However, the phrase 'American position described at British Embassy 16 June this year' might be coded as *xyin aveb oyif ceew piif noge uehy avif.*

To an experienced codebreaker, the new features in the groups must have been particularly obvious so, again, the peculiarities of the Japanese language came to the aid of the cryptanalysts. As will be seen from the illustration, the Japanese 'borrowed' even punctuation marks from English.

High level concern about the efficiency of British intelligence activities against Japan continued. The evident aggressive territorial designs of the Japanese gave the Director of Naval Intelligence, Admiral Dickens, a great deal of concern. In a minute on the subject in October 1933 he said:

> The situation in the Far East has completely changed and has left our intelligence arrangements high and dry. Unless we can have a good deal of Japanese wireless [intercepts] our Intelligence will be quite inadequate, and we may find ourselves critically at fault.[2]

This was a clear endorsement of the importance to British intelligence of the work on the Japanese codes by Eric Nave and his colleagues. However, it was felt that the current rate of effort, adequate to cope with the level of activity when the Japanese were at peace, was insufficient while the situation seemed to be lurching ever closer to war. As the main agency operating in the Far East, it was the Admiralty that took the lead in addressing the problem. As the DNI wrote in 1934:

> The more I see of the cryptographic side of naval intelligence the more I recognise its vital importance and, further, that the nucleus we have at present is far too weak on which to build up rapidly an organisation such as we would require in a war with Japan.[3]

Even before this, Admiral Dickens decided on a wholesale revamping of the Navy's capabilities, and in December 1933 he sent his deputy, Captain Tait, to the Far East to investigate and report. Tait attended a staff conference in Singapore and travelled to Shanghai, and then to went Hong Kong to record his findings. He based his recommendations on the assumption that only Japan could seriously threaten British interests in the whole of the Far East, and that it could do so 'with little or no warning'. What he proposed was the establishment of a 'Pacific Naval Intelligence Organisation' involving all the Dominions and colonies around the Pacific littoral, reporting to a central clearing house in Hong Kong.[4]

Dickens was not the only senior official concerned with intelligence collection on Japan. The Chief of the Secret Service, Admiral Sinclair, convened a conference of senior officers from all the services in late 1934 with the aim of enlisting their support in the expansion of the codebreaking activities that GCCS was trying to undertake. Eric Nave, somewhat to his surprise, was asked to attend. He soon found out why.

> C [Sinclair] made his purpose clear by his opening statement. 'We have agents in all the important cities and ports in the world and yet 90% of the reliable information we get comes from Nave here and a few people like him. What are you going to do about it?' It was obvious that all the services were fully aware of the success of my work on the China Station and the Admiral was planning the future use of codebreaking in wartime.

Meanwhile, the Japanese had made an important change in their naval attache code — it had been switched to a machine-based system. Instead of encrypting the *romaji*, as in previous versions, the machine encrypted *kana*, and it encrypted vowels as consonants and consonants as vowels. After research by Hugh Foss and others, including Eric, these facts were determined, and an attempt was made to replicate the machine on which the Japanese were encrypting the traffic.

> This was our first experience of machines; there were two wheels, one containing twenty consonants and the other the six vowels, Y being a vowel. The first trial was made in the office using a brown foolscap file folder, a collar stud retrieved from a returning laundry parcel and a piece of string and slots cut in the cover for the letters. This worked, so we asked the Signal School in Portsmouth to help and received some expertly finished models in Bakelite.
>
> To find the starting point or key the Japanese language provided a good start. Japanese is not constructed like most European languages on a consonant-vowel basis but is monosyllabic: YO KO HA MA is four syllables. The word *oyobi* was a great help, giving a sequence of three vowels.

Later we had complications. Firstly, the machine could be set to jump certain positions, but this proved a minor nuisance. More tiresome was the subsequent monthly change of the order of the letters on the wheel and later introduction of 100 keys based on the message serial numbers.

Thus, in October 1933 the GCCS Japanese Naval Section had broken the code later known by its US designation 'Orange', and it appears to have done so nearly two years before the Americans. In the US success seems to have been assisted by a theft of the code from the Japanese Consul General's office in New York.[5]

As the efforts of the US to break Japanese codes will begin to appear more frequently in this account, it would be as well to briefly recount the story of the US cryptanalytical attack on Japan. The first recorded American success was by the so-called Black Chamber of the US State Department, led by H.O. Yardley, a gifted cryptologist who had worked for the US Army during World War I. His break into the Japanese diplomatic code enabled the Americans to be aware of the Japanese negotiating position at the Washington Naval Conference — just as the British were. Despite this and subsequent successes, the Black Chamber had its appropriations severely curtailed in 1924, and the strong opposition of Secretary of State Stimson to codebreaking eventually forced the organisation to close in 1930. Yardley permanently blotted his copybook — and caused anguish for both Western codebreakers and Japanese cryptographers — when he revealed the story of the Black Chamber's exploits in a book published in June 1931.[6] This led to a series of changes in Japanese codes and in the development of more difficult techniques aimed at frustrating Western codebreakers.

The US Navy began sending young officers to Japan for language studies in 1920 at the rate of two per year, later increased to three in the period 1932–35. In all, sixty-five naval officers had acquired Japanese language skills before the outbreak of hostilities, a figure that compares very favourably with the nineteen (including Nave) that the RN had managed to train over a similar period. Then, in 1924, the Code and Signal Section of the Office of Naval Communications established a small codebreaking office under the leadership of

Lieutenant L.F. Safford, who can thus be regarded as the father of
the US Navy's codebreaking organisation.

The US Army had provided some of the funding for Yardley's
Black Chamber, but a small section within its Signals Corps also
developed expertise, largely through breaking codes proposed for
adoption by the Army. In 1929, the Signals Corps established the
Signal Intelligence Service to take up the slack left by the decline
of the Black Chamber and so, by the end of the decade, both the
US Army and Navy had the nuclei of cryptanalytical organisations
interested in the problem of Japanese codes. It is important to note,
however, that there was no American equivalent of GCCS.

In the 1920s the American cryptanalysts appear to have relied for
their successes on theft and seizures of codes from Japanese premises
in the USA. However, the US Navy had established intercept
stations in China with the key post in Shanghai, and it also had
stations on American territory at Guam and in the Philippines from
1925. The Admiralty had proposed to Commander-in-Chief China
in 1925 the tactic of putting a warship in proximity to the Japanese
fleet to collect signals intelligence, but it was the Americans who put
the idea into practice in a destroyer in 1926, and a cruiser two years
later. The collection of intelligence from these IJN Combined Fleet
manoeuvres hugely impressed itself on the US Navy's Director of
Naval Communications who said, 'it covers a line of naval information
which is very important for us to get hold of, and the value of which
we have so far failed to appreciate'.[7] In this assessment he preceded
Admiral Dickens at the Admiralty by six years.

After analysing the intercepts from the 1930 annual Combined
Fleet manoeuvres the US Navy codebreakers claimed that they had
established 'as complete an ascendancy over the Japanese navy in the
matter of radio intelligence as the British navy had over the German
navy in the Great War'. This was a somewhat premature boast;
more intriguing was the fact that the US Navy Director of Naval
Intelligence was not allowed to be informed of this.[8] During the
Shanghai Incident of 1932, US Navy officers on board the flagship
of the US Asiatic Fleet were performing exactly the same role of

intercepting and decrypting IJN messages as Eric had done in HMS *Hawkins* and was doing in HMS *Kent*.

American reports indicate that they had no trouble in solving the codes in use at the time by the IJN, which would have included the codes broken by Eric Nave at GCCS, but it does not appear that they had access to the naval attache code until Orange was penetrated. This suggests that the US Navy was not in possession of the Japanese negotiating position at the 1930 London Conference, and may not have been able to learn through this means of Japanese activities in Europe. Moreover, there was no American equivalent of the British BJ (blue jacket) system, and relationships between the two American services were such that the US Navy chose not to reveal to its Army that it had access into the IJN naval attache code system.

None of this was known in London, where Eric Nave had resumed his life as an RN officer. He was now accommodated in the west of London, in an establishment that he refers to as the Rookery. This appears to have been a superior kind of apartment complex, judging by Eric's descriptions of the other thirty residents. Around half of these dressed for dinner, because at the Rookery 'the food was consistently good and the service excellent'.

Eric's continued work on the naval attache code now had an unexpected bonus — it flushed out a Japanese spy. This was a retired officer, Major Rutland, who had been posted to the China Station in 1933. There the Japanese naval attache to London approached him when the two met in Manchuria. In *Kent* Eric had uncovered his codename — 'Shinkawa'. Rutland made it clear to the Japanese that he would not spy on Britain and he was assured that, on the contrary, their target was America. The final plans to install Rutland in the US were made when he returned to London, and these were communicated to Tokyo by the Japanese naval attache and read by GCCS. The British now had the whole plot at their fingertips.

> Instructions had been given to me to hand any messages [about Rutland] direct and personally to C and this I did in my hand writing. Summoned to a conference at which only C, his deputy and myself were present, the question was what action should now be taken. The colonel asked if we were now to

hand the matter over to MI5 to which he received the answer 'No, they will only make a mess of it, we'll handle this ourselves'. The Admiral continued, saying that the only information was from Nave and, if we arrested and charged the spy, it would be apparent that their codes were being read, when they would change their codes and we would get nothing.

The upshot was that a decision was taken to allow Rutland to proceed with the Japanese plan but under British surveillance, and the results very satisfactory to British intelligence. Rutland did go to America under the cover of operating a business at San Diego in California, with the task of watching and reporting on US Navy ships. However, one of his employees in the Portland, Oregon, office was a British agent, who had been planted by C and who allowed himself to be recruited by Rutland on the ship on the way to America.

New IJN codes continued to make their appearance, including a naval general code that was not only superencrypted but also used separate and different code and decode books, the groups having been arranged in random order. Thus, an intuitive recognition that a message might be classified Secret would no longer mean that a codebreaker could assume that the code group representing this came from the S section of the book, and so reconstruct his own version of the codebook accordingly.

> The new book was tedious in the commencement as it required a lot of indexing of code groups to find the common words. However, with a good knowledge of Japanese and particularly signalese, the abbreviated language generally used by all services, this I now had. Regularly these groups would be sent out to China to assist the interpreter in the flagship.

Eric's need for recreation soon found an outlet in tennis, where he was invited to join the club of which his director, Alastair Denniston, was a member. Denniston might have had an eye to the main chance, for when he and Eric contested the men's doubles they won. Eric also took up golf more actively, playing on Sundays. One of the fellow members of the club was the Aga Khan, whose generosity to his caddie was as striking as the beauty of his wife, a former Miss France.

In the summer of 1934, Eric's isolation from Australia was lessened with the arrival of his brother Noel in London to take up a position in the UK branch of an Australian bank. Eric arranged accommodation at the Rookery and the two brothers enjoyed following the Australian cricket team during its tour of the UK that year. Eric, by now an old hand in matters of royalty, was amused by the reaction of Noel at seeing King George V at Lord's cricket ground, meeting and chatting with the players. 'It made me conscious of the reverence and awe with which the monarch was regarded by those of his subjects in Australia who never actually saw him.'

Eric's encounters with royalty were not limited to the Palace. Eric wrote in his memoirs that GCCS had a visit during this period from Lord Louis Mountbatten, a nephew of the King. His statement that Mountbatten had just been appointed Fleet Wireless Officer in the British Mediterranean Fleet is mistaken, however. Mountbatten took up that posting in 1931, where he was renowned for his zeal in pointing out to his superiors the importance of communications and of wireless discipline. However, in 1934 Lord Louis was promoted commander and undertook a course at the Naval Tactical School before taking command of the destroyer *Daring*, an element of the Mediterranean Fleet.[9] During his visit to GCCS he was interested in the possibilities of signals intelligence in aiding the fleet's task of keeping tabs on the Italian fleet. In this he was prescient, because in November 1935 the Italians invaded Ethiopia. 'I gave him all the information I could, pointing out what a field he would have available to him with the Italian Navy in the Mediterranean.' It seems more likely that this meeting took place during Nave's previous service at GCCS, although the dates don't quite coincide, but that doesn't really explain why Eric should have been briefing the visitor on Italian Navy codes. A possible explanation is that his experience in intercept operations on the IJN in the China Fleet was of more interest to Lord Louis, rather than any special knowledge of Italian codes.

This meeting appears to have kindled a bond between Nave and Mountbatten, which took the form of occasional correspondence. When Eric later became the president of the Naval Association of Australia, the two exchanged letters relatively frequently and when Mountbatten was assassinated in 1979 Eric gave the eulogy at a

service at Melbourne's Shrine of Remembrance. Eric's role in the
service and letter of condolence sent to the Royal family drew a letter
of appreciation from the Queen and the Prince of Wales.

Despite the punishing routine of codebreaking, Eric's early
interest in the law was rekindled during this period in London by
his fellow codebreaker Dick Thatcher. The Inns of Court required
students to have some knowledge of Latin, but when he inquired this
prerequisite was waived in Eric's case because of his demonstrated
competence in Japanese. This seems an unlikely concession for the
legal profession to grant, but is probably just one further illustration
of the persuasiveness of Eric Nave. However, the pressure of his
work at GCCS did not allow him enough time to advance his legal
studies.

> In truth I found the breaking of code systems, book building and then
> translation, quite mentally exhausting at times, and I needed some relaxation
> after leaving the office. On one occasion I handed my season ticket on the
> tube [London Underground] to the collector instead of showing it. He called
> me back, as did my regular newspaper seller when I gave him half a crown
> for my Evening Standard … I was sure that if I had had an administrative
> job I would have taken up law, in which I had received excellent marks in
> my Portsmouth course.

But there was to be little spare time for Eric or any other member
of the Japanese Naval Section at GCCS. In the Far East, Japan's
aggressive tendencies were making themselves quite apparent. In
February 1933 the Japanese Government withdrew the country from
the League of Nations following the tabling of a report the League
had commissioned on the Kwantung Army's actions in invading
Manchuria. This was extremely critical of Japan and the League
accepted its findings. Then, in 1934, Japan announced that her
adherence to the conditions of both the Washington Naval Treaty
of 1922 and the 1930 London Naval Disarmament Agreement
would cease with effect from December 1936, and that she would
not participate in a second round of naval disarmament talks in
London in 1935. These moves indicated a growing distrust of Anglo-
American disarmament motives even within the IJN, which had to

that point been able to accept the outcomes of these conferences with grace if not unanimity.

Then, in February1936, Eric decoded a cable to the naval attache in London informing him of the assassination attempt by a clique of junior Army officers on senior Japanese government officials and a number of retired naval officers. They had succeeded in killing the Lord Privy Seal, the Finance Minister and Inspector General of Education. The response in Whitehall was shock, reflected in Eric's comment:

> It was staggering to me to think that in 1936 there could be in Japan, a country which had achieved so much in a short period, a group of officers expected to be responsible, who could plan and carry out assassination of their Prime Minister and senior officials close to the Emperor himself.
>
> This, described by the Japanese press as the 'February 26th Incident' had a much deeper significance … and gave food for much thought by those studying Japan's future course. It showed the lengths these Army officers were prepared to go to achieve their ends and posed a serious problem for senior Japanese Naval men whose policy and outlook was conservative. It was not good news for anyone.

Eric and others in the British Government would have been incredulous had they known that this outbreak of organised violence had been sanctioned by important sections of the Imperial Japanese Army, and that it had been anticipated by the IJN. Commander-in-Chief Yokosuka, Admiral Yonai, whom Eric had met in the Japanese Training Squadron in 1924, had approved training for squads of sailors specifically to protect Naval Headquarters in Tokyo against Army attack. He had also had kept a cruiser standing by to shell and destroy the Army Headquarters had the conspirators made any move against the Navy.[10] GCCS decrypts of cables over succeeding days revealed the truth.

This alarming news arrived at a grim period for the British at home. The hero of Jutland, Admiral Jellicoe, had died on 20 November 1935 after collapsing at the Cenotaph in Whitehall on Remembrance Day. He was followed by Lord Beattie, his successor, who died soon after Jellicoe's funeral. Worse was to follow; on 20 January 1936, King George V followed his admirals to the grave. The gloom which enveloped the nation was not lightened by rumours about the fitness of Edward VIII to rule, and the situation was not improved by the news from Tokyo.

Japanese preparations for war could also be divined in the improvements being steadily implemented in IJN codes as detected by the Japanese Naval section in GCCS. What the intercepts did not reveal, however, was that in June 1936, in a review of 'The Defence Policy of the Japanese Empire', the Japanese Government had placed Britain on its list of potential enemies, along with the USA, the USSR and China.[11]

> In the office the daily intake kept me busy. Gone were the days of simple codes. There was an awareness of security [in the IJN] which demanded constant key or systems breaking which I was able to manage. We were faced with frequent cypher changes, one of which held me up for several weeks, as it appeared that we had a transposition imposed on the existing system. However, this was revealed when a Naval Attache in Italy sent a message transposing plain language. The officer, under great emotional strain, reported that a foreign girl he had trusted was found to be a spy. Having so disgraced himself and betrayed his country, the only honourable thing he could do was to pay with his life, which he did. I was glad to have the solution but felt sad for the officer who had fallen for a 'plant'.

Espionage was, however, a game more than one could play. Eric's work on the naval attache code turned up two more potential British traitors, one an MP who was being paid a regular retainer by the Japanese Naval Attache to keep him informed of matters of parliamentary interest to Japan. Cecil Malone had been made a member of the Order of the British Empire for his services in the Royal Flying Corps in World War I. He joined the Communist Party in 1920 but in 1928 had been elected to parliament as a member of the Labour Party. C took no action against Malone because of the risk of revealing that GCCS had broken the attache code.[12] 'In view of the vast amount of information available to members, including Defence, it was a sensible arrangement from their point of view, but doubtful conduct for a member of the House of Commons.'

The other spy was a senior Royal Air Force officer, who was

similarly receiving Japanese payments in exchange for information of interest to the IJN. Nave did not reveal what action was taken on these discoveries but simply noted, with considerable understatement, that it was 'good intelligence gathering for Japan'.

Eric was cheered by the arrival in GCCS of Chief Petty Officer Flintham, who had been his telegraphist assistant in HMS *Kent* and of whom Nave thought very highly.

> I had sent an official appreciation which was read to the assembled staff where he served on return to England. Approval had been given for his secondment to me, a post he filled to naval retirement and afterwards. He copied out draft solutions for examination and was invaluable.

This is the first reference made in the Nave memoirs to a development which was to become increasingly important in the codebreakers' battle with their quarry: a lot more people than just codebreakers were needed. The assault on a code had to be backed with the intelligent assembly of a series of intercepts in that code, together with what might be generally termed 'collateral' information. In the case of a diplomatic code, this might include open source reporting on significant political or social events, things on which a naval attache might be expected to report. In the case of a military code, it would include information based on traffic analysis, reports by naval agents, and the minutiae of fleet and squadron organisation, bases, patterns of operations and so on. The staff members who assembled the collateral information were not codebreakers: in some cases they were totally unaware of the use to which their work was being put. But without their efforts the tricky and time-consuming codebreaking task would have been longer and more difficult. Flintham seems to have been the forerunner of considerable numbers of staff who played a supporting role to the codebreaking stars.

Eric's social calendar was dotted with country house weekends as a guest of his RN friends, but war was in the air and was a frequent subject of conjecture and conversation. Tom Halsey, a friend of Eric's from *Hawkins* days, returned to the Admiralty from the Mediterranean Fleet with inspiring stories of the readiness of that fleet, and particularly its destroyers under an admiral called

Cunningham, to take on the Italians. Musing on this, Eric noted that:

> It was hardly that our ships were better ... The German naval architects seemed superior to ours, as witness the pocket battleships and unsinkable 'Tirpitz'. Our strength was in people; ships were well manned magnificently led and trained and we spent so much time closed [up] at action stations at night exercises, challenging our designated 'enemy force', the Italian ships were no match for them.

Other views of preparedness for war were on display. On a tour of France with his hockey club — his third visit — Eric overheard two women declaring that they would have no babies to be used as cannon fodder against the Germans. In Switzerland on a skiing holiday, he observed a French woman member of his party spit at a dachshund, declaring it a 'Filthy Boche!' Then the Cambridge University Union passed a resolution that its members would refuse to fight for King and Country.

> Their main argument was that as Hitler and Mussolini were actively supporting the conservative General Franco, they should oppose them by joining the Left. It amounted to an unofficial declaration of war against the dictators and this led these young idealists to join the Socialist and Communist Parties and thus become a worry to their own country.
>
> This set me thinking deeply about just where Great Britain was heading. Having joined the Navy in 1917, I had served with the admirals and captains whose lives were dedicated to the service of their country. Then, of course, I had witnessed the Jubilee of King George V which showed the world how a nation revered its sovereign in the capital, London, itself the home of democracy and legal justice. However, cracks were appearing as witness the hunger march by many men in their early twenties who had never had a day's paid work in their lives. These same men were denied access to many avenues of employment because they lacked education for other than manual or factory work.

Although Britain was recovering from the Great Depression in national terms, there were plenty of jobs to be found around London and in the south. However, there remained stubborn pockets of terrible unemployment in parts of Scotland and south Wales, as well as around the Midlands and Tyneside. It was these men whom Eric had seen marching. Ironically, the collapse of the British shipbuilding industry in the early years of the decade had been triggered — in part — by the decline in naval shipbuilding orders, which cut the demand for steel and the coal to smelt it. Now efforts had to be made to revive the industry as the need to rearm was clear.[13]

Troubling though the news was from the Far East, closer to home the fascist drive to power was gaining strength and vigour. In October 1935, Mussolini had decided to invade Abyssinia, a fellow member of the League of Nations. The response from the League was a call for sanctions on Italy, only partially honoured by members. Then, in March 1936, Hitler marched his armies into that part of the Rhineland that had been demilitarised as a consequence of the Treaty of Versailles, again without effective response from the occupying powers. These incursions did get a reaction in London, especially on the intelligence front. The crises revealed the cumbersome and slow nature of the arrangements for getting intelligence from the collectors to the users within Admiralty. Analysis demonstrated that a new method was required, leading to a start the following year on the development of what was to become the Admiralty's Operational Intelligence Centre as a central clearing house of intelligence from all sources and classifications, including the products of the GCCS Naval Section. This was a bold and far-sighted move which created a model that would be reproduced and emulated — with varying degrees of success — across the Allied camp in World War II.

Eric continued to play sport as a relaxation from the daily grind of codebreaking. At this time his hockey prowess was standing him in good stead, and his Mid-Surrey team was used as a 'sparring partner' by the Oxford and Cambridge teams before their annual clash, an experience he much enjoyed. This all came to a halt when a waitress accidentally dropped pots of tea and boiling water on Eric's leg, causing severe burns requiring hospitalisation, surgery and a week's convalescence. He had another health scare when diagnosed with appendicitis.

The Admiralty doctor then ordered a trip to Chatham [naval hospital] for further medical examination; the nursing staff were delighted with my arrival, saying 'We haven't had an operation in ages. Do have it before the Surgeon Captain goes on leave. He is very good but when he has gone, heaven knows who you will get.' The Surgeon Captain said that if he could find any trace he would remove the appendix to avoid an attack overseas in an emergency, but he said 'I've had your appendix in my fingers without complaint from you, so off you go.'

Meanwhile, events in the Far East continued their apparent descent into chaos. In October 1936, the depot ship HMS *Medway*, in which Eric had sought in vain for wireless traffic from the Japanese mandates, paid a routine visit to Taiwan, which had by then been occupied by the Japanese for more than forty years. The reception given to the ship by the Japanese authorities was insulting enough for the Admiralty to suspend all further visits to Japanese ports in protest, a reasonable decision in the circumstances, but one that further reduced the British ability to gain first-hand intelligence on the IJN and its activities. The codebreakers' work became correspondingly more important. Then, in July 1937, came the Kwantung Army's attack on China proper with the manufactured Marco Polo Bridge incident outside Beijing. By September, the IJN had instituted a blockade of the entire Chinese coast. Worse was to follow, with the December attack on the British gunboats HMS *Ladybird* and *Bee* by Japanese shore batteries and the bombing of *Scarab* and *Cricket*.

At GCCS, Eric had uncovered yet another spy for Japan, this time a German national who was being despatched to Honolulu to back up the work being done by Rutland at San Diego. Again the question arose as to what should be done with this information. Furthermore, what did the Japanese interest in these two major fleet bases imply? The matter was all in the hands of C, to whom Eric gave the only copies of his handwritten translations of the relevant cables. 'I felt from my earlier conference with "Quex" [Sinclair] that the Americans would be told when appropriate.'

In many ways, 1936 was a watershed year for the British. Problems at home and abroad occupied much of the official attention that was needed for revitalising British industry and making a start on rearming the country. The abdication of King Edward VIII in favour of his brother, King George VI, in December 1936 seemed to end a long period of indecision in official life. Unknown to Eric, 1936 was also the last year he would spend in England. His codebreaking and translation work at GCCS continued, but a new technical intelligence element was added.

> It was quite a surprise to be asked to spend one hour per day in a special telephone booth where the [Japanese] Naval Attaché's telephone lines had been hooked in. The time could be of my own choosing and could be varied at will. There was another special telephone booth near mine which was devoted to German interception. Apparently Herr Hitler, when travelling in his special train, maintained regular contact with the Wilhelmstrasse [German Foreign Office] by radio telephone and we could listen in to this … There were times when the German watcher was on duty at the same time and when both had dead or no interest lines, we would chat away. On one such occasion the other watcher suddenly said, 'Shush, I've got Hitler on the line'.

With other officers from the Admiralty, Eric went to Portsmouth to witness the review of the fleet by the new King in June 1937. In the same month, the agreement he had entered into on transferring to the RN was honoured and he was promoted commander, just short of twenty years since he had joined the RAN. But, after appropriate celebrations, it was time for him to make arrangements to voyage out to the Far East again, to take up his posting on the staff of the newly established Far East Combined Bureau in Hong Kong. He was granted three months leave in which to visit Australia on the way.

> I left, far from happy at the prospect, fully aware that the climate did not suit me and knowing that as war was inevitable, I could be stuck there indefinitely. However, the time was approaching when our work was most important and its results or product could be vital to the success of our future operations. The 'Jervis Bay' took me to Adelaide to see the family. Although all my recent associations had been in England and the Royal Navy for some time now, I always drifted back to the family rather like the salmon who commences life in the northern rivers of Canada and returns there by instinct.

During his time back at GCCS, Eric had witnessed the increasing sophistication of the codes being used by the IJN and had continued to break into them. The value of his work had been demonstrated in the ability of the British to follow developments in Tokyo at a time of considerably heightened tension between the Japanese Army and Navy, and in the detection of Japanese efforts to recruit and deploy spies. His sojourn in London had allowed him to become more familiar with the British and their ways, and this had given him cause for some reflection. His personal networks in Britain had expanded and deepened. Now he was to interrupt that particular voyage of discovery and journey to a Far East, where the situation was quite different from the one he had left only four years previously.

Eric Nave aged six

Midshipman Nave, 1917

Eric with parents, 1917

Eric with Shaw and teacher in Japan, 1922

HMAS *Brisbane* at sea, 1923

HMAS *Brisbane* in Sydney Harbour, 1922

Vice Admiral Saito with Sir Macpherson MacRobertson in Melbourne, January 1924, with Eric Nave as interpreter

HMAS *Melbourne* flag staff, 1924

Eric in HMAS *Sydney*, 1925

Eric and friends in Cornwall, 1929

HMS *Hawkins*, 1925

HMS *Hawkins* in dry dock, Hong Kong, 1926

HMS *Kent, 1933*

Eric skiing in Switzerland, 1936

Eric as best man at Bouncer Burnett wedding, 1935

Helena Grey, 1939

Eric, Helena and Elizabeth, Melbourne, 1940

Monterey in South Yarra, home of FRUMEL and the Special Intelligence Bureau, 1942

Eric and Elizabeth, Brisbane, 1942

Nyrambla, Central Bureau HQ Brisbane, 1943

Captain Eric Nave, 1944

Helena and children, Melbourne, 1945

Albert Park Barracks, Melbourne, home of Defence Signals Bureau, 1949

Nave family photograph in Brighton, 1949

Eric and Helena, late 1960s

Eric presenting a medallion from
the Naval Association of Australia
to the chairman of the *Dame Pattie*
America's Cup syndicate, Emil
Christensen. July 1967

Eric and Margaret, wedding day,
December 1970

Eric and Margaret, 1992

(*Left*) Eric as Federal President of
Naval Association of Australia, 1970

Eric's eightieth birthday, 1979

6 Far East Combined Bureau, 1937–40

Eric Nave wrote his memoirs many years after the events he was describing and he had, naturally, the advantage of hindsight in being able to put significant passages of his long and eventful life into perspective. The situation towards which he was now travelling would mark a critical phase in both his professional career and in his personal affairs. He may possibly have been aware of the former as his ship sailed north from Australia towards Hong Kong, but the latter seems to have come as a complete surprise.

Once again, Eric was leaving his family and voyaging to the Far East where he realised that things were markedly changed from his days in HMS *Kent*. For one thing he was now of a senior rank, and he was aware that his posting this time was a complete change from those he had previously filled. It must also have been a little daunting to be about to join an organisation about which he had heard much, one where he would not be in charge, and in which he would not be left to his own devices as he had previously been.

> I arrived in Hong Kong late October 1937 to take up my appointment on the Commander-in-Chief's staff but this time located in his shore office in the Dockyard. This was my 4th commission in the Far East and when the ship from Australia entered the harbour it was to see that many ships, over 20 vessels, had been blown ashore by a typhoon.

It was a fitting omen for Eric's last posting to the China Fleet — a stormy period indeed.

Readers will recall that the DNI, Admiral Dickens, had sent his deputy, Captain Tait, to China in 1933 to see what could be done to improve the collection and collation of intelligence on the Imperial Japanese Navy. Tait's recommendations were that there should be a sizable increase in the intelligence staff to man new intercept stations — some of which would be in the colonies and dominions fringing the Pacific — and to increase the rate at which IJN codes could be attacked and broken. It wasn't only the Admiralty that acted upon these recommendations. The other two British services and the Secret Intelligence Service decided to throw in their lot with the idea, and the result was a completely new kind of organisation called the Far East Combined Bureau (FECB), set up in the Hong Kong Naval Dockyard in April 1935. It was the prototype of the all-source intelligence centres that were to be set up in Allied commands in the coming war, and it was unique in several ways. Personnel from all three services manned the bureau, although the Admiralty always provided the officer-in-charge, who went by the amorphous unclassified title of Captain on the Staff C-in-C China. Internally, he was referred to as Chief of Intelligence Staff (COIS). The Royal Navy also provided the bulk of the personnel and the real estate for FECB. 'The office was organised on a 3-service basis, the cryptographic [*sic*] work being all done by the Naval party, including W/T intercepts. We had liaison officers from Army and Air ... with Captain Rushbrooke Royal Navy in overall command.'

FECB absorbed the majority of the intelligence agencies the British Services operated in the Far East. It took under its wing the head of the Army's Shanghai Intelligence Office and the naval intercept and DF station at Stonecutters Island in Hong Kong. Interestingly, the Deputy Chief was an RAN commander, and the RAN was to be a principal collaborator with FECB in the collection and analysis of intelligence on the Japanese. When Eric Nave joined FECB, the RAN officer was Commander Arthur Spurgeon, who kindly offered the share of a flat in the Mid-Levels on Hong Kong Island. Eric accepted gratefully.

The major role of FECB was to give timely warning of

impending hostilities. Should war break out, it was to support the Far East command organisation and to keep London informed of developments on the intelligence scene. The organisation had several sections, of which 'Y' did the cryptanalysis. This was headed by a commander and had three lieutenant commanders on the staff, as well as a large body of male non-commissioned officers and other ranks, and Women's Royal Naval Service ratings. Nave's friend and colleague, Harry Shaw, now a captain in the Royal Naval Reserve, had established the cryptanalytical section of FECB, and he had been joined by Dick Thatcher. Now it was Eric's turn to lead the organisation. His use of the term 'liaison officers' to describe the Army and Air Force members of the staff shows a degree of naval bias, as the Army certainly resented the idea that they were a mere appendage to FECB's naval core.[1]

An early issue between the Y Section and the Chief of Intelligence Staff was that of the 'ownership' of the intelligence that Shaw and Thatcher generated from decrypts. In the past, they and Nave had communicated this directly to the Commander-in-Chief and to Admiralty, but the first captain of FECB disagreed. Intelligence from decrypts had to be evaluated alongside other sources so that its reliability could be assessed before it was passed by FECB to higher authority. As can be imagined, the cryptanalysts, who had previously enjoyed personal access to the most senior levels of the China Fleet, were not pleased with this development, but the captain was adamant — and correct. As it transpired, FECB was to rely for a major proportion of its intelligence on signals intelligence, but there were other sources of information and these needed to be used to validate the intercepts. The codebreakers too benefited from collateral intelligence from other sources.

The other change in Eric's role was that codebreaking was now much more a team effort, involving more than a lone cryptanalyst sweating over red message forms in the cabin of a cruiser. The reasons are obvious — there were a lot more intercepts to be worked on, the Japanese were introducing more and more codes, and the codes themselves were becoming more complex.

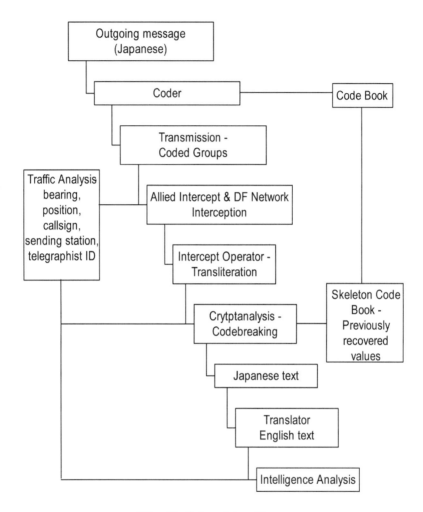

The Codebreaking Process

The main Japanese Naval Code which I had been reading in London became my main responsibility. It was a 'hatted' code, that is the groups were in random order and it was necessary to break 100 keys set by the message number which governed the transposition of code groups into columns. This code gave us our best information of future operations and was a complicated procedure.

Again, the experience Eric and others had gained of the IJN's signalese and the internal arrangement of its routine messages played a big part in defeating this code.

> But I found an aid to solution as the Japanese Admiralty reported the departures of convoys and individual ships though the Straits of Shimonoseki [at the southern end of the Inland Sea] en route to Shanghai. The signal always followed the same form e.g. *Nagasaki Maru* (No. 4267) passed Moji 0800 date bound Shanghai. E. Base. I now wrote out the message as the coder did and by rearranging the code groups obtained the order of columns for this message and others in that serial number. This also established the number of columns for messages with other serial numbers.

Eric said that it was he who instigated the 'borrowing' of Japanese diplomatic and commercial messages passed via the British cable company in Hong Kong to replicate the process followed at GCCS. This is possible, but Harry Shaw had used the same procedure in Shanghai before he moved ashore into FECB in Hong Kong. Shaw's initiative had uncovered a startling piece of intelligence — there was a Japanese spy within the highest levels of the British armed forces in the Far East. This was revealed by a verbatim account of the main points made by Admiral Dreyer at a conference on the Singapore Naval Base, a meeting attended by a select few senior officers and officials. The spy had a friend who was a shorthand typist in the Governor-General's office in Singapore.[2] With this discovery clearly emerging from an inspection of the Japanese Consul General's cables, it would be surprising if Shaw had not made similar arrangements in Hong Kong. However, Eric made the following claim:

> I saw the Head of the Eastern Extension Telegraph Company who sent for the previous day's cables which I placed in my Hong Kong basket, a wicker basket used by most Europeans for carrying a variety of things from bathing togs to shopping. Next day these were returned after we had copied the Japanese Consul General's code messages, and the next batch was brought to the office. Having started the service I had to be one of the staff keeping it going. This proved to be a most fruitful source of information, and I read a message which obviously referred to me. The Consul General reported to Tokyo that the Intelligence staff had been strengthened by the arrival

of a Japanese speaking expert. Later, other messages were sent referring to the strengthening of the staff at Stonecuttters, where our intercept unit was located.

So much for FECB security! Having made the discovery of a Japanese agent who had access to that kind of highly classified material, it now fell to Eric to try to determine who it might be. The source had to be highly placed, but shortly it transpired that the leakage of information was occurring at the very pinnacle of the bureau — from the Chief of Intelligence Staff himself, Captain Rushbrooke.

> I had sat next to an Italian woman, the Baroness married to a French banker, a baron, at a dinner party given by the Chief of Intelligence Far East — (Captain R.) I suspected this lady as the source but Captain R. would not believe it, since she was a friend of his wife, even when these reports stopped on her departure to Europe on leave. He did agree that if these reports recommenced on her return it would be too much of a coincidence. This in due course happened and we found she had been recruited as a spy by Edda Ciano, Mussolini's daughter, and wife of Count Ciano [later Italian Foreign Minister] when the Cianos were on duty in Shanghai. She was one of the Chiari sisters, very beautiful and well known.

Eric surmised that Captain Rushbrooke had been indiscreet in keeping his wife informed of events in FECB, and that she had passed the information on in turn to the Baroness. This lady had contrived to develop a close friendship with Mrs Rushbrooke on the instructions of her controller. Bad as the discovery was, a more sinister aspect was the revelation that there existed such a formal intelligence-collection arrangement between Italy and Japan. In November 1937, Italy had acceded to the 1936 Anti-Comintern Pact between Germany and Japan, which was designed to present a united front against communist aggression in Europe and Asia. Until Eric Nave's decryptions, the British had not suspected that the bonds between the three countries were as far-reaching as that.[3]

During this period, Hong Kong was a hot bed of intrigue, with a great many people of interest passing through on their way to and from China. Eric noted that 'a real cloak and dagger atmosphere existed'. Amongst the various foreigners serving in a range of different advisory positions to the Nationalist Chinese forces was an Australian known as 'Mr Perkins' who was close to the head of the Chinese Air Force. Another had the role of 'advisor' to the Generalissimo, and there was a one-armed Canadian arms manufacturer who provided mortar ammunition to the Chinese Army. In contrast, the newly commissioned Lieutenant Ian Fleming, Royal Naval Volunteer Reserve, was very subdued when he visited the colony for familiarisation. 'We saw no sign of the future James Bond,' said Eric.

The British could be confident that their efforts in setting up FECB had paid off. With only slight exaggeration, the situation was summed up by James Rusbridger's description of the state of cryptanalytical affairs:

> As far as Japan was concerned, by the end of 1937 GCCS could read all its naval attaché messages passing between Europe and Tokyo, diplomatic traffic sent on the Red machine (this was handled by Hobart-Hampden and Parlett), and signals sent in the general naval code (the Blue Book), used by all ships of the Japanese Navy in home and foreign waters.[4]

The daily grind of decoding and translation demanded some compensating relaxation. Eric continued with his cricket, becoming captain of the Navy team in 1938, but he also took up golf with more determination and application, playing at Happy Valley, where the course crisscrossed over the race track, and at Fanling in the New Territories.

> When work permitted we could take a Wednesday afternoon off. I played on these days with James Warburton, an Air Force officer on my staff. He was fascinated with the dicing game Liar Dice greatly used in deciding who pays for drinks … We played it for everything, drinks on the train [to Fanling], rickshaws from the train to the golf club, the honour from the 1st tee etc. He later took a house on the mainland en route to the golf club and named it 'Lyah Dyce'.

However, there were not to be very many occasions for Wednesday afternoons off. With the Japanese forces now engaged in fighting along the entire eastern seaboard of China, the volume of military traffic being intercepted quickly outstripped the capacity of the FECB Y Section to decode and translate it. Decisions had to be taken on

which messages were to be processed and which were to be left until
— some time in the future — there might be sufficient breathing
space to attend to them. Clearly, operational traffic attracted most
FECB attention and, fortunately, the order of transmission of IJN
messages followed a set pattern.

> Although we could read all the codes, we had no time to read the daily
> situation reports made by every ship and command each night. However,
> on the operational side we had prior knowledge of every landing made
> by the Japanese. The first advice came immediately following the meeting
> of the War Cabinet in the Commander-in-Chief's cypher. It would read
> 'Instructions have been issued for the capture of Canton, it will be known
> as Operation "Y". Details will be promulgated by the Chief of the Naval
> Staff.' The first signal would be from the Minister but the follow up from the
> CNS would give the most complete details e.g. the number of transports,
> sometimes close to 100, and names of escorting warships, Army Divisions
> involved, the landing place, route to be taken by attacking forces, villages
> they would pass through and so on.

This was first class intelligence, but its distribution had to be
closely controlled so that the Japanese would not suspect that the
British were reading their codes. Not all senior officers authorised
to receive the intelligence from FECB decrypts were circumspect
with their handling of the information. The Japanese, in fact,
postponed the assault on Guangzhou [Canton] because details of
the operational plan appeared in the Hong Kong press. They had
been briefed to media representatives by Army public relations, who
thought it would make a good story! The Governor of Hong Kong,
on hearing of the planned operation, had phoned the Consul General
in Guangzhou so that the British ships in that port could be got clear
before the invasion force arrived. He had used an open line through
exchanges manned by Chinese nationals! Remedial action ensured
that, when the assault was relaunched in May 1938, there were no
leaks from Hong Kong and it went ahead as scheduled.

There is a passage in *Betrayal at Pearl Harbor* about the effectiveness
of FECB W Section that demonstrates, once again, James Rusbridger's
misuse of information provided by Eric Nave. Following the quote

above from the Nave memoirs, it continues: 'Not a single message escaped the listening post in Hong Kong. The powerful intercept station at Stonecutters Island sucked up everything transmitted from Japan and from every ship at sea.'[5] This is a misinterpretation — or oversimplification — of what Eric said, in a rather contradictory way, in a BBC interview in 1989 on the subject of interception in Hong Kong:

> The reception there in China, and particularly from Hong Kong, Stonecutters, was excellent. We could read Tokyo [Radio] 24 hours a day; and the possibility of missing an important dispatch, I think, just didn't exist. Atmospherics, of course, was one thing; but we generally could overcome that. We could get static very bad at times. It was difficult, yes; but for the most part we were not in a position where you could miss a certain period during the day, or a whole message at any time. You had confidence that you could read all the traffic.

The Rusbridger statement has transformed the Nave discussion of reception of Tokyo Radio — a very powerful transmitter optimised for its task — with 'everything transmitted from Japan and from every ship at sea'. It could not possibly be true, for four reasons. First, the vagaries of radio transmission at the frequency bands then in use make it highly unlikely that every IJN transmission would even reach Hong Kong to be intercepted, a point which impelled the British to accelerate their program of building intercept stations around the Pacific. Second, the station at Stonecutters Island did not have unlimited receivers or telegraphists to man them. Watch would have been kept only on those frequencies likely to yield the most important messages — those from commanders ashore and afloat, which was why so much emphasis was placed on Tokyo Radio.

The third reason why the statement is misleading is that, as has been seen, there were simply not enough codebreakers and translators to decrypt every IJN intercept. Fourth, the British never fully recovered all code values in the books used by the IJN. Even without garbles or corruptions in the telegraphists' intercept attempts, there were always gaps in the decrypts or perhaps guesses at what an unrecovered group might mean. Rusbridger was, of course, building his case that the

British knew all there was to know about the IJN, and were thus aware of the plan to strike Pearl Harbor. He clearly made up much of this bit of his 'evidence'.

Eric had now been in FECB for nearly two years, and he began to experience health problems related to the weather, but undoubtedly exacerbated by the pressure of work he was experiencing.

> The summers were very trying with quite high humidity and air-conditioning non-existent. When Harry Shaw, now back from England, arrived in the office in the morning, having come by car from his flat garage the first thing he did was to change his shirt in the office, it being wet through in that short time. This was known as Shaw's Strip Tease. It was quite normal for us all to make three changes of clothing each day.
>
> The situation was deteriorating and it was now a very strenuous life with no day off at all and with Sundays in the office as usual but mornings only, unless it was a very busy day. In the humid heat this caught up with me and I started to suffer severe attacks of vomiting. I could say that the tropics never did suit me. After 2 years I always became jaded and needed a cool climate to restore my health. With the war pace increasing this was not possible. I was in hospital for a period for investigation but unfortunately the medical expert was on vacation and I was discharged with no diagnosis being made.

In this part of his memoirs, Eric makes no mention of a most significant event that came to pass because of his hospitalisation — he met his future wife. Helena Elizabeth Gray was a nurse at the Queen Mary Hospital in Hong Kong who, Eric said, 'had been trying to get some expert medical advice on my complaint so far undiagnosed'. Eric's daughters recall their mother telling them that she met Eric through a fellow nurse at the hospital. Born in January 1909 in Walsall, Staffordshire, there was a suggestion that she had decided to volunteer for duty in Hong Kong because of an unhappy relationship in the UK. True or not, Helena clearly took her naval patient's welfare seriously and romance blossomed.

However, the military and political situation was indeed getting worse. In China, following the fall of Nanjing in late 1937, and the attacks by aircraft and artillery on British and other foreign shipping in the Yangtse River, the Japanese had assaulted and captured not only

Guangzhou but Xiamen [Amoy] and Hangzhou south of Shanghai. In effect, Hong Kong itself was now isolated from land contact with the Nationalist Chinese. Shipping to and from the colony had to pass through an IJN blockade. There began to be concerns in London about the security of its Chinese possessions, and preparations were made for evacuating the bulk of the precious FECB resource to Singapore, including an expansion of the RN intercept station at Kranji outside the naval base there.[6]

Meanwhile, in Europe the growing military power and diplomatic intransigence of the resurgent German nation were clearly signalling the imminent likelihood of war. British codebreakers, aided by the Poles and the French, had established that the German armed forces and the vast majority of its other state instrumentalities were using variants of one cypher machine — known as Enigma — to encrypt their communications. Work was also proceeding on breaking Italian codes and ciphers. GCCS was rapidly expanding and, as a consequence of the exercise mobilisation of British headquarters staffs following the annexation of Austria by Germany in May1938, and the Munich Crisis in September of the same year, the decision was taken to move GCCS from central London. The organisation was re-established at the country manor of Bletchley Park in Buckinghamshire, fifty miles north of the capital, which had been previously purchased by C, Admiral Sinclair. Bletchley Park thenceforward became the centre for all British codebreaking, and took the major responsibility for attacking Japanese Army code systems, while Eric Nave and his colleagues in the Y Section of FECB had the major responsibility for IJN codebreaking.

While codebreaking was certainly a primary intelligence source for FECB on the activities of the IJN, it was not the only one. Readers will recall from Chapter 2 the illustration of traffic analysis provided by the message transmitted by Leading Telegraphist 'Scrubby' Forrest from the RAN flagship *Australia* in 1922. Technology had made some startling advances since then, especially in the field of direction finding.

Very briefly, some ground-breaking work by two Italian scientists,

Bellini and Tossi, had shown that if an antenna array of two loops arranged at right angles was tuned to the required frequency, by comparing signal strengths in the loops, then it was possible to establish the direction of arrival of a signal with some degree of accuracy. This discovery led to intense work to perfect an operational direction-finding system operating at the most common radio frequency bands in military use, and by the early 1930s workable solutions to most of the problems had been found. Now, not only could the message be intercepted but the direction in which the transmitter lay from the intercept station could be determined.

If the bearing of the transmitter could be taken by two — but preferably more — direction-finding stations at different locations and the results plotted, an approximate position of the transmitter could also be determined. If a series of these direction-finding fixes on a mobile transmitter were to be gained, then the course and speed of the target could be established. Part of the Pacific Naval Intelligence Organisation arrangements made by Admiral Dickens was the establishment of a network of direction-finding stations around the Pacific rim, and these stations began to become operational in 1937. Interestingly, the first US Navy direction-finding station opened in Guam in the same year. A trial conducted by the China Fleet in early 1939 showed that tracking accuracy depended on having multiple direction finding sites reporting on the target, and a drive was begun to build more stations. By 1940 the Pacific Naval Intelligence Organisation could boast eleven stations, with more coming on stream in the near future.[7]

The invention of the cathode ray oscilloscope opened the way for another technological advance in signals intelligence. In 1922, the foreign intercept operator listening to Scrubby Forrest's transmission recognised the sender by his distinctive way of sending Morse code. It was now possible to display the characteristic waveforms of Scrubby's Morse code dots and dashes on the screen of an oscilloscope, and to photograph them. If a library of these was built up, then a particular operator could be identified by non-telegraphists too, simply by comparing the transmitted waveform and the library photograph. The

British gave this process the codename 'TINA', and it was deployed to FECB. On a similar basis, by using an oscilloscope it was also possible to recognise differences in the transmission characteristics of individual radio transmitters, a technique that was known as 'radio fingerprinting'.

Traffic analysis was known by the British as Procedure W, and it quickly became apparent that a marriage between Procedure Y and Procedure W was made in intelligence heaven. A target ship could not disguise its identity by changing callsigns, as its radio fingerprint would give the change away. Telegraphists associated with particular naval commanders, who generally preferred to take their own operators with them when they transferred between flagships, would disclose the shift of flag as soon as they transmitted from their new site. To the codebreakers, these events created cribs with which they could attack codes. If they did break a message, like that for the assault on Guangzhou, then the traffic analysts could confirm that the operation had commenced and could track the convoy on its way to the target. When a change in code rendered the Y Section temporarily in limbo, the W Section could divine target activities from traffic analysis.

These intriguing possibilities were tested and refined by FECB and trialled on live targets, both British and Japanese. The results demonstrated that under good conditions with well-located direction-finding sites, a close correlation between a target's reported and decoded position and the position obtained from bearings obtained by direction finding was possible. But the trials also showed that that direction-finding coverage of the China Sea was patchy, and that more stations were needed to improve the performance of the network as a whole.

As intercept capabilities improved, it became possible for the codebreakers to increase the rate of recovery of codebook values. Eric Nave said:

> With a wealth of information our codebook was rapidly filled and it was a great source of amusement and satisfaction when a Japanese recipient couldn't read the message and asked for a check and repeat. I had discovered

the mistake made by the encoder and read the first message.

More formally, Harry Shaw reported that:

> Book building on the 4-*kana* code General Code went on steadily and progress was made on the Flag Officer's Code, which mainly concerned local politics in China. A new naval *kana* code came into use between Japanese naval bases and hence was known as the Dockyard Code. The book was alphabetical but the vocabulary, being largely technical, was slow to build up.[8]

Japanese communications security was, however, making advances of its own. On the diplomatic front, from the end of 1938 the Japanese Foreign Office introduced a new machine cypher for use between Tokyo and thirteen selected diplomatic posts overseas. This immediately shut the British (and the Americans) off from communications between the Japanese Foreign Office and posts like London, Washington and Berlin. The system, known as Type B by the Japanese, was dubbed 'Purple' by the US Army and solved only after considerable frustration by a stroke of inspired cryptologic genius in 1940, but it was never solved by the British. The remaining posts continued to use the original Type A machine code, known by the Americans as 'Red', so that it was possible for FECB to uncover a series of Japanese spies in Hong Kong and Singapore from intercepting the traffic of the consul generals.

> We intercepted messages which referred to information the area commander received from a spy in Hong Kong but had no idea of the identity of the individual for, with its mixed population, this was an easy place for any country to infiltrate a spy. I had my suspicions of a rather superior type of Japanese barber who operated in the Hong Kong Club, a place patronised by local senior people and used by most naval officers.

Section Y's travails were, however, about to become more serious. In November 1938 the IJN's four-*kana* General Code was replaced by another, and decrypts revealed that yet another change was in the offing. It came in June 1939, with the adoption IJN-wide of Naval Code D, a general operational code of five-figure groups. This family of codes is better known in history by the title it was given by the

US Navy – JN-25. Code D intercepts referred by FECB to GCCS were examined by the section struggling with the IJA operational code, which noticed some similarities with the Army system. The first break came because Code D was used to encode ships' daily positions, which contain a lot of numerals — typically made up of a date and time, a position in latitude and longitude, a course, a speed and percentage of fuel remaining. Some even contained estimates of the same information twenty-four hours in the future. The repeated use of numerals provided an entry into the code, because it was discovered that numerals and months of the year were arithmetically linked. As well, the Japanese codemakers had incorporated, perversely, another source of insecurity in its construction: all the code groups were divisible by three. Nevertheless, these did not — of themselves — present the British with a solution. There were 30,000 values in the codebook, and it was used in conjunction with an additive table, a matrix of ten columns by ten rows comprising five-figure additives.

> In the early stages it was easy and we built up the book at a terrific rate, which was good, as it was the main naval cipher. I felt they must cover this weakness by introducing a hatted book [which the Japanese did.] However, the very important signals such as the new landing operations continued to come in the C-in-C's transposed 5 letter book and I read these personally as key breaking was necessary.

The landing operations Eric referred to were those on Hainan Island and in the Spratley Islands in the South China Sea, bringing the Japanese ever closer to South East Asia and Singapore. Curiously, while Eric was having some success in mastering the Flag Officers' Code, the US Navy cryptanalysts at the naval base at Pearl Harbor (Station HYPO) were having no luck at all with it.[9] This was the major codebreaking task HYPO had been set. The attack on Code D (JN-25A) was being undertaken by the Naval Security Group in Washington (OP-20-G), an outgrowth of Safford's Code Section, and, at the end of 1940, by the cryptanalysts assigned to the US Asiatic Fleet based in the Philippines, codenamed Station CAST. CAST was situated first at the Cavite Navy Yard near Manila, and later at Corregidor, the fortress island at the mouth of Manila Bay.

Code D (or JN-25A and its succession of replacement variants) was the main IJN operational code used for a majority of IJN messages throughout the Pacific War, and it thus attracted the expert attention of both Japanese cryptographers and Allied codebreakers. From 1941, the IJN introduced a number of additional complications to Code D. One was a table of grid positions to obviate the need for coders to delve into the numerical values of the codebook when encoding geographical positions. The second was a table of geographical designators. Instead of obliging coders to spell out the names of common geographical features which, as has been demonstrated, had the propensity to assist codebreakers, the Japanese assigned one-to three-letter designators for these instead. Thus 'R' indicated the New Guinea area, while 'RZP' was assigned to Tillage in the Solomon Islands. This systematic association of geographical features was, however, another source of insecurity — the designators should have been chosen at random. The third complication was a separate table for enciphering dates.[10] To decrypt a message the codebreaker had first to strip off the additive table values to reveal the code groups, attempt to match the code groups with those in the skeleton codebook painstakingly built up, solve the grid code, the geographical designators and the date code, and then translate the message.

By then the bulk of FECB, its equipment and personnel, including Eric Nave, had been relocated to Singapore.

> It was clear that trouble with Japan was getting closer, but we had excellent reception and facilities which were too good to sacrifice. As we came through the [northern] summer [1939] the situation in Europe grew steadily worse and we commenced getting the earlier war warning telegrams [messages issued as codewords in a gradually ascending order of seriousness instructing that preparations be made for war]. It was clear that London was preparing for war. In August I was told that I must leave Hong Kong in HMS *Birmingham* [heavy cruiser] for Singapore and was requested to maintain output on the way, which was not practicable. We had four of our own interpreters with back up staff, these being specially selected retired Chief Petty Officers.

Although this order must have been anticipated, and preparation of facilities in Singapore to accommodate FECB had begun in late 1938, it caused considerable disruption to FECB staff and dependents. Leases had to be terminated, furniture disposed of and arrangements made for families either to return to the UK or to transfer to Singapore under their own steam. Space for personal effects on board *Birmingham* would be strictly limited, with FECB personnel and equipment crammed in on top of the normal ship's company, so that even bachelors were obliged to shed prized possessions. There were a large number of memorable parties around Hong Kong, at which all the surplus liquor accumulated was disposed of in the usual way. Eric remarked:

> Coming back to the flat one day there were no Angostura Bitters, a customary requirement with [pink] gin. The Chinese boy, on being questioned, apologised for the oversight and ordered a quart bottle of bitters. I have wondered what use the Japanese made of the almost full bottle when they occupied the island.

The move was made on 24 August. Despite the time allowed for preparations for the reception of FECB in Singapore, all was still not in readiness when *Birmingham* discharged her precious cargo at the new naval base three days later. Elphick suggested a reason for this. While the Government and populace of Hong Kong had clear evidence of the expansionist military activity of the Japanese, and were happy to support a sizable British military presence, quite the opposite was true of Singapore. There, China and the Japanese forces were a long way away, and the colony smarted from the impost of having to pay for a proportion of the costs of the naval base's construction and maintenance. New military burdens were not welcome.[11]

And FECB was a considerable entity. Its strength had grown to over 150 personnel, nearly one hundred of whom were associated with Section W. Section Y comprised about twenty-five personnel of all services, but they were predominately RN. Eric was one of four naval cryptanalysts/translators with Shaw, and another RN officer and Malcolm 'Bouncer' Burnett, who joined in mid-September.

> Captain H.L. Shaw arrived from England and he was very welcome as he took over the Consular code, leaving me free to concentrate on the very

important naval messages ... The situation was steadily deteriorating in Singapore and when an important Japanese was summoned for questioning this became impossible, as only a dead body arrived; he had taken a pill in the car. Whilst we were working extremely hard every day, there seemed no sense of urgency in Government circles with no apparent organisation or mobilisation of the large civil population on a war basis.

The pressure of their work was not their only problem. 'Accommodation at the Singapore Naval Base was very bad. No air-conditioning of office or sleeping quarters. The latter was in small cabins extremely hot at night in this season, Singapore being within one degree of the Equator.'

It was certainly not the kind of climate likely to resolve Eric Nave's health problems, but there was better news on the codebreaking front. With the break found by GCCS in Code D, progress was rapidly made in building up a skeleton codebook. By 7 September GCCS was able to outline the weaknesses of the code and on 18 September Burnett set out from London for Singapore with this and additional material to assist in breaking it.

> Malcolm Burnett now arrived from the UK bringing with him the breaking methods for the new 5-figure cipher the Japanese Navy had introduced. We had to farm this task out to London where they had a section dealing solely with breaking systems. Our task on the spot was clearly the provision of intelligence urgently needed to meet operational requirements.

GCCS had discovered Code D's structure and how it was used, but the recovery of groups for numerals left the British with most of the hard work still to be done. This was a massive task but by 11 December GCCS was congratulating the FECB Y Section on its decryption of more than one thousand Code D messages, and by the end of the year there was general satisfaction in the British camp about their capability to read Japanese messages. According to Commander Denniston: 'To sum up the situation of the Naval Section [of GCCS] in 1939, including the Japanese branch in Hong Kong: they exercised a very fair measure of control of all Italian and Japanese naval cyphers.'[12]

In the Nave narrative there now appears another inconsistency.

Although FECB in Singapore and OP-20-G were both working to recover values from JN-25, there were no links between the two. The Americans knew of the existence of FECB, because a US Navy liaison officer had joined the organisation in December 1939, but it is unlikely that its codebreaking activities had been revealed to them before Eric Nave left Singapore in February 1940. It was not until November 1940 that approval for this step came from London, following an American approach to the British in August with the offer of a Purple decoder as part of a broader signals intelligence exchange. Similarly, the British may have surmised that the Americans were working on Japanese codes, but the existence and purpose of the US Navy's Manila station CAST was probably not known. However, Eric said that:

> FECB flew an officer, Malcolm Burnett from Singapore to the US unit at Corregidor to give them the means of breaking and reading these five cipher messages which they categorised as JN-25. He reported that they were not reading operational messages but relying on their extensive DF network for information on the Japanese Fleet. This important step enabled Singapore, Corregidor and Honolulu to exchange solutions and recoveries.

In December 1940, the IJN replaced JN-25A with the B variant. This comprised a new codebook, containing the same systemic flaws as the first, but the earlier additive table was retained. Broadly speaking, this exchange did take place as described above — although at that point HYPO at Pearl Harbor was not working on JN-25 — but the visit did not occur until well after Eric Nave was in back in Australia. I conclude that the appearance of the above account at this point in Nave's narrative is an oversight, and Burnett may have passed this information to Eric privately. There is no evidence that an arrangement between FECB and CAST was forged before the capitals had given their blessing. A visit by Commander Wisden, the deputy chief of FECB, to Manila did take place in November 1940 but Burnett is confirmed by US sources to have made a visit to CAST in April 1941.[13] The first exchange of Code D/JN-25B material between FECB and CAST took place on 28 February 1941.

But in the midst of the gathering gloom, on 2 September 1939

Paymaster Commander Theodore Eric Nave and Sister Helena Gray
were married in Singapore's Anglican Cathedral. Eric's best man was
Bouncer Burnett and Harry Shaw gave Helena away. Consider that
the FECB party only embarked in *Birmingham* on 24 August and
that the ship arrived in Singapore three days afterwards. A week
later Eric was waiting at the altar for his bride. Somehow, amidst
all the turmoil of the movement of a considerable number of people
and their equipment at relatively short notice from Hong Kong
to Singapore, the couple had managed to make all the necessary
arrangements for a wedding in a place neither had ever more than
visited — a considerable achievement.

There are some clues in the Nave memoirs as to how this might
have been done. Eric had a friend of long standing who had settled
in Singapore and established a number of successful businesses,
including a racecourse in the Cameron Highlands to the east of
Kuala Lumpur, in what is now Malaysia. He offered the Naves his
house, established in the mountain coolness, for their honeymoon,
an offer they gratefully accepted. Later, Eric's friend was also to make
available to the newlyweds a house in Singapore at a competitive rate
of interest, a most generous concession in the over-heated housing
market of the time.

In the possession of the Nave children is a charming letter written
by Helena to 'Father and Mother' — Thomas and Ethyl — soon after
the marriage. It is difficult to judge how much they may have known
about Helena, but she wrote as if she had satisfied any criteria that
Thomas in particular might have stipulated to his son. Judging from
the letter, there is no doubt that Helena had all the social graces that
Thomas had worried about when Eric was considering proposing to
Miss Barry in 1930.

War had broken out between the British Commonwealth and
Germany on the day after the wedding, but Eric found the authorities
in Singapore strangely apathetic in the face of a growing Japanese
security threat that his daily work uncovered. Codebreaking disclosed
that there was no shortage of Japanese agents active in the colony, but
the authorities seemed slow to act, which must have been a source of

much frustration to Eric. For exercise and relaxation he returned to golf, joining the Island Golf Club.

> The membership was a mixed one, but most Europeans belonged to the Royal Singapore, but I never met any members, for I found little pleasure in the golf. It was more a case of keeping my body fit for duty as I was now in my 3rd year of the tropics with virtually seven days a week pressure of work.

Eric was also invited to join the Johore Club across the causeway in Malaysia (then the British colony of Malaya), but there the members got even less satisfaction from their golf. The Sultan, on whose land the course was constructed, had become enamoured of a petty officer's vivacious singer-dancer daughter, who appeared 'sparsely clad in the outfit supplied for her turn at a place of entertainment'. He divorced his Scottish wife of many years in accordance with the Muslim custom, using the thrice-repeated word *Talaq*, and married the showgirl. The British community was scandalised and cut the Sultan's new wife dead whenever she appeared at the club. 'His retaliation was swift and dramatic,' Eric noted. 'When the members arrived for their customary round of golf they found a shrub or tree planted in the centre of each green where the hole would normally be.'

It was the period of the 'Phony War' in Europe, although the RN was kept busy around the world, particularly combating German commerce raiders. In Japan there seemed a ray of hope for peace when Admiral Yonai became Prime Minister in January 1940. Yonai was known to oppose war with the Western powers, but his appointment was bitterly opposed by the Japanese Army and his government fell in July.

> Although Indian troops were now arriving in Singapore it was impossible for us to feel optimistic about any war in the Far East when we knew so much about Japanese strengths coming into the area, both Army and Navy, and particularly in Siam [Thailand].

There is ample evidence that through the work of FECB, including Sections Y and W, the British were very well supplied with intelligence on Japanese military capabilities and intentions, as well as information on strengths and dispositions. A question frequently asked in the light of the complete military debacle that ensued in early 1942 is, 'How could they have been so unprepared?' Very broadly speaking, the two major schools of thought on the answer can be considered as the 'incompetence' theory and the 'confusion' theory. The former points to evidence that the military commanders simply could not bring themselves to believe that a mob of 'little yellow rice-eaters' could defeat British forces, let alone field superior technology and apply it with consummate skill. Thus they took few steps to prepare to meet the Japanese.

The 'confusion' school believes that although there was some incompetence displayed, senior British commanders were so confused about Japanese objectives that they simply dithered until it was too late to take effective action. Perhaps the best brief summation is the one offered by the British historian of the Far East in the period leading up to the war, Anthony Best, whose penetrating studies of the intelligence background of this whole period are major sources of important insights into the British view of the Japanese. He said: 'The picture which emerges of Malaya in 1941 is therefore one in which the FECB did not speak with a clear enough voice to an audience that was already profoundly deaf. Conditions in London were not that different.'[14]

By now, the pressure of unremitting codebreaking work, the enervating climate and, possibly, the knowledge that so little notice was being taken of the warning signs being detected by Section Y, all affected Eric's health and his bouts of sickness became more frequent.

> I was again hospitalised in Johore Hospital. Various tests were carried out and I was subjected to every indignity the profession could devise but the Superintendent could not find the answer and called the senior Surgeon. He asked me a number of questions and as I answered each one in the affirmative he said 'No doubt about it, its "Sprue"'.

Tropical sprue is a malabsorption syndrome that is prevalent in tropical and subtropical areas. The cause of the disease is unknown, but could be related to ingestion of infectious organisms. Common symptoms include diarrhoea, indigestion, abdominal cramps, weight loss, pallor and irritability and the treatment involves a strictly controlled diet low in fat. Folic acid is a corrective and nowadays treatment with antibiotics is recommended, but there were none available in 1940.[15] In Eric the disease had been accelerating all the time he was in the Far East but had not been diagnosed, let alone treated. The doctors recommended a period of leave in a cooler climate. Normally, sprue cases were invalided out of the tropics but, as Helena was told, 'He is key personnel and we want him back'. Eric was to be sent on leave to Australia.

> This was most unsatisfactory from my point of view as if invalided we would be sent back to England at Admiralty expense. Instead I had to pay our fares and all other expenses and then return to a climate my body could no longer tolerate ... I knew I was worn out and needed permanent relief from work in the tropics, but the Administration in London was clearly unaware of this.

Despite this remark, the decision on leave was probably taken by the naval authorities in Singapore rather than referred to London. Nobody is truly indispensable, but FECB apparently thought sufficiently highly of Eric Nave that the Chief of Intelligence Staff was prepared to intervene in local medical judgments and to influence the doctors away from the more common invaliding decision. So, in February 1940, the Naves embarked in a Dutch ship for the voyage to Australia, Eric travelling in civilian clothes and equipped with a passport that described him as an accountant because of uncertainty over Dutch feelings about the RN.

It was an anticlimactic end to an extraordinarily fruitful period of Eric's life. He had led the attack on a number of key IJN and diplomatic codes and had made a good start on filling in the skeleton codebook for the new Code D. Later, when the Americans discovered the depth of FECB's penetration of Japanese codes prior to the war, they were surprised. Indeed, Rusbridger's case for a Churchillian conspiracy over Pearl Harbor is partially constructed on the success that FECB and its GCCS colleagues had enjoyed. With the Flag

Officers' Code Nave seems to have had personal success in attacking it that was denied to the US Navy group in Pearl Harbor. On top of this he had discovered a number of other codes, including what was known as the Dockyard Code. The value of the information being coded in this system at a time of accelerating IJN preparations for war can be imagined.

Again it must have been with mixed feelings that Eric set sail for Australia, this time with his new bride. He must have had a sense of pride in his achievements mixed with a dread of having to return his ill body to Singapore to continue the battle on completion of his leave. On a more positive note, he had begun a much-needed period of rest to regain his health, as well as the welcome anticipation of seeing his family again and of introducing Helena to them. He was not to know that he was sailing towards a remarkable change in his professional life, or that the organisation he was leaving would shortly disappear in the flames of war.

7 Australia Revisited, 1940–41

The passage from Singapore took only nine days, and on 22 February 1940 Eric and Helena, now four months pregnant, arrived at the port of Fremantle, twenty kilometres south of Perth. The couple was met by the Resident Naval Officer, who shepherded them through the formalities of Immigration, Customs and Health, which Eric observed were 'necessarily thorough'. Their onward passage to Adelaide was by train 1800 kilometres to the east across the huge empty Nullarbor Plain. The train only ran twice a week but, by chance, there was one departing on the evening of their arrival. Eric was able to book seats and the Navy provided a car to take the couple, and luggage, to Perth to catch it. They must have sunk into their berths gratefully after a long and trying day.

The trains may nowadays run more frequently and at higher speed, but the Nullarbor hasn't changed much since 1940. Eric and Helena had three days of travel ahead of them before they reached the junction at Port Pirie in South Australia and changed trains for Adelaide. It was not a pleasant trip.

> The train progressed steadily eastwards. It was summer and hot water came from both taps in the wash place. The aborigines came begging at a few stops which made one feel rather sad for them. My father had arranged a reserve carriage from Port Pirie, being unsure of how sick I was. The whole family came to the station in Adelaide to meet us and now my 'leave' was to start, in the cool weather mentioned in Australia. The temperature was over the century [Fahrenheit] where it remained for 10 days, with the top of 116F, not falling very much at night.

One can only wonder what Helena Nave made of this introduction to Australia.

An early priority was to have the Singapore diagnosis of Eric's condition verified. By coincidence (or was it the Nave luck again?), the specialist consulted had served in the RAN and had travelled from Adelaide to Melbourne in 1917 with Eric when he went to join the Navy. Moreover, he had recently treated a patient with the same condition in the UK. After several tests, the diagnosis of tropical sprue was confirmed, and the specialist added strawberries to the diet of liver extract, Melba toast and oranges that Eric had been prescribed in Singapore. It wasn't much, but it was something.

Eric's condition was of some concern and he was placed in the care of the District Naval Medical Officer in Adelaide. The RAN's Director of Naval Medical Services in Melbourne advised the Naval Board of this and commented that Eric appeared 'to have been a semi-invalid for the last 11 months'. The medical survey report one month later stated that the sprue had been contracted in April 1939 and had persisted, with intermissions, ever since. While Eric's condition had improved, further attacks of diarrhoea were likely and 'he is totally unfit for further service in the tropics.'[1]

When Eric's leave, or more properly convalescence, had expired he reported to Navy Office in Melbourne, where the whole naval adventure had begun only twenty-three years previously. Of course, he was a commander now and an officer of the Royal Navy as well, and he did not want to be sent back to Singapore, so there was some discussion about what should be done with him. Luck was, however, again with him as the Chief of Naval Staff at the time was Vice Admiral Sir Ragnar Colvin CB RN.

> He had been Naval Attaché in Tokyo in 1922/23 when I was studying Japanese. He was quite sympathetic to my condition, particularly as he recalled that I had bought credit to the Naval Service in obtaining record high marks in my Japanese Interpreters examination.

The Australians duly informed the Admiral Commanding Malaya —Eric's superior officer — of the results of the medical examination. It seemed pretty clear that FECB were not going to get him back.

But the RN had not abandoned attempts to regain the codebreaking knowledge and experience of Eric Nave that easily. On 8 May the admiral responded tartly with a message saying: 'It is observed that this officer's services would be urgently required for duty in United Kingdom should he not become fit for further service in the Far East'.

But the medical world was adamant that Commander Nave could not even travel through the tropics just yet so, in the end, Eric was assigned to work on intelligence duties. Commander R.B.M. Long, known familiarly as 'Cocky' (short for 'cockatoo'), had been appointed Director of Naval Intelligence in August 1939, the first to hold the post as a separate staff director since 1923. As Long and the RAN Naval Intelligence Organisation had key roles in the next episodes in Eric Nave's career, this is an appropriate point at which to provide some background.

The work that has since become known as Procedures W and Y were features of the RAN's contribution to World War I. The first recovery of an Imperial German Naval codebook took place in Port Phillip Bay in 1914, and it was an Australian break into another code that ensured that Admiral von Spee and most of his squadron would meet a violent end at the Battle of the Falkland Islands at the hands of the Royal Navy. The RAN Wireless Service, as it was known, tracked German ships in the Indian and Pacific Oceans throughout the war. The British saluted the overall performance of this very small but dedicated and skillful group and the future of naval intelligence in Australia seemed assured.

Peace and the perception that the 'war to end all wars' had just been fought led to a rapid decline in naval manpower and Intelligence ceased to be a separate RAN staff division. Instead, it became the responsibility of the Assistant Chief of Naval Staff, a very busy officer. Understandably, the maintenance of an intelligence organisation, its manpower and standards became a relatively low priority. There were, of course, exceptions. The idea of the famous RAN Coastwatcher Service, first mooted in 1913, was voiced again in 1919, and by 1928 the bones of the wartime organisation were in place. Sydney became the de facto centre of intelligence in the RAN, where the flame was kept alive by a succession of dedicated and innovative district intelligence officers.

While the organisation unravelled, the concept of interception and breaking codes continued to receive some attention from the RAN. The directive that fleet telegraphists were to learn *kana* Morse, the loan of Eric Nave to the Admiralty for service in *Hawkins* and 'outside Admiralty', and a series of letters between Melbourne and London on the subject, led to the development of good working relationships in Procedure Y between the RAN and the China Fleet. All RAN cruisers were required to practise Procedure Y, and former RAN telegraphists in outposts as isolated as Nauru were encouraged to retain their *kana* skills. Over time, the RAN developed a cadre of experienced *kana* operators with a good knowledge of the IJN's communications architecture and procedures, but they were few in number. Moreover, they did not break IJN codes, this being left to GCCS and people like Eric Nave and, from 1935, to FECB.

In April 1934, the Naval Board agreed to boost the RAN's Procedure Y capacity by allowing in the personnel budget for eight telegraphists specifically for this duty. Their assigned target was the Japanese Mandated Islands. In 1938, plans to send two of these operators to FECB in Hong Kong for training and experience could not be fulfilled because of an acute shortage of qualified operators. However, by January 1939 the Naval Board could offer FECB twelve fully trained Procedure Y telegraphists with fifteen more in the training pipeline. Plans were also put in place for three direction-finding stations to be established in Australia. This Australian part of the Pacific Naval Intelligence Organisation network — HMAS *Harman* in Canberra, HMAS *Coonawarra* in Darwin and a third station at Jandakot near Perth in Western Australia — was not fully completed until 1941, but the stations were desperately needed to fill gaps in the reception coverage from other British sites in the Far East.[2] Other Australian stations were also involved in the interception of Japanese radio transmissions, including Park Orchards twenty kilometres east of Melbourne from 1939, and Townsville from June 1941. The point to note here is that the Australian commitment to interception and direction finding of Japanese signals was both of long standing and of a size quite substantial for a navy as small as the RAN. The British certainly welcomed and benefited from its output.

As the signs of a crisis in relations between the West and Japan began to emerge — and many Australians, including those in high places, were sure that hostilities were only a matter of time — the need for intelligence assumed a higher priority in RAN planning and activities. The close ties with the China Fleet resulted in the RAN being offered and accepting the post of Deputy Chief of Intelligence Staff at the rank of commander in 1935. That a small navy like Australia's would find an officer to send to Hong Kong from its quite meagre supply of commanders speaks volumes about the importance it attached to the organisation. And it was also in 1935 that Cocky Long made his appearance in RAN intelligence circles as officer-in-charge of the District Intelligence Office in Sydney.

Long had joined the RAN in the first entry into its new Naval College in 1913. His career had followed a familiar pattern for the day, including several postings to billets in RN ships. Although he was by specialisation a torpedo officer, he had shown an interest in intelligence but the Naval Board had not responded to his requests for training in that direction. When the British cruiser *Dauntless* in which he was serving was sent to join the China Fleet in early 1927 he made the acquaintance of one Paymaster Lieutenant Nave RAN, of whom he formed a very good opinion.[3] However, Long's steady progress up the ranks of the RAN officer corps came to an abrupt halt in 1935 when he was not selected for promotion to commander at the appropriate juncture. No sufficient explanation has been found for this but, although undoubtedly hard on Long, it was a godsend for the RAN and Australia's wartime allies, because Long was an absolute genius at Intelligence.

Urbane, erudite and well connected through family and marriage ties with the top echelons of Australian society, Cocky Long exercised influence well outside the range of the normal naval officer, and he was able to persuade people of all walks of life to become involved in the intelligence empire he proceeded to construct. From his Sydney office he established links with the kinds of agencies that would be useful in the collection of intelligence — ships' masters, airline pilots, customs agents and businessmen who travelled into areas of intelligence interest. He ran most of these agents personally: it is said that after the end of the war he destroyed hundreds of files on them, as they did not appear, or need to appear, in official records.

Long's father-in-law, for example, was the owner of Australia's largest inter-island shipping company, whose ships were ready collectors of information on what the Japanese were doing in their mandated territories in the Pacific, and what Japanese trading companies were up to in other areas of interest to Australia. When Australia established a consulate in the strategically important Portuguese colony on the eastern half of the island of Timor, the consul and his deputy were both Long's men. He even used his own staff innovatively. One was sent on his honeymoon to visit South-East Asian cities of intelligence interest, while another took up a vacant position in a trade office in Shanghai.

Long's talents naturally drew him to Navy Office, where he was successful in having the Directorate re-established as a separate entity. There, as part of the Pacific Naval Intelligence Organisation, he had access to a lot more sensitive information, as well as separate communications channels between his office and his fellow directors in the Admiralty and other dominions and colonies. Although the British were still inclined to regard intelligence flow as a one-way matter — the 'colonials' would be told only what the Admiralty thought they needed to know — Long was not deterred. Possibly by discussing the issue with returning deputy commanders from FECB, and certainly in consultation with the RAN Director of Signals and Communications, Commander Jack Newman, Long became an enthusiastic supporter of and advocate for an Australian signals intelligence organisation.

Newman had also been a member of the first Australian Naval College entry and it's interesting that Newman, who started his professional career as a submariner, became a communicator, while

Long started as a torpedo specialist and wound up in intelligence. Nave had started as a paymaster and become a cryptanalyst. In March 1939, Newman had represented Australia at a conference in Singapore on wireless intelligence in the Far East. By the end of that year he and Long convinced the Chief of Naval Staff, Admiral Colvin, to make a formal proposal to the heads of the Army and Air Force and the Government that a 'cryptographic' organisation be set up in Australia.[4]

The Army was interested, the Royal Australian Air Force (RAAF) less so (its own directorate of intelligence had only just been established) and the Defence Committee and Government dithered. It was not until April 1940 that Prime Minister Menzies officially sought the opinion of London, which did not come back until October that year and said, in effect, 'if you want to, but we'll be in charge'. Meanwhile, both the Army and the Navy set about achieving the aim without waiting for government sanction. The Army first took a leaf out of the Navy's book and established an intercept detachment as part of the 3rd Australian Signals Division at Park Orchards, which concentrated on Japanese and foreign news broadcasts. As well, in January 1940 a 'cipher-breaking group' was set up by Headquarters Eastern Command in Sydney. Prominent academics in the fields of classics and mathematics at Sydney University were approached and encouraged to take an interest in the problem, which they did. However, although this had proved a successful ploy in GCCS, at Bletchley Park the academics had recourse to the long experience and cryptanalytical expertise of the existing staff. The same was not the case in Sydney. Nevertheless, they studied the codes used in Japanese diplomatic cables, including 'LA', which they broke easily. A report by the command headed 'Cryptography' and dated 18 October 1940 said:

> With further reference to the above subject you are advised that the work of the cipher-breaking group continues and that exceedingly good results are either anticipated or in view. Work has been concentrated on an attempt to break down the Japanese commercial and diplomatic codes by reducing the cipher groups to a Romanised-Japanese text which could then be read freely

by Japanese interpreters. Three definite codes have been identified in use and in the case of one of these it has become apparent that a new code was brought into operation on 1 Oct 40.[5]

There is only circumstantial evidence that any other diplomatic codes were actually broken by the Army, although a valiant *ab initio* attempt was being made. But in the same report quoted above, the group was able to record success in breaking a coded letter between an eminent British official in Shanghai and a lady in Sydney, which turned out to be 'personal and salacious'. With a nice sense of irony, the report concluded: 'From this you will be able to appreciate to some degree the nature and value of the work that can be accomplished by this cipher-breaking group'.

The RAN already had the intercept and direction-finding stations, but it had no codebreakers. Then, in May 1940, Eric Nave appeared in Melbourne looking for work, and preferably not in Singapore. One can only imagine the delight with which he was greeted by Newman and Long. In a minute written in November 1939, Long had identified the critical missing link needed in setting up his 'cryptographic organisation' in Australia:

> For some years prior to the commencement of the war every effort was made to locate Cryptographers, but apart from one or two amateurs who are obviously of no value unless trained, no professional Cryptographer has been located. In this connection, Dr Frederick Wheatley of Sydney obtained some fame during the Great War for 'cracking' the code used by the 'SCHARNHORST' and 'GNEISNAU' when in the Pacific. This gentleman is now over 70 years of age and although he possesses a profound knowledge of the German language he is probably quite unable to deal with modern Codes and Cyphers.[6]

Nave was, therefore, nothing short of manna from heaven. An experienced cryptanalyst, an accomplished linguist, and an expert on Japanese diplomatic and naval codes, he could hardly have had better qualifications to lead the new group. And he was an Australian, despite holding a Royal Navy commission. As Eric Nave saw the situation, however, it was far from a gift.

I was attached to the Signal Division, the director being Commander J.B.

Newman. The RAN had a transmitting station at Belconnen outside Canberra and nearby the receiving station called HMAS *Harman*. There was no interception of foreign wireless and no operators trained in reading Japanese *kana* [this is incorrect]. Commander Newman was most obliging in arranging for the basic qualification. The other drawback was their inability to get a clear signal of Japanese stations. There was no interception of Japanese W/T, no skeleton codebook and no means by which I could follow the work I had been doing for years. Even if I had raw material from a W/T station, without the basic codebook I was out of action.

The FECB in Singapore signalled that they wanted me back to solve a change in the Flag Officers' Code which carried the most valuable intelligence but nobody else could do it at FECB. However, after specialist reports they were advised that the state of my health made this impossible.

It was in May 1940 that the Germans launched their *blitzkrieg* through Holland, Belgium and into France, overrunning these countries and driving Britain's major ally out of the war in only six weeks. This was a grim period for British forces around the world and Eric recalled that

> It now seemed that the strong voice of Winston Churchill voicing the defiance of the British people was our main weapon, and how well he expressed that defiance! At this time he sent a personal letter to officers of Commander and equivalent rank. I kept this historic letter.

And so he did, for a copy appears in his memoirs, addressed 'Commander T.E. Nave RN c/o Navy Office, Melbourne' and dated 4 July 1940. The letter exhorts its recipients that 'on what may be the eve of an attempted invasion' it is 'their duty to maintain a spirit of alert and confident energy'.

Against this sombre background of a succession of bad news from Europe, Eric Nave set about the creation of what was euphemistically described as the 'naval organisation', comprised of himself, another paymaster and a small clerical staff. He must have had a sense of *déjà vu*, as his situation was not dissimilar to that he had been obliged to confront in HMS *Hawkins* in 1925. There were obvious differences. He himself was by now an experienced codebreaker, and he could be assured of a steady supply of intercepted messages to work on. But

he was, once again, by himself when it came to cryptanalysis with
great things expected of him, and rather more pressure for results to
emerge from his work. In addition, he was physically unwell. These
circumstances must have been something of a comedown for him
from his days as ace codebreaker in FECB, and his frustration showed
in the following comment about this hiatus in his career:

> Since mid-1925, when loaned to *Hawkins*, I now had fifteen years experience
> of Japanese codes and in that time had been in continuous production of
> intelligence, other than for very brief periods during system changes. Reading
> code messages involves two distinct operations, the first and dominating
> stage being the solution of the system used. Being the first on this work
> since 1925 and entirely self-taught, I had to do everything myself, but in this
> phase I was virtually the only person in FECB with that competence. Once
> the system was broken and in the second phase the clear text emerged, it
> was merely translators' work and such were easy to find.

Eric had, in fact, undertaken training courses while at GCCS as
he himself noted. Furthermore, the last phrase regarding the ease
of finding translators was not true of Australia at any time, and
certainly not in 1940. Language training is not the main plot of this
story, but some background is instructive in acquainting the reader
with the parlous state in which all the codebreaking organisations in
Australia found themselves. It will be recalled that Japanese language
instruction had begun at the Royal Military College Duntroon near
Canberra in 1916, which provided a trickle of young officers assessed
to have the aptitude to undertake studies in Japan. In 1937, the Army
decided to abandon this program on the grounds that 'this language
is of little cultural value', an intriguing observation. The same year
a part-time instructor of Japanese at the University of Sydney was
relieved of this duty, 'as it had interfered too greatly with his duties as
Quartermaster and Adjutant, Sydney University Rifles'.

At least the Government was puzzled by these decisions and, in
July 1938, the Minister of Defence called for a review of the policy on
language training by the Defence Committee. The response from the
services was slow; a sub-committee on which DNI Long served was
established only in March 1939, and not until January 1940 did it table

its report identifying the need for seventy-five Japanese interpreters and 'double that number of personnel with some knowledge of the language'. In February, the Defence Committee took the report, noted that at that time the Services had no first class Japanese interpreters, and then pigeonholed it because of the war in Europe.[7]

As an historical aside, the Japanese Government was also keen to find out the state of Australia's facilities for training Japanese linguists. In late July 1936, the Consul General in Sydney sent a flurry of letters to academic institutions and commercial language schools across Australia, in which he asked for details of qualified language instructors, student loads and courses taught. It was a prime example of overt intelligence collection and the absence of responses on the file held by the Australian Archives might indicate that it was recognised as such by the recipients of the inquiry.[8]

Because of the lack of accommodation in an overcrowded wartime Melbourne, Eric and Helena were obliged to take a suite of rooms in the Majestic Hotel in St Kilda, just south of the central business district and a short tram ride to naval headquarters at Victoria Barracks. On 27 July 1940 their first child Elizabeth entered a very sombre world, but brought great delight to her parents. A snapshot taken when Elizabeth was a few weeks old shows a gaunt and emaciated Eric, still enduring the effects of his illness. Shortly afterwards, they were able to move in with Eric's brother Lionel, sharing a house in Hawthorn, a suburb east of the centre of the city. Bouncer Burnett became Elizabeth's godfather.

At Nave's 'naval organisation', attempts to solve codes based on material forwarded by airmail from FECB in Singapore had been given up. In response to a question asked by a researcher on why he didn't take up the struggle with JN-25 in Melbourne, Eric replied simply that 'We could not intercept Japanese main naval traffic and moreover, as the only Japanese linguist and cryptographer, I could not handle the complicated processing'.[9] This was perfectly true: as Eric knew from his Singapore days, attacking JN-25A was a task for a large team. Instead, Nave's efforts were restricted to studying the codes used in the mandated islands traffic being intercepted by

Australian stations, and the commercial shipping traffic originating from Japanese merchant ships. The importance of the merchant ship code came from analysis of the traffic originated by Italian merchant ships in the days leading up to Italy joining the war in June 1940, which had demonstrated that commercial traffic could be an important intelligence source on national intentions.

There is almost an exultant note in the follow-up message sent by the Naval Board to Admiralty in July 1940 on Eric's medical and employment circumstances.

> Paymaster Commander Nave will not be medically fit to return to Singapore during the current year. Ultimate fitness to return in doubt. Meanwhile his services are being fully employed in establishing special intelligence organisation here. Good results have already been obtained particularly in connection with Japanese Mandated Islands codes and Merchant Ship Codes. These results have been communicated to Singapore Bureau which has been kept fully advised of Nave's activities. Hope to expand local organisation and Naval Board consider Nave can continue to be very usefully employed here.[10]

This message, incidentally, at a classification of only Secret, violates all the rules for reporting and discussing codebreaking activities. Fortunately, it was sent by cable rather than by radio. Had the Japanese intercepted and decoded it, there could have been serious consequences for the work of Allied codebreakers.

Meanwhile, the Japanese progression towards war continued. In July the Yonai Cabinet fell, leaving the war faction in unchallenged control of the Japanese Navy and Army and, therefore, of the government. Then, in September, Japan pressured the Vichy French regime in Indochina into permitting Japanese forces to be stationed in the northern part of the country. In the same month Japan joined Germany and Italy in the Tripartite Pact, by which it agreed to make common cause with the other Axis members.

A naval conference in Singapore in October 1940 provided the Australians with an opportunity to advertise their home-grown signals intelligence capability and to seek closer links with FECB. This prompted an invitation for a visit to Australia by the chief of on Intelligence Staff, Captain F.J. Wylie, in January 1941, hosted by DNI Long. The post-visit FECB message to the Australians, summed up in a minute circulated by DNI on 10 January 1941, was both comforting and confusing: Wylie appreciated the help that the 'naval organisation' had already provided him but he also wanted it to take on more responsibility. And he was firmly of the view that it ought to be under his control in Singapore.

These remarks must have given Eric Nave much to ponder. While it was flattering that his organisation was well regarded by Captain Wylie after such a brief existence, it was difficult to see how it could possibly take on more responsibility without augmentation by cryptanalysts and interpreters, neither of which were offered by the British. Wylie merely undertook to inform DNI of any applicants to FECB for Japanese interpreter positions, but had no further suggestions on how these skilled personnel might be found. Wylie himself seems to have had time to reflect and reconsider the issue of the 'naval organisation', which he termed a 'Y' bureau, before he prepared his own report on the visit to Commander-in-Chief China on 17 January. His hard line on FECB control, pushed in talks in Australia, had been modified somewhat.

> The question of assistance from Australia in the form of a subsidiary 'Y' bureau under Paymaster Commander Nave was discussed. Captain Wylie stated that the FECB's opinion favours concentration of effort in one place in order to take full advantage from pooling of knowledge and experience. It was obvious, however, that in wartime there were certain advantages in avoiding having all the eggs in one basket and, in view of the necessity for Paymaster Commander Nave to remain in Australia, considerable value should be obtained from a subsidiary organisation in that country. It was agreed that Paymaster Commander Nave should endeavour to obtain suitable assistance.[11]

In January 1941, Eric suffered a recurrence of his disease and was sent on two-weeks' convalescent leave. Nevertheless, he was back at work before Jack Newman left to attend a communications conference in Singapore in March, following which he followed up the matters raised during Wylie's visit with FECB. Nave briefed Newman on what questions to ask, and Newman's report on this contains the following observation under the heading of 'Cryptography':

> At the request of Paymaster Commander Nave it was suggested that copies of Consular and Diplomatic codes, and any of the codes regularly intercepted in Australia, should be made available to him. The head of the 'Y' Section stated, however, that the Consular and Diplomatic codes were now so complicated that a large staff of experts is required to obtain results, and that anything of interest read from this or other codes or cyphers would be forwarded to Naval Board. This did not appear to me to be an ideal arrangement, and it is suggested that Paymaster Commander Nave makes further request for codes and cyphers which are regularly intercepted and which he considers may be of value in Australia.
>
> Head of 'Y' section emphasised the great importance attached to breaking the 45 sign code; and stated that he would be most grateful for any help Paymaster Commander Nave gives in this matter which is now of great urgency.

This was an odd kind of backhanded compliment to Eric. Consular codes were too difficult for him and his organisation to handle, but could he please solve one that nobody at FECB could crack. His response was very muted indeed:

> Cooperation from Australia depends on the material available, and it seems that if the Australian 'Y' duty remains as largely Mandated Islands interception that the best assistance would be rendered by assuming responsibility for call signs and W/T Intelligence of stations in that area and special work on codes in general use there.[12]

Nave's reaction to the FECB refusal of his request for assistance might have been tempered by reflections on the situation in which Britain now found itself. It came following a further recurrence of his tropical sprue in May and another medical survey on his condition, which had found Eric fit for shore service in a temperate climate only.

> This illness I had contracted was most unfortunate, coming at a time when the country was in need of the knowledge required, and rendered me quite unfit to serve in the area of operations. To return to Singapore would only mean further hospitalisation and destroy my chance of recovery. I was

comforted by the knowledge that here in Australia, the land of my birth and education, I could do very useful work while starting on the slow process of rebuilding my own strength, being still on a restricted diet.

There was one other fascinating detail to come out of the Wylie visit. The British and Americans had become aware of Japanese efforts to use South American countries as bases for espionage and subversion. There they could be protected from the ministrations of the US Federal Bureau of Investigation and like agencies. Nave's group had discovered that it could get clear intercepts of consular traffic to Japan's posts in South America and asked whether these were of any interest to FECB. They were: Wylie's report of his visit highlights traffic to and from Lima in Peru, Santiago in Chile and Sepetiba in Brazil, and copies of these messages can be found in the US Naval Security Group histories in the national archives in Maryland. FECB was also interested in Australian intercepts of Russian Far East traffic saying that 'Little is known of Russian Far East W/T organisation and procedure and any assistance in interception and analysis would be greatly appreciated'.[13]

The month of May, however, marked a crucial juncture in the development of Australia's signals intelligence organisation and capability. Brought together by the realisation that neither could individually apply the necessary capabilities to solving their cryptanalytical problems, at a series of conferences largely engineered by DNI Long, the Army and Navy decided to pool their resources to set up a combined attack on Japanese codes. The existence of the 'naval organisation' was acknowledged, as were the expertise of Nave and the RAN's links with FECB. At the same time, the need for Australia to develop a capability independent of Singapore was a prominent consideration in the changes which were agreed. The solution was to combine the Eastern Command 'cipher-breaking group', and the 'special intelligence section' at Park Orchards, with the 'naval organisation' to produce a Special Intelligence Bureau, headed by Eric Nave.

> The Military Intelligence [MI] people had told me that M.I. Sydney had a small group at the University who were studying Japanese cable messages.

This showed most commendable planning by the Army and also an excellent spirit on the part of the University staff who gave their time in the interests of their country.

I met the gentlemen concerned; they were Professor T.G. Room, a distinguished mathematician, Richard Lyons, mathematician, Professor Dale Trendall, a linguist of many talents and A.P. Treweek, from the language area. All agreed to come to Melbourne and the necessary arrangements were made by the Army with the University.

The new organisation was established in July 1941, initially within Naval Headquarters in Victoria Barracks in Melbourne. By August, the cooperation of three of the Sydney academics had been enlisted. The bureau now consisted of Nave, an RAN cryptanalyst — Lieutenant Miller —, translators Lieutenant Jamieson, RAN Volunteer Reserve, and Army Lieutenant Longfield-Lloyd, Professor Room, Mr Lyons and Major Treweek, a classicist. Treweek held the rank of major, having been a member of the Citizens Military Forces before the war. Professor Trendall joined the bureau in January 1942.[14] Although considered at the time, applications for commissions for the other three academics were never processed. Using the good offices of DNI Long and his liaison officer attached to Dutch naval headquarters in Jakarta, Nave arranged for Professor Room, accompanied by an Jamieson, to travel to the Netherlands East Indies for discussions with the Dutch cryptanalytical section at Bandung known as *Kamer 14* (Room 14). The codebreakers of *Kamer 14* had made considerable progress on Japanese diplomatic and naval codes independently of the British and Americans, but by 1941 there was a good liaison established with FECB. From there, the party travelled to Singapore, arriving back in Australia in November after a three-week trip.

This is an appropriate point to raise the question of why scholars of the classics and mathematicians seemed to have been favoured in the selection of potential codebreakers. Unfortunately, there are no firm answers about classics scholars. It is perhaps their mastery of arcane and often dead languages that heightens their awareness of, and sensitivity towards, the structure of a language. As Eric Nave discovered, knowledge of the orthographic rules of Japanese was a great help in breaking codes. Mathematicians are adept at establishing numerical relationships and probabilities, and they came into their own when the attack on codes and ciphers became mechanised. But a lack of classics or mathematics in one's education was not a barrier to codebreaking. After the attack on Pearl Harbor, when the Honolulu signals intelligence centre, Station HYPO, was desperately seeing additional resources, the US Navy reassigned them the band of the battleship USS *California* — now resting on the bottom of the harbour. At HYPO the musicians showed a remarkable aptitude for the art of codebreaking.[15] In Britain, recruiters for Bletchley Park were also interested in candidates' ability to play chess and dexterity in solving cryptic crosswords.

The Special Intelligence Bureau was working on a number of Japanese codes. From June 1940 Nave's 'naval organisation' had been taking an interest in what became known as JN-20. Traffic levels were comparatively light, and it was not until November 1941 that a full break was made into the 'C' version, when it was discovered to be a code used by a naval civil engineering bureau covering stores, personnel and shipping matters. This was not wildly exciting perhaps, but the break did establish the depth of Japanese militarisation of the mandated islands, and the bureau was the only agency to have broken the code. In June 1942, a later version came into use by the IJN's Fourth and Eight Fleets, the latter based in Rabaul, and it became a source of much interesting intelligence. Eric Nave had started the research into JN-20, and he and the staff he had trained continued the work until the Japanese abandoned the code in 1944.[16]

In July 1941 the Special Intelligence Bureau began its attack, which was ultimately successful, on JN-4, four-*kana* series. JN-4 and its brothers — JN-14 and JN-147 — were operational codes normally used for the protection of short-term tactical information. These were to become of particular importance in the fighting in the Solomons when the main IJN code, JN-25, became unreadable for a critical period. At that juncture, JN-4C, which was reserved for the use of the IJN Sixth Fleet and its force of submarines, was the only code accessible to the Allies. Breaks into this system enabled the cryptanalysts to decode the instructions from Commander Sixth Fleet to his boats and their after-action reports back to headquarters. Such messages were particularly valuable in keeping important convoys up the Australian east coast clear of IJN submarine operating areas.

A third example of the work undertaken by Eric Nave and his bureau at this time was that on the Merchant Ships Naval Liaison Cypher, later known as JN-11. In June 1941, SIB received a photocopy of a JN-11 codebook obtained by the US Navy. As Japanese preparations for the southward advance gathered pace, so did the traffic intercepted in this system The Special Intelligence Bureau read this until a new system was introduced in the middle of August.[17]

The problem always confronting Nave's organisation was a shortage of skilled personnel, as is elegantly described in the post-war analysis of its operations — the 'Red Book' — when it describes the situation that existed in 1942:

> the RAN Unit, when an independent unit, lacked the necessary experienced personnel, equipment and staff to handle adequately the recovery and reading of the main Minor Systems ... Research work was necessarily restricted to such as could be handled by one or [two] officers with one or two assistants, but the standard of achievement was high.[18]

Eric Nave could have used any help he could find from any sources. The need for an effective organisation along the lines of FECB was underlined by the ultimatum issued in July 1941 by the Japanese Government to the Vichy regime, demanding access to French air bases and ports in southern Indochina. The French caved in to this demand, which they were not position to resist. Japanese forces were in occupation by 21 July. They could now readily interdict the entire South China Sea, and all British and Dutch territories in South-East Asia were now within range of Japanese aircraft. The IJN had a major forward base for its ships at Camranh Bay.

This advance to the south triggered an immediate response from the Western powers with an embargo on the export of strategic materials, including oil, to Japan. The United States first imposed this on 26 July, followed by Britain, the Dutch and the Australians. The

Australian Combined Operational Intelligence Centre, established under the auspices of DNI Long in October 1940, and given the task of watching Japanese activities in particular, would henceforward be an avid customer for all the information the Special Intelligence Bureau could supply.

Despite the problems which beset the Special Intelligence Bureau, it was now officially established, and had access to almost all the resources that Australia could lay claim to in the area of codebreaking. Moreover, it was making some progress. On 28 November 1941, the Defence Committee recorded the strength of the Special Intelligence Bureau as ten — three naval officers, two Army officers and five civilians. It was Australia's first national signals intelligence organisation and virtually home-grown. Nave was to provide the training and the bureau was given the authority to requisition 'further additions to staff as they become necessary'. Eric had already introduced some changes to intercept procedures, with the diplomatic section now gaining access to Japanese diplomatic traffic from the cable company, as was the practice in GCCS and FECB.

The qualification of 'almost' all resources is an important one. In June 1940, the Australian Army had established the No. 4 Special Wireless Section with the task of intercepting and evaluating French and German wireless transmissions. Captain Jack Ryan, who had been a telegraphist in HMAS *Sydney* at the time of her battle with SMS *Emden* in November 1914, led the unit, and he favoured those with a maritime background in selecting his troops. In January 1941, the section arrived in Egypt and, after a period of training with a unit of the British Royal Signals, it was despatched to Greece with the British Expeditionary Force. After service monitoring German communications in the Greek campaign, the unit went to Syria for the campaign to eject the Vichy French regime and to monitor the German advance into the southern USSR. Considerable experience had been gained in all aspects of the Procedure W world, and the unit also had the capacity for translation of plain-language traffic in French and German.[19]

While serving in the Middle East theatre, No. 4 Special Wireless

Section was, to some extent, under the direction of GCCS and its signals intelligence establishment at Sarafand in Palestine. In December 1941, when the section's attention switched to Japanese, Sarafand was able to provide instruction and training material in *kana*. The section returned to Australia in March 1942 and its second-in-command, Lieutenant A.W. 'Mic' Sandford, who had received some briefings from and training with GCCS agencies in the Far East, was to play an important part in the next segments of the Eric Nave story.

The benefits of having an organisation like the Special Intelligence Bureau began to manifest themselves very quickly in Australia, although not all had the necessary faith in its product. When Italy entered the war in June 1940, Japan agreed to assume responsibility for the conduct of Italian diplomatic and consular relations with the Australian Government. Then, in September 1941, the bureau intercepted and decoded a Japanese consular message instructing the Japanese Consul General in Melbourne to find another neutral country to look after Italian interests.

> I took this message to show the Admiral [Colvin] and had great difficulty convincing the Admiral's Secretary, Captain Foley, of its importance and therefore had to explain that the reason could only be that Japan would no longer be in a position to handle Italian interests because they would be at war with us. It amounted to a prior warning of some months. This was the only channel I had and I asked that it be passed on to government with adequate security for information of the Prime Minister. In British circles such a message would have gone immediately to War Office, Air Minister, Foreign Office and Prime Minister, but Foley took no action.

As in GCCS and FECB, Special Intelligence Bureau decodes of Japan's diplomatic traffic provided further indications and examples of Japanese intelligence gathering in Australia. 'We also discovered that the Consul General in Sydney regularly reported to Tokyo the departure of the *Queen Elizabeth* and *Queen Mary* carrying troops. Doubtless this intelligence was duly passed on to their Axis partner.'

In December 1940, three German auxiliary cruisers had attacked Nauru, destroying the phosphate loader and the radio station and sinking five British phosphate carriers. The German ships used Japanese names, disguises and flags in this raid, a fact which prompted the Australian Government to protest through the British Embassy in Tokyo. Furthermore, in mid-1941, the Government passed legislation authorising the Navy and Air Force to intercept all neutral ships, including Japanese, on the high seas so as to protect the Australian coast from similar raids. The Japanese Government in turn protested, but to no avail. The Special Intelligence Bureau was able to support the surveillance effort with its intercepts of traffic to and from Japanese merchant ships.

> During one period of tension with Japan the regular merchant ships on the Australian and New Zealand runs failed to keep their scheduled arrivals and we were able to tell DNI that they were idling 60 miles or so off Sydney and Auckland pending further instructions from Japan

Now occurred a curious incident in the relationship between Nave and Newman. Readers are reminded of the close association between the DNI and the Director of Communications in their joint efforts to get SIB up and running. From the evidence of many pieces of Navy Office correspondence in the Australian Archives, each kept the other informed of developments and proposals, and they invariably supported each other in seeking the approval of higher authority. Long does not appear to have 'trespassed' into Newman's bailiwick, and in his official reports leaves all reference to the work of the RAN's W/T Intelligence Section to Newman. Needless to say, he was a crucial recipient of the product of both Nave's bureau and Newman's section from which the Naval Intelligence Directorate would produce processed intelligence to support the Australian Naval Staff and to pass on to other Pacific Naval Intelligence Organisation authorities. All this is what makes the following passage in Nave's memoirs so difficult to credit.

> About this time the Director of Communications, Commander Newman, suggested to me that we keep DNI out of these matters and handle them ourselves. This would have meant that the DNI could be in ignorance of matters he needed to know. I could not possibly agree to this, it was contrary to all practices both in London and in the Far East where we worked for the

Combined Service Intelligence Branch and they were trained to handle such matters with proper security. This was most unfortunate and it coloured my relations with him from that time on. He lost no opportunity trying to undermine my position but I was far too busy to allow this to intrude on my work, and as I was the only experienced body available, I had to do practically everything myself.

It would be an extraordinary suggestion for Newman to have made, and it must be remembered that Eric was writing well after the event and had other scores to settle with Newman. The use of the phrase 'with proper security' is telling, as the Americans were later to allege that Nave was guilty of not observing the rules for proper security.

It must also be borne in mind that Eric was also working under some pressure. He gives few hints in his memoirs about this, apart from throwaway lines like 'I had to do practically everything myself' but, fortunately, there was a contemporary yardstick against which his workload can be estimated. In the US Navy's codebreaking group — OP-20-G — in Washington, during the latter half of 1941 the translation unit alone had a staff of one officer, two yeomen (clerks) and six translators, three of whom were still in training. The officer in charge worked a sixteen-hour day, seven days a week. He did have more material to translate than the RAN Special Intelligence Bureau, but translating and evaluating the result were his only duties.[20] Eric Nave had to do all of that, including the training task, as well as most of the codebreaking until his new trainees could shoulder some of the load. The goad at his back was the understanding that unless intercepts were decoded as quickly as possible and then translated accurately, the intelligence they contained would be of little value.

But Eric's heavy workload and the falling-out with Newman were completely overshadowed by the ominous trends in Japanese military developments. Admiral Nomura had been despatched to Washington in September in an attempt to bargain away the trade embargo, talks which dragged on until 7 December. On 15 October, the Japanese Cabinet resigned and General Tojo became Prime Minister. The intentions of the new Japanese government began to become clear from intercepts made by Western cryptanalysts around the world, but soon there came an indication that the long drawn out period of waiting for a Japanese move was coming to an end. Let Eric Nave tell of it in his own words:

> No doubt the most important pieces of information I was able to provide in Melbourne came in November and early December 1941. On 19 November 1941 a circular message was sent out from Tokyo which we received, it being a clear indication that Japan was on the point of declaring war. All overseas posts were informed that in the event of a national emergency involving the breaking of diplomatic relations and the consequent interruption of overseas communications, a warning would be broadcast in the middle of the Japanese shortwave broadcasts as follows and this would be repeated at the end :-
>
> The breaking of international relations with America — *Hibashi no Kaze ame* —East wind, rain.
> With Russia — *Kita no Kaze humori* — North wind, cloudy
> With Britain — *Nishi no Kaze hare* — West wind, fine
> This warning was to be repeated at successive broadcasts

This 'winds message' was to be at the centre of the controversy over the lack of warning of the attack on Pearl Harbor. A copy of the decode on which Eric's account is based is in the Australian Archives dated 19 November 1941. This time there was no repeat of the difficulty with Captain Foley, although it would appear that it took until 28 November for the message to be decoded and for the detail of its contents to get to the Secretary of the Defence Department, Frederick Shedden.[21] But the letter covering the decode shows that the Prime Minister did see it on that same day. As Eric observed, 'This news created quite a stir in defence circles'. One outcome was that the Army intercept station at Park Orchards was put on high alert to listen to the Japanese short-wave news broadcasts.

The message had been transmitted in several Japanese diplomatic codes, because different missions were served by different systems. The consulates in Australia used the TSU code or J-19, with which the Special Intelligence Bureau had received assistance from FECB. It is interesting that the same message was intercepted in Washington in J-19 code and was not decrypted until 26 November, because this

was a lesser priority than traffic in the higher level Purple code. At
the subsequent inquiry by the US Government, officers of the US
Navy codebreaking unit in Pearl Harbor revealed that even with
the Purple machine in their possession, some decodes of Purple
messages occurred on the day of transmission, some took a few days,
but other messages were not decoded until fifty-nine days after their
transmission by Tokyo.[22] Other US cryptanalytical organisations
reported the same 'winds message' on 26 November, so, given the
relative strengths of the US cryptanalytical effort and the Special
Intelligence Bureau, the Australian organisation did well.

Then, on 2 December, an intercept from Tokyo was decoded
instructing all overseas authorities to burn all their codes and ciphers.
This was a dramatic development.

> The Chief of Naval Staff was in Canberra at a War Cabinet meeting, so I
> took this to the Second Naval Member, Commodore J.W. Durnford. He
> read it and remarked 'This is a very important piece of information, Nave'
> and immediately rang Canberra on the secraphone to pass it on to the
> meeting. He asked 'How long do you think we have?' My opinion was '3 to
> 4 days which takes us to the weekend.'

On taking the necessary action, Japanese diplomatic posts were
to report to Tokyo with the one-word message, *Haruna*. Special
Intelligence Bureau also detected this message from the consulates
in Australia. Durnford advised Shedden formally of both pieces of
information on 4 December.[23] Then everybody began the nervous
wait for whatever the consequences of this series of dramatic messages
might be.

One other event in Eric Nave's life quite possibly had more
significance for him at the time than even these cryptanalytic triumphs.
On 25 November 1941 son David was born to join Elizabeth. It was
an inauspicious time to born. Not only was Australia about to be
confronted with an onslaught by the Japanese, but the following four
years were to see Eric continually busy and, for most of the time,
operating under considerable operational pressure. It is likely that
he saw very little of his family during this period, and David recalls
his father as being somewhat distant and not particularly friendly

towards his son. Some indication of Nave's attachment to and regard for his personnel can be seen in the fact that Richard Lyons became David's godfather.

But if Eric Nave had had the opportunity at the time to reflect on this period of his professional life, it must have given him some satisfaction. For the second time in his codebreaking career he had been given the responsibility for building a competent signals intelligence organisation, and had done so. The times had not been propitious, the available resources scanty or — as in the case of cryptanalysts — non-existent, and he had had the difficulty of convincing his superiors that the intelligence the Special Intelligence Bureau was producing was not only important, but could also be trusted. On top of that, he was not a well man: convalescence from sprue involved a long-term program on a strict diet, which was hardly conducive to doing one's best work under trying conditions. But he had achieved what had been asked for, and his information was making a difference. There must have been some ironic chuckles over the fact that the government, which had been so unimpressed with the proposal by Admiral Colvin to set up such a unit in November 1939, was now a grateful recipient of intelligence from the organisation he never believed he needed.

These achievements are worthy enough, but the real triumph of Eric Nave's period in command of the Special Intelligence Bureau was that he had melded together a group of service officers and civilians into an Australian national signals intelligence organisation. Although it was not a large agency and it had a number of deficiencies, it was a sound foundation on which to build the edifice that was to succeed it. Above all, its products had attracted the attention of the British and given Australia an international bargaining chip it had not previously had to play.

8 Pearl Harbor and the Arrival of the Americans, 1942

The event that Nave's Special Intelligence Bureau diplomatic decodes had foreshadowed revealed itself in dramatic fashion on 7 and 8 December 1941. First Malaya was invaded, then the US Navy's main Pacific base at Pearl Harbor was attacked by Imperial Japanese Navy aircraft, and then General MacArthur's forces in the Philippines felt the striking power of the IJA and IJN air forces operating from bases in Taiwan. Intelligence analysts had warned about the possibility of attack on the first and the third targets, but not the second. Why were there no warnings? Who was responsible for this oversight? Who should wear the blame?

It can be confidently stated that Eric Nave and the Special Intelligence Bureau had nothing at all to do with the alleged intelligence 'failures' that might have given warning of Japanese intentions to attack Pearl Harbor. In fact, there would be no need to make any but a passing reference to this episode in this book were it not for the fact that James Rusbridger chose to make Eric a key actor in their book, *Betrayal at Pearl Harbor*. So the issue must be examined and disposed of.

There are two central allegations underlying the many investigations and inquiries that Pearl Harbor spawned. The first is that the information on Japanese intentions, like the 'winds message', ought to have alerted all the appropriate authorities to the likelihood of a Japanese attack, but it did not. Therefore the authorities concerned were clearly incompetent. The second allegation is that Allied (and that term can be used from this point on) codebreakers had made sufficient progress in breaking the main Naval Operational Code — now JN-25B — to know that Pearl Harbor was a target for the IJN Combined Fleet under Admiral Yamamoto Isoroku. The corollary is that 'somebody' had the information but, for various nefarious reasons, did not pass it on to allow it to be acted upon — the classic conspiracy theory.

The first allegation can be dismissed promptly. The trend in Japanese preparations for war was clearly understood, and intelligence agencies in the USA and the Far East had warned their superiors. Receipt of the 'winds message' did alert Allied commanders, and the Army and Navy commanders in Hawaii were informed of this. For example, the US Navy Chief of Staff, Admiral Stark, advised all his Pacific commands and London on 27 November that

> This dispatch is to be considered a war warning. Negotiations with Japan looking towards stabilisation of conditions in the Pacific have ceased and an aggressive move by Japan is expected within the next few days. The number and equipment of Japanese troops and the organisation of naval task forces indicates an amphibious expedition against either The Philippines, Thai or Kra Peninsula or possibly Borneo. Execute an appropriate defensive deployment preparatory to carrying out the tasks assigned in WPL [War Plans List] 46. Inform district and Army authorities. A similar warning is being sent by War Department.
>
> Spenavo [Special Naval Office — in UK] inform British. Continental [US] districts Guam, Samoa directed take appropriate measures against sabotage.[1]

There is room for doubt that the actual 'winds execute' message was intercepted by US stations, although it was received by the Australian Army intercept station at Park Orchards, but the implications were clear to all.

The second allegation forms the central theme of books like *Betrayal at Pearl Harbor*. Rusbridger's main argument was that the 'somebody' was Churchill, whose codebreakers had uncovered intercepted signals pointing to the impending attack, and that his 'nefarious reason' was to ensure that America entered the war. His basis for much of this is information he claimed to have extracted from Eric Nave — that FECB was freely reading IJN operational codes in 1940 before Nave departed for Australia on sick leave. In interviews with the Australian media after the manuscript attracted British D-notice attention in 1989, Eric skillfully evaded answering questions on this point although, possibly with an eye to sales, he did not protest the claim too strongly. He agreed that 'British security officers' had broken Japanese codes before Pearl Harbor, and responded to the suggestion that Churchill had sufficient information to have deduced Pearl Harbor was a target with, 'I think you could say that, yes'. But he did not assert that this information came from British codebreaking. Churchill's reticence in passing on this information he ascribed to matters of 'national diplomacy'.[2]

Nor did Eric make this claim about Churchill's alleged perfidy in his memoirs. Instead, he suggested of the Americans that:

> With complete knowledge of Japanese negotiating instructions [derived from Purple decrypts] and other related intelligence, any element of surprise should have been impossible. In Australia with only meagre means we were never in doubt and action was taken to recall aircraft from Ambon.

The last phrase has been added in penscript, suggesting that Eric realized that in making a claim that Australia knew that Pearl Harbor was to be attacked he was stretching the truth. The clarification shows only that Australia was aware that an attack by the Japanese was likely, and that the thrust was expected to be directed southwards.

The cryptanalytical facts are as follows. By late 1940 the IJN had introduced a new codebook for Code D, which was designated by the Allies JN-25B, different from the one Eric was familiar with. When Jack Newman visited FECB in March 1941 he was told that 'most Japanese codes' could not be read, and that FECB was depending on W Section to keep track of the Japanese fleet. By the time of Pearl Harbor, even with the cooperation between the US Navy's Station CAST in Corregidor and FECB, and by the Dutch *Kamer 14* through FECB, only about 30 percent of the code had been recovered. [3]

This might have sufficed to give an inkling of Japanese intentions against Hawaii, except that all the detailed orders issued by

Yamamoto for the operation were passed by hand or landline, and that on 1 December the IJN again changed the JN-25 edition in use. Even an order by Admiral Yamamoto in late November 1941 for his Combined Fleet to 'test communications setup required upon opening hostilities', although intercepted, could not be decoded from the few JN-25B recoveries made by that time.[4]

There were other indicators which, considered with the benefit of hindsight, might have given analysts a reasonable idea that Pearl Harbor was of interest to the Japanese, but what else would the major base of one's enemy be? There has been nothing revealed by the many investigations that would have clearly indicated that the IJN was to launch a pre-emptive strike to destroy the US Pacific Fleet. This will do nothing to convince the conspiracy theorists, but they have nothing to do with the story of Eric Nave. Once he had realised the use to which Rusbridger had put his account of the work of FECB, Eric repudiated it in the strongest terms. One can argue that he should have been more careful than to let his good name be associated with Rusbridger's revisionist theory, but he was eighty-seven when the book was published and, as will be revealed in a later chapter, the circumstances leading to its publication were very complicated.

In the post-war analysis of Japanese war plans, it has been alleged by Japanese commentators that the Allies, and the US in particular, might have misinterpreted Japanese intentions because of inadequate translation of Japanese texts into English. Eric Nave was peculiarly alert to this issue but it is worth stressing now. The Japanese language is notoriously imprecise and words and phrases might carry quite different meanings depending on the context in which they are set. I do not wish to belabour this point, but an illustration of this problem would be useful. In a book written to cast doubt on the US understanding of the Japanese position before hostilities commenced in 1941, Professor Komatsu Kenchiro drew attention to the special difficulty of coding, decoding and translating the diplomatic language used by the Japanese Foreign Office of the time — the *Bungo-tai*. He illustrated this by re-translating Purple decodes used by the US in determining its negotiating position with Admiral Nomura, an exercise which demonstrated considerable variances to the American translation. In the professor's own words:

> Although *Bungo-tai* was officially abandoned after the war, in fact it remains in use today because it is relatively concise. This style uses both Japanese and Chinese word order (which are quite different) depending on the terms being used ... Consequently, only Japanese with a high level of education can read this telegraphed diplomatic language properly, and in addition, the translator needs to know Latin and French technical terms used by diplomats.[5]

Professor Komatsu, I believe, overstated his case. Most military messages, needing to be understood by all addressees, did not employ *Bungo-tai*, but is true that a lack of suitably qualified and experienced translators was to bedevil the Allied attack on Japanese codes throughout the war. The codebreaking represented a technological and intellectual triumph but the translation of even military Japanese into English was fraught with difficulties.

However, Eric Nave was personally involved in the Allied effort and it is a pity that his memoirs become less coherent and almost peter out after his account of the attack on Pearl Harbor. It is as if he recognised that all the encouragement he had been receiving from Rusbridger was focused only on getting him to that point. He gives accounts of several major battles in which the role of signals intelligence is raised, but he says very little about what work he was engaged on and what was achieved by it. This gap is unfortunate because his role in generating the intelligence upon which the Allies relied was an important one, but his recollection might have been coloured by his treatment at the hands of the US Navy during 1942. Fortunately, there are many surviving records that allow the story to be told in part; the clash of personalities that was at its core can only be inferred.

The Japanese attack almost immediately made Australia a place of much more strategic importance than it had been. As the Allied defence of what was termed the 'Malay Barrier' crumbled under the Japanese onslaught, Australia came to be seen as a bastion in which Allied forces could regroup and gather their strength before launching a counter-attack to recover their lost territory. In fact, the country was hardly a bastion of any kind and there would need to be a lot of regrouping and reinforcement before any kind of effective defence and counter-attack could be mounted from its shores.

For the FECB, however, Australia offered a secure base from which it could continue its activities. At the end of December, the Chief of Intelligence Staff sent a message to the RAN asking if Australia could provide the facilities necessary to accommodate the majority of his W and Y Section staff. Without consulting either Nave or Long, Commander Jack Newman, as head of the RAN's W/T Intelligence unit, replied that the required intercept positions and other facilities could not be found. This was a grievous error with long-term strategic consequences and it affected not only the British contribution to the attack on Japanese codes and cyphers but also the capability of Australia to service its own needs in the signals intelligence war. On 6 January 1942, the British withdrew FECB to Colombo in Sri Lanka and then to Kilindili near Mombassa in Kenya. Nave commented:

> The FECB in Singapore had signalled Navy Office Melbourne asking if a wireless interception station could be made available to them if they moved down to Australia. A reply was sent that none was available. I only saw these messages after despatch; this was a great pity. Had they signalled the Defence Department accommodation would have been provided. Now this highly experienced unit would have to vacate the Singapore location and would largely lose its effectiveness

Why Newman acted in this way is not at all clear. It was probably true that there were not the receivers and antennas that the British required readily available, but these could have been found or cobbled together. The experience of the FECB operators and their numbers would have made a welcome addition to Australia's hard-pressed resources. Was he worried that his own unit might be overwhelmed by FECB? During his January 1941 visit, Captain Wylie had certainly made no secret of his belief that he ought to be in charge of all British Y and W activities in the Pacific Naval Intelligence Organisation. In that case, perhaps Nave should have congratulated Newman rather than condemning him for forestalling a British takeover of the

Australian signals intelligence operations. But the incident could not have improved the situation between the two men.

Meanwhile, the war was going badly for the Allies. On 23 January the Japanese invaded Rabaul, Australia's northernmost military outpost, and dispersed the defenders. The 'impregnable bastion' of Singapore fell on 15 February to a Japanese force outnumbered more than three to one by the defenders. It was a serious blow to British military prestige, but worse was to follow. On the same day, the Commander-in-Chief of the Allied forces charged with defending the Netherlands East Indies advised London that his task was hopeless. On 19 February, the IJN launched a massive coordinated attack by carrier aircraft and land-based bombers against Darwin — the first hostile attack on Australia in its history — and virtually destroyed the town and its infrastructure.

On 27 February, in the Battle of the Java Sea the IJN destroyed or drove off the last Allied naval force in the region, and on 1 March the Australia cruiser *Perth* disappeared, the victim of an invasion force attacking the western extremity of Java. The Netherlands East Indies government surrendered on 14 March, leaving only General MacArthur's army still resisting on the Bataan Peninsula, and a small group of Dutch and Australian troops fighting a guerrilla campaign on Timor. On land, sea and in the air, the Japanese had been devastatingly triumphant. The Allied Combined Chiefs of Staff in Washington decided to place MacArthur in charge of the defence of Australia and he was ordered there to assume his new command. He arrived in Melbourne on 21 March 1942.

The Special Intelligence Bureau was decoding Japanese traffic and contributing to the Allied cause, especially in the field of Japanese diplomatic traffic to and from South America. In February, Nave had set up within his organisation a small Diplomatic Section which, at its outset, consisted of Professor Trendall, Mr Cooper — a GCCS 'refugee' from Singapore — and two senior members of the British Consular Service as translators.[6] One of a series of histories of World War II signals intelligence activities published by the US National Security Agency contains a number of decoded messages recorded as originating from 'ACNB', and commencing in February 1942. ACNB was the signal address of Navy Office and the decodes were from the Special Intelligence Bureau. They show Japanese diplomatic manoeuvrings before the war commenced (because decoding had been delayed), reports on the movements of Allied warships, and suggestions that a demonstration of force by the IJN in South American waters would bring many Latin governments off the fence and into the Japanese orbit.[7]

Eric Nave's pressing requirement was for interpreters. Evacuated consular officials from Japan and stragglers from FECB were helpful but nowhere near enough to handle the workload. Then an offer of assistance arrived from a quite unexpected direction. On 19 February the Australian naval attache in Washington cabled the Chief of Naval Staff advising that the US Navy was going to evacuate Station CAST from Corregidor to Australia, and suggesting that 'ACNB should undertake an investigation of where and how these key personnel might be most advantageously employed'.[8]

> In Melbourne we had a visit from Commander 'Rosey' Mason, dynamic head of OP-20-G, the US Navy codebreaking unit, who told me that he had come on behalf of ComSouWesPac [Commander US Naval Forces South West Pacific —Vice Admiral Leary, US Navy] to raise the possibility of their unit from Corregidor under Lieutenant Fabian operating from Melbourne.

Eric was mistaken. Lieutenant Commander Redfield Mason was neither the head of OP-20-G, the cryptanalytical section of the US Navy's Communications Security Group, nor a codebreaker. He had been on the intelligence staff of the US Asiatic Fleet and was at that time a Japanese interpreter attached to the Office of Naval Intelligence in Washington. How he came to be in the Philippines is not clear, but he was evacuated with the first group of CAST personnel from Corregidor via Bandung. On arrival in Australia he was thought by Admiral Leary, at first Commander ANZAC Force and then Commander Allied Naval Forces South West Pacific Area, to be the officer in charge of the unit. That position was actually held by Lieutenant Rudolph Fabian US Navy, but Jack Newman and

Eric Nave negotiated in good faith with Mason. This cannot have sat well with Fabian who, along with many of his fellows, had a low opinion of the British, although he had certainly benefited from the work done at FECB. However, Fabian's recollection of the visit by Bouncer Burnett to Cavite in April 1941 and the value of subsequent exchanges was somewhat different from the FECB version:

> There was a visitor from GCCS Singapore, a RN Lieutenant Commander whose first name was Malcolm. I do not know what his peace offering was or even if he had one, but I do remember he was greatly impressed with what we had been doing in the way of cryptanalysis at the time. We received little if anything from the British in Singapore.[9]

Even the official National Security Agency history of the period notes that 'The British, in turn, provided valuable information about JN-25, which was, for COMINT purposes, the most profitable Japanese naval system'.[10] Fabian clearly had a grudge against the British, which blossomed on his arrival in Australia.

Station CAST members had had an interesting war to date. Bombed out of the Cavite Navy Yard, they were moved to tunnels in the Corregidor fortress complex on the south-west corner of Manila Bay. On 5 February, Fabian and sixteen others were transported to Java by submarine to assist the Dutch cryptanalysts at *Kamer 14*. Then, as the Japanese closed in on Java, a second submarine took them to Fremantle. A second group of thirty-six was evacuated from Corregidor on a third submarine to Fremantle on 16 March, and a third group left Corregidor on 10 April, also by submarine.

The arrival of the Station CAST personnel made essential a move of the Special Intelligence Bureau out of Victoria Barracks, and the combined group took over a three-storey block of flats in South Yarra named Monterey. Designed as a thirty-two single bedroom apartments, the building soon became a codebreaking rabbit warren, with Newman's W/T Intelligence group on the ground floor, Fabian's CAST group and the uniformed cryptanalysts of the Special Intelligence Bureau on the first floor, and Nave's diplomatic codebreaking group on the top. Armed guards patrolled the exterior, and security passes were required to move from one part of the building to another.

It was a uniquely talented group of men, assisted by a large contingent of members of the Women's Royal Australian Naval Service (WRANS), who collated and processed Japanese naval and diplomatic decrypts. Monterey was filled with American and Australian naval personnel, academics and diplomats from the Special Intelligence Bureau, Japanese linguists from three countries, who as collators, punchcard operators, cryptographers and translators all worked together under intense pressure. The level of this extempore international cooperation was, generally, high. Collectively, the group eventually became known as Fleet Radio Unit Melbourne (FRUMEL) in December 1942. Before that it had several names including Station Belconnen, but I have used the FRUMEL title throughout.

Fabian was a complex character. Only thirty-two when he arrived in Melbourne, and nine years younger than Nave, he was a 1931 graduate of the US Naval Academy. Although he had personally selected a career as an ordnance officer, he discovered that OP-20-G had intervened and he was co-opted into cryptographic school in 1938. A cryptanalyst, and intensely partisan on the primacy of that skill in the signals intelligence field, he spent a year in Washington after completing his cryptanalyst course before being posted in command of Station CAST in 1940.[11] Fabian was certainly a glutton for work and he drove his men hard. One remarked that he was 'a tough cookie. Once you understood him, however, he was not too bad.' Fabian also told his men that they had to work hard in Melbourne because the US Navy had no men to send out to help them; consequently the enormous size of the workforce at OP-20-G astounded FRUMEL people returning Stateside.[12] Smith remarks that Fabian was 'to create a number of ripples within the as yet undeveloped Australian Sigint community and the greater field of Anglo-American collaboration'. Smith also suggests that his genius was for administration rather than for codebreaking, an opinion seemingly supported by some FRUMEL personnel and more senior cryptanalysts.[13] But Fabian also had friends in high places and was highly regarded by his superiors, surviving a purge of US Navy cryptanalytic officers in June 1942.

What exactly was the role of Fabian and his team? Station CAST had operated under the general guidance and direction of OP-20-G in Washington in its tasking and in the exchange of technical material on IJN codes. It also operated one of the four Purple machines then in existence to attack high-level Japanese diplomatic traffic. But Station CAST worked for the Commander Sixteenth Naval District, who was a subordinate of the Commander US Asiatic Fleet — Admiral Hart. Its product went to that officer, who could and did direct that some of the decrypts be shared with General MacArthur in Manila. With the dissolution of the US Asiatic Fleet command organisation in February 1942, Station CAST became an organisational waif, but Admiral Hart directed that it operate in support of the local US Navy command in what became the South West Pacific Area. Fabian executed his orders with meticulous precision, even though the organisation he was now working within was not a US Navy operation but a joint Australian/US unit.

Lest the uni-directional service mandated by Fabian for FRUMEL seem an item of military minutiae, consider that the Special Intelligence Bureau had provided a service to all three Australian services and the Australian Government through DNI and the Chief of Naval Staff. The decisions on who could see what information were not made by Eric Nave, but by the appropriate intelligence authorities in each of the services: this was the substance of his earlier dispute with Newman. Nave's experience in London and in his various postings to the China Fleet and FECB had instilled in him respect for this clear distinction between codebreaking and intelligence. It was ingrained in him to pass on the products of his labours to the relevant Intelligence office.

Unfortunately for Nave, the US Navy had taken a different route. In a series of coups in Washington, the communicators had staked their claim to control signals intelligence and been awarded the prize. OP-20-G was not subordinated to the Office of Naval Intelligence, but had the right to decide who got the information it derived from intercepting and decoding Japanese traffic, to the point of sometimes cutting the Office of Naval Intelligence out of the loop altogether. The Fabian interpretation of this arrangement, as it applied in Melbourne, was that he would pass his information to Admiral Leary and let him decide what to do with it. If Leary directed that it was to be shared with General MacArthur and other Allied commanders then it would be done but, if not, they would be left in the dark.

To make this arrangement watertight, Fabian attempted to operate his part of FRUMEL, which was much larger that the Special Intelligence Bureau, independently of Nave. Eric might have had hope that his undoubted talents would be applied to the codebreaking issue of the day — JN-25B — but Fabian jealously reserved this for his group. Initially, there was to be no cooperation on high-grade codes, period! Eric and his team, now steadily expanding with the addition of new RAN codebreakers and with Lieutenant Commander Merry RN from FECB, were relegated to the task of attacking lower grade codes — the minor codes. 'Minor' denotes their degree of cryptologic complexity rather than their importance for intelligence purposes, and in a minute to DNI Long on 28 July Eric deplored the shortage of translators but reported good progress on this type of code.

> Naval Section. Payr.[Paymaster]-Lieut. Commander Merry is the only qualified interpreter here and he handles an operational code. The daily traffic keeps him fully occupied and at times of pressure he can cope with only part. Payr.–Lieut. Jamieson deals with 3 low-grade codes which provide useful intelligence, particularly of movements. My own part, in addition to the general direction, is the solution of unknown codes and working them up to a stage for other translators; one will be ready very soon and another is waiting.
>
> Anticipated new work. Work is proceeding on several unknown codes in London Washington and here, and we are in close touch. The codes include the Submarine Code and the Flag Officers book. Results are encouraging and we shall need a minimum of one officer for each.[14]

There was, however, some joy for Newman in the new arrangements, as it became apparent that the existing intercept network would not provide sufficient material to allow the IJN codes to be put under serious attack. A new antenna array and

receiver site were erected at Moorabbin on the southern outskirts
of Melbourne. Here, there was a far higher degree of inter-Allied
cooperation, with the site manned jointly by the US Navy and
RAN, the majority of the latter personnel being WRANS.

The first five WRANS in Moorabbin were given three weeks to adapt
to the USN methods and worked day and night to complete the task,
sometimes working eight-, nine-, and ten-hour watches ... Gradually the
WRANS took their places on full-time watchkeeping duty, alternating
on all frequencies, and slowly the USN operators began to adapt to their
presence of which they had been very suspicious in the beginning. Even the
democratic USN was wary of having women it its ranks.[15]

If the Australians were having some difficulty coming to terms
with the way the US Navy cryptanalytical organisation distributed
its product, another complication was to follow. General MacArthur,
now the Commander-in-Chief South West Pacific Area, had been
used to receiving signals intelligence from the US Army Signals
Intelligence Service unit in the Philippines, as well as from Station
CAST courtesy of Admiral Hart. In Melbourne, however, he had
only snippets from FRUMEL, mostly courtesy of Admiral Leary. He
shortly declared that he wanted his own signals intelligence unit to
service his new General Headquarters. It was a reasonable enough
request and, as General Headquarters was a combined tri-service
organisation, the expectation was that the Central Bureau would
be the same. The early minutes of conferences held to discuss how
the Commander-in-Chief's wishes might be met show that all three
Australian services were represented, as well as the US Army but, as
the US Navy representative, Fabian attended only the first meeting
on 6 April 1942. After that, the US Navy seems to have ignored
Central Bureau.[16]

The Central Bureau was now set up in Melbourne, but it was not possible
for us to amalgamate. The reason was that the US Army under General
MacArthur in Australia could not cooperate directly with the US Navy
units which took their orders from Washington; the division here was
necessary because the Intelligence units were an essential part of their own
service.

The problem was one of long standing and this was merely its latest manifestation. The joint nature of the Special Intelligence Bureau was now forfeit to the struggle between the US Army and Navy over signals intelligence, to which some applied more vigour than to the fight with the Japanese. The naval and civilian (until October 1942) elements stayed with FRUMEL while the Australian Army and Air Force joined Central Bureau, and set up the organisation in a large house in South Yarra — Cranleigh, not far from Monterey. The RAN maintained its helpful attitude, and responded to requests for assistance, training and material for the new bureau. Even after it moved to Brisbane in July 1942, Newman continued to offer assistance, not directly and officially, but either through DNI or by private correspondence with Major Mic Sandford, head of the Australian Army component.

Training in codebreaking was vitally important and the task fell to Eric Nave. As an Australian Army cryptanalyst recalled after the war:

> One of my indelible memories of those early days in Central Bureau was of the scene in Captain Nave's room upstairs in 'Cranleigh', with the winter sun slanting through the lead-paned windows. There in a class-like atmosphere, Captain Nave taught a small group of us how to unravel the Japanese Naval Air codes so effectively that when we were posted to field sections, we were able to read them continuously. Thanks to his instruction also, when the codes changed, we were able to reconstruct them with the minimum of delay. The atmosphere of excitement and discovery that marked our first encounters with the Japanese codes has never left me.[17]

Nave's active involvement in training Central Bureau personnel of other services can only have heightened the mistrust that Fabian had for Nave's commitment to FRUMEL, although it was Newman and Long who were most closely associated with the new Central Bureau. A British officer visiting Melbourne in May/June 1942 made the following observations on the disharmony between Nave and Fabian:

> In my capacity as a 'Visitor' I was able to observe quite a lot concerning the internal working of the organisation and I am convinced that Nave is wasting

his time 'running' a separate section which is redundant in that it might be incorporated in the U.S. Section. Nave is an excellent cryptographer and we should be far better off if he were able to devote his whole time to work of this nature. I think he is inclined to see the matter in this light himself, although he is naturally loath to giving up charge of his own show.[18]

As the new Allies attempted to find a way of working harmoniously together, the IJN and IJA were having their own difficulties in agreeing on the next step in their war — Stage Two, as it became known. Elements within the IJN were keen to invade Australia, but the IJA, which had borne the brunt of the fighting and the casualties so far, was not convinced. The military and logistics problems were too large for the IJA to contemplate, although they did agree that the Allied conversion of Australia into a base for attacking the newly expanded Japanese Empire presented a challenge that would have to be faced. Admiral Yamamoto, for his part, wanted to strike eastwards against Hawaii. The compromise reached between these positions was for a campaign to isolate Australia from the USA by establishing bases along the lines of communication between the two countries and to sever contact. Port Moresby and the Solomons were two of several locations selected for the new Japanese bases. Yamamoto would get his second chance at annihilating the US Pacific Fleet in June after these objectives had been achieved. The IJN was to take the lead with the Army in support.

There is a charming codebreaking story from about this time. Allied cryptanalysts were finding that the IJN used a code within a code to conceal its geographical coordinates, a *kana* grid which the coder used to transform the latitude and longitude of positions before applying the main code, be that JN-25B or another. Allied bewilderment continued until it was discovered that the grid was a poem taught to Japanese schoolchildren because it contains all the syllables of the Japanese language used only once. The poem begins *I-ro ha-ni-ho-he-to*, which is how it got its Allied name, the I-RO-HA code.

To organise its South Pacific campaigns, the IJN needed to generate an enormous volume of radio traffic, which did not go unnoticed by the Allies. The cryptanalysts had had a stroke of good luck in the discovery that the change introduced in JN-25B before Pearl Harbor was modest in character, and that breaking into it was relatively easy. So the main IJN operational code became almost transparent to the cryptanalysts at FRUMEL. Second, the traffic analysts of Newman's Wireless Intelligence unit had a field day. It was soon clear that a major realignment of air, land and naval forces was under way, with most of the activity centred on Truk (Fourth Fleet) and Rabaul (Eighth Fleet). The codebreakers, probably Minor Systems, solved the digraph/trigraph system used by the Japanese for designating geographical features on 23 March, so that it became apparent what the IJN's targets were. Despite Japanese radio security and deception measures, the Allies had a clear picture of a massive operation, directed principally against Port Moresby, with Tulagi in the Solomons a secondary target, although the detailed plans for individual task forces were not quite as distinct. A joint US Navy/ RAN task force centred on the carriers *Enterprise* and *Yorktown* was positioned to intercept the assault and the ensuing clash has since been known to history as the Battle of the Coral Sea.

Most accounts of the cryptologic struggle to divine the Japanese intentions and of the battle that ensued in the Coral Sea have been written by Americans about Americans. Dominant though the US role was, the contribution of the junior partner is frequently ignored. It was Rear Admiral Crace's cruiser force that absorbed much of the land-based bombing effort which might have been directed against the American carriers, and his presence in the heavy cruiser *Australia* off Jomard Passage decided the invasion convoy commander on retirement rather than attempting to force his way into the Coral Sea. Eric Nave didn't even mention Coral Sea in his memoirs, but there is some recognition of the part played by the Special Intelligence Bureau and the Wireless Intelligence unit in the individual accounts given by US personnel who were at FRUMEL before and during the battle. The Moorabbin WRANS were much admired for their work (as they were later when they took duties within FRUMEL) and the US Navy appreciated the translation assistance that Special Intelligence

Bureau officers provided. A name missing from those mentioned is 'Nave'. How was it that Eric Nave, with his long experience and superior grasp of the IJN's signalese, could not have been involved in the vital effort to decode and translate the Japanese messages before and during the Battle of the Coral Sea?

Could it be that Fabian took steps to deliberately exclude him, for he clearly made use of other Special Intelligence Bureau officers in the task? The British officer's report of May/June 1942 that suggested that Nave himself declined to work on the problem is clearly wrong. There was probably an element of professional jealousy — the eager young pup and the old bloodhound each convinced that he knew the best way of breaking Japanese codes. Fabian may well have expressed the view that translation was the least important of the processes in codebreaking, a view that Eric could not share. Then there was the fact that the American interlopers had taken over, in deed if not in name, an organisation that had taken all Eric's charm, wit, intelligence and contacts to construct virtually single-handedly over a period of almost two years. Perhaps Fabian did not appreciate the need for tact in what he saw — correctly — as a matter of life and death. Even so, there would have been some latitude for common courtesy had Fabian chosen to take it. Alternatively, Eric may simply have expressed a typical Australian resentment of the period of the Americans coming in and throwing their weight around. The British report notes that 'Nave is not good at cooperation with anyone'. History has recorded that the same observation could well be made about Fabian.

There were certainly technological issues at play. Station CAST had the Purple machine and, later, the 'IBM equipment', the latter a punched card reader that assisted cryptanalysts by sorting and finding matches in coded groups. As the US Navy operator of this equipment said of his arrival in Melbourne, and his discovery that the machine evacuated from Corregidor was incomplete, 'I could not order parts from the Australians because they had nothing; they did everything by hand'. Fabian ensured that it stayed that way, making no machine time available to the Special Intelligence Bureau cryptanalysts, even though WRANS began to take over the tasks of ministering to the needs of the IBM equipment very quickly. Eric was aware of the use by GCCS of the British equivalent — the Hollerith machine — but he would have not had any opportunity of using one or even studying its utility for his minor code work.

Whatever either man might have wished the Special Intelligence Bureau–FRUMEL relationship to be, the record shows that there was considerable and continuous tension between the Americans and the Australians on JN-25 until Nave's bureau was closed by the Holden Agreement in October 1942. The UK National Archives contains a most interesting file listing chronologically messages exchanged between GCCS, OP-20-G, Nave and Shaw on JN-25B.[19] There was a marked decline in recoveries after FECB was withdrawn first to Colombo and then to Kilindili, but progress picked up again in June 1942. GCCS asked Nave whether progress in Melbourne might be 'speeded up by the transfer to you of the Crypto Staff now in New Zealand'. Eric declined the offer, pointing to the lack of codebreaking experience in the New Zealand unit. On 20 June Shaw confirmed that Kilindili was exchanging codebreaking data with Nave.

In July Nave referred to the contretemps with Fabian over security of codebreaking communications. 'In US Navy Special Intelligence Centre such material is always handled by their own staff, and officer in charge is reluctant to have such coding [on Melbourne–Kilindili circuits] by other than my staff'. The matter resurfaced in an August message from Fabian to OP-20-G, which was forwarded to GCCS. 'I have refused to permit latter [code values] to be handled in practically public ACNB code room where over 200 civilian clerks are employed'. As became evident, this was all part of a campaign orchestrated by the US Navy to seize control of the attack on Japanese naval codes, and GCCS had no choice but to concur with Fabian's edict.

On 15 September Nave informed GCCS and Kilindili that 'I have loaned two mathematicians for work with US party for 5 figure cipher'. The next sentence was electrifying. 'Professor Room has produced a method whereby given a depth of 12 the additive can be determined in three hours … Would you like details. They are being supplied to the U.S. Party for transmission to Washington by air.' Further details of the Room solution were signalled on 21 and 29 September. These messages appear to effectively counter the suggestion, put around by Fabian that, 'When we moved to Monterey he [Nave] and a couple of others worked in a room topside and he was working on a minor cipher of some sort. I can't remember what it was.'

It now seems that Nave and his Special Intelligence Bureau were providing important support to the Americans in continuing the struggle to break into and decrypt JN-25B messages. That he had to accept this assistance may have galled Fabian and, if not dealt with resolutely, it might have somewhat tarnished the image he was so assiduously cultivating of FRUMEL's success being an all-American affair, attributable to his leadership. Not being able to assail Nave on cryptanalytic grounds — although the smear quoted above suggests he tried — he turned instead to Nave's alleged insecurity in the handling of cryptanalytic information.

> The building we were in had a common switchboard and we hadn't gotten our direct service, so he would pick up the phone and Christ, he would violate every rule of security in the book talking about this stuff. Until one day, I told him to shut up and I went up there and bawled the hell out of him. He was in the clouds as far as his work was concerned. He just forgot these simple little other rules that governed people.[20]

There is no record of how Commander Nave with seventeen years experience in codebreaking reacted to being 'bawled the hell out' by Lieutenant Commander Fabian with less than three. It cannot have improved US–Australian relations. However, despite Fabian's best efforts — and arguably no less a level of security awareness on the part of the Australian staff at Monterey — somehow the business of FRUMEL became public knowledge. Some WRANS who worked at FRUMEL were startled one morning to hear their tram conductor announce to all and sundry. 'See that building over there? It's a big spy place. That's where they break all the Japanese codes.'[21]

An interesting summation of the contretemps between the Special Intelligence Bureau and FRUMEL was offered by one of Fabian's men.

> He [Fabian] said that Nave was handling comint [communications

intelligence] insecurely. Fabian was known to be a fanatic about comint security (he had discussed shooting all 60 men in the unit in Corregidor to avoid their capture and interrogation by the Japanese) but I think it could have been a way of getting rid of a rival who was the logical candidate to put in charge of a combined US and Australian comint unit. Nave was senior, older and more experienced at solving Japanese Naval codes and a better Japanese linguist.[22]

Reduced to its essentials, the clash between Nave and Fabian was most probably about sharing information. Fabian's view was that he was not in Australia to help Australians: his job was to support his admiral. This might seem an odd attitude for an ally to take, but Fabian had support for this from the highest quarters. No less an authority than General MacArthur broke the same news gently to Prime Minister Curtin at their first Prime Minister's War Conference on 8 April 1942.

> The Commander-in-Chief added that, though the American people were animated by a warm friendship for Australia, their purpose in building up forces in the Commonwealth was not so much from an interest in Australia but rather from its utility as a base from which to hit Japan. In view of the strategical importance of Australia in a war with Japan, this course of military action would probably be followed irrespective of the American relationship to the people who might be occupying Australia.[23]

So long as something that Australia could offer was useful to US forces, then it would be supported, but only to the extent that the US saw fit to do so. Any concept of partnership was premature. As will be seen, Australia contributed far more to Allied intelligence in South West Pacific Area than its relative size would suggest, but this conditionality of American support was a constant backdrop to Australian decisions.

And always at issue was the responsibility Eric felt towards the Special Intelligence Bureau's cryptanalytic partners — GCCS and Central Bureau — and to former clients in the Intelligence world. It was a matter which aroused strong passions. There is a statement in the British report that Nave was passing 'a copy of all translations' to the Chief of Naval Staff, but Fabian was sending 'a daily digest of all special and W/T intelligence' to Admiral Leary. Nave may also have been sending decrypts to Long, which would be in contravention of Fabian's instructions. Fabian's view was that if the Australian Chief of Naval Staff and DNI were to receive intelligence from FRUMEL it would be as a result of a decision of Commander Allied Naval Forces, disregarding the fact that a proportion of the intelligence being generated was produced using RAN resources. One could easily appreciate how irksome such a restriction would be to Eric Nave, and how challenging Nave's defiance of it would be to Fabian.

Others felt as Nave did. For example, Long found that DNI New Zealand was receiving information from the Americans that General Headquarters refused him, so he arranged to have it supplied via the Commonwealth route until direct supply was resumed. The Chief of British Naval Intelligence, Eastern Theatre, Captain Alan Hillgarth RN, in whom Long confided, reported to Churchill that:

> Long is forced to have recourse to underground methods to obtain some of the information he must have in order to discharge his job adequately. This is, in my view, entirely the fault of the Americans, who make the fullest use of him and his people but give only limited trust in return.[24]

Nor was the RAN alone in feeling left out in the new arrangements imposed by the US Navy. In October 1942 the assistant director of Military Intelligence, Lieutenant Colonel R.A. Little, who was the link between the General Staff and the codebreakers, recorded:

> My feeling is that since the advent of the USN Crypto Sec[tion] under Lt. Comdr. Fabian Army have not been treated fairly as although Army provide about 1/3 of the staff and all the intercepts the Army was allowed to have was a precis of the diplomatic material. More recently we have been permitted to read through in the presence of an M.O. some of the diplomatic messages that Comdr Nave was good enough to pass to us. These were taken away as soon as read.[25]

Before returning to the controversy and its outcomes, it would be remiss not to acknowledge the role of FRUMEL in three other campaigns in 1942. The first was the unit's part in intercepting and translating the messages to and from IJN submarines operating off

Australia's east coast. As General MacArthur husbanded his meagre forces in defence of Papua New Guinea against the Japanese invaders, knowledge of the presence of these undersea predators was an important advantage in the efforts of the RAN to get the vital convoys of men and material to the battlefront. The second was FRUMEL's support for the Allies in the Solomons campaign. Although a change in JN-25C had delayed decoding of messages which would probably have avoided the costly naval losses at the Battle of Savo Island on 8/9 August, the unit provided plenty of intelligence in support of later parts of the campaign.

However, the jewel in FRUMEL's crown was arguably its role in assisting the US Navy to prepare for the Battle of Midway in June 1942. Of the many pieces of information on Japanese movements and intentions gleaned from its activities, the single most important was its identification of the target of the campaign 'AF' as Midway Island. FRUMEL was also the first to read Admiral Yamamoto's fourteen-part operation order for Midway.

Set against the backdrop of these strategically important events, the Nave–Fabian clash seems petty indeed, but it is worth considering two accounts of the controversy from third-party viewpoints, one American, the other Australian. In his official history of US communications intelligence during the war, Robert Benson of the National Security Agency's Center for Cryptologic History makes the following comment:

> This disagreeable controversy [between FRUMEL and Central Bureau] may be attributable to other factors too. It seems likely that there were serious personality problems involving the relationship of certain British and Australian personnel with FRUMEL. Hopefully this had been solved when, by terms of the Holden Agreement of November [*sic*] 1942, FRUMEL was placed solely under the USN.[26]

David Jenkins, an Australian investigative journalist who researched and wrote a fine book on the IJN's submarine attack on Australia between 1942 and 1944, offers another view of Eric Nave at the time. Jenkins reconstructed the operation of FRUMEL, probably largely from interviews with Treweek, and painted a portrait not flattering to Nave from these. Treweek seems to have not got on well with Nave, and these feelings might have coloured his judgment. While acknowledging his capabilities and achievements, Jenkins claims that Nave had an 'obsession with secrecy':

> Nave was a man of intelligence and dogged perseverance, with a number of strings to his bow … he had the skills that were needed to overcome most of the bureaucratic obstacles he found in his way. He had a good sense of humour. All the same, he was not an easy man to get on with. One major drawback was his obsession with secrecy. Nave would not always advise his staff when the British or Americans passed on the keys to a new code, but would leave them to work it out for themselves … 'He was great on security for its own sake,' Dr Treweek said. 'There were all sorts of things he wouldn't tell us.'

This is ironic in view of Fabian's remarks on Nave's lack of security, but perhaps the two commentators had different ideas on what 'security' meant. In Jenkins' account it seems to have been applied to Eric's rigid enforcement of the 'need-to-know' principle. But he continued:

> Nave also had difficulties with his superiors. He seemed to have a prickly relationship with Commander Long, the Director of Naval Intelligence, whom he considered a man of no great ability … At forty-three Nave was ten years older than Fabian and conscious of his more exalted rank. But that could not disguise the fact that Nave was not playing in quite the same league as Fabian. Nave had grown up in the days of simpler codes. They [CAST] were working on JN-25, Nave was handling the important but less glamorous Mandated Islands merchant shipping traffic and the like.[27]

As far as I have been able to establish, Jenkins was wrong about the Nave–Long relationship, which seems to have continued harmoniously during and after the war. Jenkins offers no documentary or other evidence to support other elements of his case, which also contains some errors of fact. JN-25B was no more complicated than Code D, on which Nave had successfully worked in 1939/40. But there is another consideration that should be explored. Despite his RN commission, Nave was an Australian and he believed passionately in the need for Australia to have its own national signals intelligence capability. This view was common amongst those who were cleared for access to the decrypted Japanese traffic, and it had been the catalyst for the initial approach by Long and Newman to the Chief of Naval Staff in 1939.

Despite other disagreements they might have had, both Nave and Newman retained this as a goal to be realised with the contingent assistance of the Americans. Newman evidently saw the route to this goal in cooperation with Fabian, who needed Newman's unit to keep his cryptanalysts supplied with live traffic. Nave might have chosen the same route had it been open to him, but he possibly did not envisage subordination to the US Navy as a strategically sound option. This stubborn streak of independence would not have suited Fabian. As events turned out, both Nave and Newman were right and they both made a vital contribution to Australia's signals intelligence future. This Australian national ambition was not a secret, as a 1943 account makes clear:

> But the Australians foreseeing the possibility of separation of Australian and American interests and possibly forces at a later stage of the war, have insisted on keeping a complete setup of their own which could function separately if the need arose. They also retained the right to communicate directly with other parts of the British Empire and not solely via Washington.[28]

Just how important this foresight was can be understood from the salutary tale of the Royal Canadian Navy's wartime codebreaking experience. The Canadian west coast signals intelligence establishment was at Esquimault, outside Victoria on Vancouver Island in British Columbia, and not far from the US Navy unit at Bainbridge in Washington State. This proximity turned out to be a curse, as the Canadians quickly came under control of the US Navy, upon whom they relied for their codebreaking. The Canadians were not allowed to develop their own expertise and at war's end, when the US Navy withdrew, they were left with very little on which to build an independent national capability.

However, as the Benson quote above presaged, events on the wider stage in 1942 also held disappointment in store for Eric Nave. After considerable discussion, on 2 October 1942 GCCS and the

US Naval Security Group signed an agreement that the US Navy would take the primary responsibility for IJN traffic decryption. The agreement specified

> (b) The British to disband the British–Australian naval unit at Melbourne and turn over to the U.S. unit there such personnel as the U.S. may desire, except for Commander Nave, who is to be recalled. Requests for any particular individuals from Kilindili or Melbourne will be entertained by the British. The future status of the diplomatic party at Melbourne will depend on the wishes of the Australian Government and the senior naval and military authorities in that area, which the Admiralty will ascertain.[29]

It is intriguing that the British signed this agreement with such a clause included. The phraseology suggests an incomplete understanding on the part of both GCCS and OP-20-G of the nature of the Special Intelligence Bureau, which had never been 'British–Australian' and over which neither the Admiralty nor GCCS had any executive authority. Of course, at the time the US Navy had the British over a barrel because it was impossible to provide signals intelligence support to the British Eastern Fleet without their cooperation. But it was extremely high-handed of the British to be disposing of Australian organisations and their personnel. However, on 11 November, and after having 'consultation with the US Naval Commander in this area', the Naval Board agreed to the disbandment of its Special Intelligence Bureau and the dispersal of its personnel.[30] The one accurate point in the whole clause of the agreement was that the Admiralty certainly did have the right to direct Eric Nave wherever it wanted to.

So the reorganisation of FRUMEL in accordance with American demands went ahead. Not all was lost. The diplomatic section of the Special Intelligence Bureau that Nave had created was taken over by the Australian Army and continued operations throughout the war. Newman and his W/T Intelligence organisation were retained by Fabian and served out the war intact: in fact Newman became the officer-in-charge of FRUMEL in December 1944. However, with no more role to play in FRUMEL and his organisation 'requisitioned' by the US Navy, Eric's future looked bleak. If he was 'prickly', as one of his critics described him, it would seem to have been with good reason.

The Admiralty wanted him back and they had a job lined up for him at GCCS. His medical condition offered no protection from this recall to the UK, and it was a move he was eager to avoid. He had a young family now, and the prospect of a transfer from Australia, away from his family and professional connections, back to a very different Great Britain from the one he had left in 1937, held little appeal. As GCCS had apparently surrendered its interest in Japanese codes, he could assume that the position being offered would be in another field and, with Australia still absorbing Japanese bombing and submarine attacks, Eric clearly felt that this was not the time to leave the cryptanalytic front line. But how could his departure be prevented?

The ejection of Eric Nave from FRUMEL quickly reached the ears of the Australian Army. At Central Bureau, now located in Brisbane, the cryptanalytic task was proving beyond the capabilities of the former members of the Australian Special Wireless Group and Mic Sandford was on the lookout for any means of augmenting its capabilities.

> Major Sandford of the Army Central Bureau heard the news of my recall and telephoned me to ask if there was any possibility of them getting my services on loan. He pointed out that they had a W/T and intelligence unit but no Japanese linguist and nobody trained in cryptography. I promised to consider the matter and advise him the next day.
>
> The situation was that I was an Australian transferred from RAN to RN because of my specialist knowledge of Japanese communications. Owing to the Japanese penetration the RN was now out of this field, while the Australian Army now fighting the Japanese had a very serious deficiency in my field. The Admiral, Sir Guy Royle, was in favour so I told Mick [*sic*] Sandford that if it could be arranged I would be agreeable. To go to England and work on research seemed a poor alternative, research being an area in which I was not experienced. My health had been slowly but steadily improving, and this could continue better in this climate.

There followed two months of frenzied efforts to induce the Admiralty to change its mind. The first approach was made on 3

November, in a signal to the Australian Army Staff in London from the Chief of the General Staff:

> RAN also had special section for naval material under CDR T.E. Nave RN but now this section has been placed under control US Navy releasing Nave who is under orders to return Admiralty London shortly. In view Naves long experience of cryptography particularly in regard Japanese ciphers and his specialised knowledge of Japanese language I am most anxious obtain loan of Nave whose services would be invaluable to Central Bureau at Brisbane. No other person is available here to fill this urgent need.[31]

At first the British were adamant, but when figures as august as the Australian Chief of Naval Staff and finally even General MacArthur threw their weight behind the struggle, the Admiralty began to give ground. In early January 1943, they gave an indication that they might be prepared to rescind Eric's recall if Australia would agree to release some of the diplomatic translators who had been working at the Special Intelligence Bureau. There followed even more frenzied exchanges, as the Australians were not willing to give up any of their scarce Japanese linguist resources, but eventually a deal was struck. Two diplomats, who had reported to Melbourne in December 1942, only to find that the Special Intelligence Bureau for which they were destined had disappeared, were traded for Paymaster Commander Nave. It was to prove a very good bargain for Australia and the Allies.

What of the subject of this international tug-of-war? Eric went on leave in November and returned to duty in December, still posted back to the UK. The RAN supported the Army's efforts and made arrangements to delay Eric's despatch until the Admiralty decision was final. In fact, Eric was posted to Brisbane on 18 December 1942, well before the Admiralty's decision was known. Could it have been that DNI Long had established through his private channel with DNI London that the request would be approved? It was not until 20 January 1943 that his fate was decided: he was to join Central Bureau in Brisbane. His comment on this decision was enigmatic: 'Approval was given and I was loaned to the Australian Army and proceeded to Brisbane, having sent my family to Adelaide'.

'Prickly' he might have been to his detractors, but Nave stood by his personnel. He endeavoured to persuade Professor Room and Richard Lyons, two of his mathematician codebreakers, who were also surplus to Fabian's requirements, to go to the UK to join Bletchley Park. Lyons remembered:

> However, before Commander Nave, the head of the Bureau, left I had the satisfaction of receiving from him what may be called a contingent invitation to go to the Foreign Office [GCCS]. When the decision was made to transfer control of the Office to the Americans Commander Nave told Room that if he were willing to go to London he could get him placed at the F.O. I was not surprised to hear this, because Room's intellectual power is phenomenal, but I was exceedingly gratified when he announced that the offer included me, adding that this was for my part in some spectacular success we had had earlier in the year. Room's immediate response was to accept enthusiastically and for one thrilling morning I thought we were in for a super experience. However, when Room had weighed all the pros and cons of the proposal, he decided that much as he would have liked to go to London, his gifts could be used more effectively in Australia, and the offer lapsed.[32]

Arguably, 1942 was the toughest year of Eric's career. Having created and trained the Special Intelligence Bureau, he had to endure its dismantlement at the hands of the Americans. The lack of recognition of his unit's contribution to the 'main game' — the pursuit of JN-25B — must have rankled deeply, and the US Navy's perception of its duty obviously came as a personal affront to his instincts and training as an intelligence officer. Ejection from the organisation he had built must have been a supreme disappointment, and his looming transfer to 'research' duties in London a further indication that his skills were possibly no longer valued in his specialist field. The three-month long battle with the Admiralty over his disposal would have added insult to injury. By year's end he was destined to join a conglomerate organisation run by foreigners and to work under the auspices of the Australian Army — perhaps not a welcome career change. It must have been a very thoughtful Eric Nave who set out for Brisbane and a new phase of his codebreaking life.

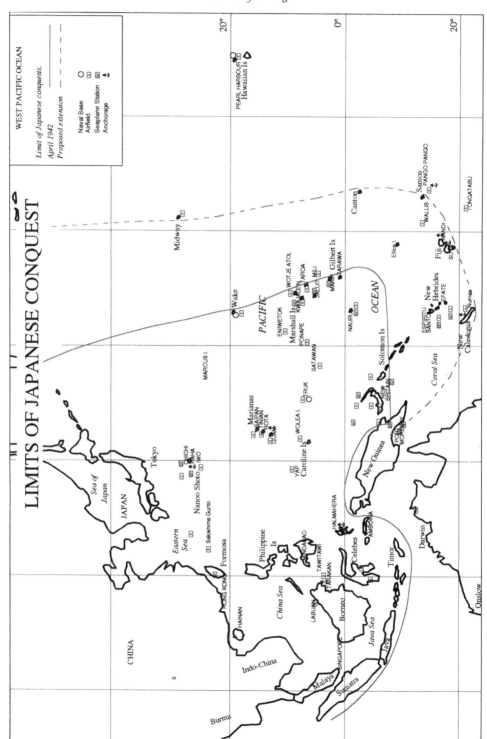

LIMITS OF JAPANESE CONQUEST

WEST PACIFIC OCEAN

Limit of Japanese conquests,
April 1942
Proposed extension

Naval Base ○
Airfield ⊞
Seaplane Station ⊞
Anchorage ⬧

9 Central Bureau, Brisbane, 1942–45

> Investigation discloses that a central Allied signal intelligence section is required for the interception and cryptanalysing of Japanese intelligence. The time delay and transmission uncertainties incident to sending intercepted material to Washington and elsewhere dictate that this work be handled locally. Allied forces here are organising such a bureau.[1]

With this proclamation, Central Bureau was activated in Melbourne by General MacArthur on 15 April 1942. The first meeting of the potential participants in this new venture had taken place on 6 April. The Australian Army's Chief Signals Officer chaired the meeting; Eric Nave and Jack Newman represented the RAN and Fabian, then still a lieutenant, the US Navy, but that was almost the last meeting of the group he attended.[2] Newman, in particular, and DNI Long supported the new organisation. Long was almost always represented while Newman provided practical assistance and material like callsign books and instruction on radio fingerprinting and TINA, the system for identifying an individual operator's transmitting characteristics, which was useful in tracking the unit he was assigned to.

Manning the new bureau was a problem. At first it comprised only personnel from the Australian Army's Special Wireless Group, a British signals detachment evacuated from Singapore, some untrained RAAF operators, survivors of the US Army's Manila signals intelligence unit, and the US Army's 126th Signal Radio Intelligence Company. Central Bureau was placed under the command of Major

General Akin, MacArthur's Chief Signals Officer, and the organisation was tasked with a fourfold mission. First it was a cryptanalytical agency, second it was responsible for radio security, and third Central Bureau was to work closely with the US Army's Special Intelligence Service at Arlington Hall near Washington DC. Finally, the unit was to exchange intelligence with the British and the US Navy.

The initial director of this polyglot little community was Colonel Joe Sherr on General Akin's staff. There were three assistant directors responsible for the three major service components — Lieutenant Colonel Abraham Sinkov of the American Army's Special Intelligence Service, Major (later Lieutenant Colonel) A.W. Sandford of the Australian Military Forces and Wing Commander Roy Booth of the RAAF. When General MacArthur moved his headquarters to Brisbane in July 1942, Central Bureau went with him and, in September, was established in Nyrambla, a large house at 21 Henry Street that still stands. On 1 May 1988 a plaque was attached to the front of the building bearing the words:

> Central Bureau, an organisation comprising service personnel of Australia, USA, Britain, Canada and NZ, both men and women, functioned in this house from 1942 until 1945. From intercepted radio messages the organisation provided intelligence which made a decisive contribution to the Allied victory in the Pacific War.

Barracks and work facilities for the unit were built on Ascot Racecourse, with the unit's equipment transported by train from Melbourne under armed guard. The change of railway gauges, and the consequent need to move the equipment from train to train, was much remarked upon by the US personnel. Field intercept units of the US Army, Australian Army and the RAAF were placed under command of Central Bureau and detached to appropriate intercept locations. Initial success was registered with the detection of IJN messages preceding aircraft attacks on Townsville, which commenced in July 1942. At this early stage of its development, however, Central Bureau was largely reliant on signals intelligence from other agencies — from the British, from the US Army in Washington and from the US Navy, especially FRUMEL. This last relationship was soured by Fabian, who refused to have anything to do with Central Bureau because 'it had nothing to offer FRUMEL'.[3]

Another unique feature of Central Bureau's operations — although not an issue for the bureau itself — was that its products were not offered to MacArthur's Intelligence Chief (G-2), Major General Willoughby. Indeed, Intelligence exercised no control over Akin's Central Bureau at all until 1943.[4] Despite this, Willoughby later felt able to comment on the signals intelligence distribution arrangements in South West Pacific Area command, and the sins of omission of the US Navy in particular, in an affidavit submitted to an inquiry into the Pearl Harbor attack:

> In an otherwise meritorious desire for security (though every modern nation knows that crypto-analysis is going on) The Navy has shrouded the whole enterprise in mystery, excluding other services, and rigidly centralising the whole enterprise. At this date for example, this same system is still in vogue: as far as SWPA is concerned, the crypto-analysis is made in Melbourne, forwarded via 7th Fleet DNI; The Melbourne station is under direct orders of Washington, is not bound by any local responsibilities, forwards what they select and when it suits them. The possibility of erroneous or incomplete selection is as evident now as it was in 1941. The only excuse the [US] Navy has is that its field is primarily naval intercepts, but there is a lot of Army traffic or other incidental traffic. This collateral traffic is not always understood or correctly interpreted by the Navy, in my opinion.
>
> The solution to this vexing and dangerous problem is a completely joint, interlocking intercept and crypto-analysis service, on the highest level and with the freest exchange of messages and interpretation.'[5]

There is a lot of truth in Willoughby's complaint — and his proposed solution — although the situation was never so black as he depicted it, and relationships between the two codebreaking agencies in Australia did improve following Fabian's recall to Washington in 1943.[6] But this quite ludicrous situation was another manifestation of the internecine struggle fought between the US Army and the US Navy over signals intelligence, which seemed to some officers to be of more immediate importance than the war against the Japanese. The Australians, who provided half of the staff of Central Bureau and the majority of its field units, were innocent bystanders caught in the crossfire.

The big problem for Mic Sandford and Roy Booth was that neither they nor their staffs had any experience in breaking Japanese codes, a task which had to be left to the Americans. This was not a good situation for a budding national cryptanalysis organisation, and the opportunity offered by the disbandment of the Special Intelligence Bureau came as a godsend. As he had for Long and Newman in May 1940, Eric Nave appeared at the exactly the right time for Central Bureau. Nor, this time, did he come alone: Professor Room, unwanted by Fabian, decided also to transfer to Brisbane.

The circumstances of Central Bureau probably came as no surprise to Eric, as he had been kept informed of its progress through Long's network. But this time he was not to be working on his own, and he found himself in very good company. Abe Sinkov, the US Deputy Director, was a bird of similar feather, having been co-opted into codebreaking in 1931 by the legendary William Friedman, under whose direction the American Army broke Purple. A professor of mathematics by training, Sinkov had become an important civilian member of the US Army's Special Intelligence Service and had been chosen for the US delegation that went to London in early 1941 to confer with GCCS, taking with it a copy of the Purple machine to trade. At that stage he was commissioned into the US Army as a captain.

It was the discussions with the Sinkov mission that led the British to authorise full exchange between FECB and CAST. At the time of General MacArthur's formation of Central Bureau Sinkov had, in fact, been head of the Special Intelligence Services Italian Section, and he was selected for the job in Australia apparently because he was 'unmarried'. Whatever the reason, Central Bureau gained a very experienced and highly competent cryptanalyst, who also proved to have a knack for melding the polyglot national elements working there into a cohesive and happy group.

In contrast to the Special Intelligence Bureau/FRUMEL set-up, Central Bureau was organised on functional lines and operated in a corporate manner. Compartmentalisation along the lines of

Bletchley Park's 'hut' system ensured that the 'need to know' principle was maintained, but there were few restrictions on the movement of personnel from one hut to another when the workload or the relative importance of a break dictated this. Skills were applied to the area of work that required them.

> In Central Bureau, people shared information with each other. We were a small enough organisation that people in different sections could talk to each other to solve problems … As the supervisor of the cryptologic section I spent much time showing the IBM people what our problems were and what we wanted to do to solve them. Major Zach Halpin, the head of the IBM section, was able to rearrange punch cards so that we could sort traffic by time interval, [which] was important in finding the solution to the Japanese Army Water Transport Code.[7]

At the time of Eric's arrival, Central Bureau was labouring under a number of interrelated difficulties, the first one strategic. While the Allies and the Japanese fought fiercely in the Solomons, a smaller campaign but of comparable bloodiness was being waged in Papua New Guinea. Deterred from seizing Port Moresby by the Battle of the Coral Sea, the Japanese had launched an incredibly courageous attempt to seize the town by an overland assault from bridgeheads at Buna and Gona on the north coast, across the steep mountain spine of the island along what became known as the Kokoda Track. Their advance was checked by Australian troops only fifty kilometres short of the target, and the Japanese commenced a fighting retreat, their signals being intercepted by the Australian Army's 55 Wireless Section at Port Moresby. In August, a Japanese amphibious assault on the strategic Allied base at Milne Bay on the eastern extremity of the island had been repulsed, again by Australia troops. Now General MacArthur had deployed Australian and American units to recapture Buna and Gona.

The strategic problem was that the South West Pacific Area had only a very small naval force led by the heavy cruiser *Australia*, which could not effectively support this operation because to do so would have required the ships to operate in largely uncharted waters with no air cover. In contrast, the skies over the whole theatre were dominated by IJN and IJA aircraft. The Allied air forces were in poor shape, with major unservicability problems and too few aircraft to meet the needs of the operational forces, yet air power was the only offensive weapon that could be used against the Japanese at the time. The sole advantage MacArthur held was that he was receiving signals intelligence on Japanese movements and intentions from the US Navy, which enabled him to provide seaborne supplies and reinforcements at minimal risk to his few resources. Extremely valuable though this was, his headquarters needed intelligence on the Japanese Army's movements and intentions, and this it was not getting, except through traffic analysis.

The cryptanalytic problem facing Central Bureau and all other Allied codebreakers was that the Japanese Army's mainline code was proving very resistant to attack. Unlike the IJN, where all ships had access to JN-25 because of the need to deploy them from theatre to theatre at short notice, the IJA cryptographic architecture was very different. It was organised around military divisions, with each division having a different code for communicating vertically to and from its superior Corps headquarters. Where two divisions were operating together, there was no horizontal cryptographic path for them to use — messages had to go in separate codes through corps. This might have been operationally cumbersome but it was an excellent means of protecting codes. It reduced considerably the volume of traffic in each system, which frustrated the Allied codebreakers. The low power on which Japanese Army transmitters generally operated in the field complicated the intercept problem as well. Importantly, the IJA codes were much better designed than those of the Navy. The least secure, such as the Water Transport Code, was more sophisticated than the earlier versions of JN-25 had been. According to Sinkov:

> Central Bureau's mission was the whole range of Army communications including air traffic because apparently – in the Japanese structure – the Army was responsible for air traffic. In terms of cryptanalytic study we had an air-ground section, a mainline army communications section, and a water transport section because it too was a Japanese army responsibility. We studied both Japanese army and Japanese navy air-ground, but they

were not two distinct sections. Because of his experience, the air-ground problem was under the control of the Royal Navy Officer, Captain Nave, who produced a good deal of useful intelligence.[8]

Not surprisingly then, the main focus of Central Bureau's codebreakers, all from the US Army Special Intelligence Service, was on the IJA mainline code which left few, if any, resources to be applied to the breaking of the so-called minor codes. Eric Nave's reputation in breaking these had been well established by his work at the Special Intelligence Bureau, and through his instruction of Central Bureau personnel in Melbourne. He was the ideal person to take charge of the task. Because the main source of Japanese aircraft operating in support of the ground forces in New Guinea at the time was the IJN, the main priority was to break the naval air-ground code.

> Enemy activity in this region was largely by Japanese naval aircraft, so this was the wireless traffic intercepted. A party, including Abe Sinkov, a capable US cryptographer was working on its examination. I joined this task, a drastic change for me, from reading a vast volume of traffic in high level codes to be faced with unreadable material of apparently low grade. It was clear that Central Bureau lacked Japanese linguists and code breakers. With my experience of naval codes I soon had results and the others left me to the task. In this I was spurred on by the US Air Commander [General Kenney] who said 'If we are going to lose our aircraft on the ground as we did up North [the Philippines], it is going to be too bad'.
>
> The task seemed extremely difficult, bearing in mind the speed of aircraft, allowing little time for action. However, one had in mind the chilling recollection of the devastation of Japanese bombers at Pearl Harbor and on the 'Repulse' and 'Prince of Wales'. It was vital that a serious attempt be made to find a solution.

Eric approached the task in the usual way — by examining volumes of traffic intercepted by Central Bureau's field units. By this stage, the RAAF had trained and formed several field intercept units known as 'wireless units', and two were deployed forward to Port Moresby and to Milne Bay, while a third was in Darwin. The coverage of their intercepts was very broad. Assisted by material recovered from downed IJN aircraft, the naval air-ground code soon began to provide some important intelligence on air operations. Eric also discovered another vital clue to impending Japanese attacks.

> I found similar routine messages from bases such as Rabaul, Ambon, Kendari etc. transmitted every 2 hours; 0600, 0800, 1000. These were weather reports to all bases in the vast area of operations. Messages at irregular intervals covered weather reports and personnel transport.
>
> I now discovered an occasional such weather report to different call signs of operational units. They were few but I thought there must be some reason. There was: on one of these occasions, an air raid by Japanese planes on Milne Bay. Testing this thought showed the report preceded an air raid on Allied facilities at Oro Bay. Switching to another area, such a special weather report preceded an air raid on Darwin. In each case the time of the report allowed the bombers to fly from base to the target area. It was clear that a recce [reconnaissance] plane was sent over the target area to give the bombers the weather on take off. I found a report which said 'cloudy, 9/10ths, there is a gap in the southeast' to confirm this.

This information was immediately passed to the Central Bureau field units who were alerted to listen for these special reports. Because this intelligence was of immediate tactical significance, they were authorised to pass this information directly to the command headquarters they were supporting, so that the target could be warned of an approaching raid and countermeasures could be taken.[9] Thus, the arrival of Eric Nave in Central Bureau was one small step in redressing the imbalance of skills between the Allies. His contribution was soon registered and appreciated, and the official account of Central Bureau's activities — the Technical Records — dryly records the facts:

> A programme of concentration on Naval Air-Ground was initiated and a special section was formed. The operational codebook was solved giving a much wider range of information. These Naval Air-Ground codebooks were the first solved by the Bureau. From then onwards these codes were read continuously.[10]

For the Australians it was a wonderful fillip to morale. In a letter written to Colonel Little on 20 February 1943, Mic Sandford made the following statement:

Domestic progress has been tremendous. Nave is quite invaluable. We are now reading air operational traffic of the utmost importance. Hitherto, however, while a certain amount had been done in the field, a good deal reaches us too late to be of any but historical value. Ryan has arranged to institute two watches on this traffic in the Brisbane area and we are having a teletype line installed. This should enable our air headquarters to receive the information simultaneously with the Japanese.[11]

However, as Sandford noted, the problem with these air-ground codes was a matter of timeliness. The time taken to intercept and copy the Japanese transmissions, code them, send them to Brisbane, have them decoded and the results coded and then passed back to the intercepting station for decoding and transmission to the relevant authorities was longer than the applicability of the information. Eric found a way around the problem and the Technical Records show how this worked.

As a result, personnel trained in the handling of these systems were sent to the field stations, where they were able to treat intercepted messages and decypher them on the spot. The intelligence was then passed at once to the local headquarters for immediate action

A lot more value could be wrung from this code, as the Japanese had the habit of supplementing surface ship convoys with air cover against Allied air, submarine or surface attacks. The intelligence gained was employed to direct Allied submarines into attacking positions and to plot the progress of individual Japanese convoys. A further bonus from reading this code was that Japanese reports of Allied attacks could also be monitored. Claims made in the heat of battle by Allied pilots or submarine commanding officers could be validated or modified by Japanese reports of losses or damage inflicted, thus providing General Headquarters with a far more reliable estimate of the enemy's order of battle and its readiness for operations.

I found a few messages from planes to base which fell into no known pattern and were unreadable at first sight as the groups used seldom appeared elsewhere. However, experience in this field was a most valuable thing, and identifying first a few numerals, I found the aircraft was reporting to base its position. It was a valuable discovery to read 'Have taken up position over convoy, Latitude, Longitude, course and speed given'.

These messages proved most difficult, which was accentuated by the fact that every time a bomber was lost the code book was changed. With the build up of American strength, the code book changes became more frequent, some lasting only a few days. Almost invariably I could get sufficient of the whole message to be able to give this to our US Navy contact whence it was passed on to the submarines.

Probably the most significant illustration of the value of signals intelligence in this phase of the war in the South West Pacific Area was the Battle of the Bismarck Sea in March 1943, which broke the stalemate between the Japanese and Allied forces in New Guinea. Alerted by US naval intelligence on the assembly of forces to reinforce Lae from Rabaul, the Allied air forces were able to launch strikes simultaneously on the convoy and on the air bases from which the supporting air forces were scheduled to fly cover for it.[12] The result was horrendous loss of life for the Japanese Army, and the loss or damage of all the convoy's surface escorts. Not only did the outcome of the battle prevent Japanese reinforcement of their troops in New Guinea, and cause the loss of urgently needed supplies, but it also established Allied air superiority over the contested region, a control never afterward lost.

General Kenney followed up this success in August 1943 when cryptanalysis from both Central Bureau and naval sources pointed to the build-up of Japanese air forces around their base at Wewak. It was the intelligence gained from reading the air-ground codes that allowed the Allied air forces to plan and conduct a series of devastating air strikes on the crowded Wewak airfields, some of them newly constructed for the purpose.[13] This loss of air control and the destruction of hundreds of aircraft at once limited the scale of Japanese attacks on Allied positions and shipping, while seriously crippling the IJA's ability to support its troops. It was a defeat from which Japanese air power in the South West Pacific Area never recovered.

The so-called convoy codes were also an important break by Eric Nave's section at Central Bureau. Allied air forces and submarines were now contesting Japanese control over the seas around and to the north of New Guinea so successfully, and the attrition rate of IJN destroyers had been so high, that troop and logistics convoys were often escorted only by aircraft. These used a special code to communicate with their bases and with other supporting aircraft.

> It was in the closing days of Rabaul's importance as a [Japanese] naval air base that regular convoy positions were first intercepted by 1WU and 2WU [RAAF intercept units]. Protection for convoys coming down from the north was provided from Kavieng. Convoy positions would be given either by the aircraft reporting back to base or the base giving a recent position to an aircraft attempting to locate the convoy. As soon as a convoy position message was intercepted and processed by the intelligence section, details were telephoned, teletyped or signalled direct to the relevant naval or air operations centre. The submarine or air group nearest the convoy would be contacted and attacks carried out.[14]

There were other important breaks into these minor codes. Central Bureau and the Special Intelligence Service cryptanalysts at Arlington Hall combined to decode the Water Transport Code. The IJA Shipping Transport Command coordinated the sea movement of its units, their equipment and resupply, and did so using Army codes. The first breaks were made into the code by Central Bureau in April 1943.[15] Now it was possible for the Allies not only to know that a convoy was sailing and the route it would follow, but what was embarked in its ships. By August 1944 this minor code had produced 75,000 significant pieces of intelligence on Japanese shipping and convoys.[16]

The solution of the IJA's place-name code was an early success claimed jointly by Central Bureau and Arlington Hall.[17] This enabled intelligence analysts to determine the originating region — Palau for example — and the area addressed — perhaps Rabaul. The identities of the individual units originating the messages and their addressees was encoded in yet another system, which was eventually broken by Arlington Hall, but now Central Bureau could say that Palau was originating a lot of traffic destined for units in Rabaul. This increase in traffic volume usually preceded a reinforcement of troops to Rabaul.

The inference was that a convoy would shortly be formed, and this information would alert those working on the air-ground codes

The foregoing is not intended to diminish in any way the significance of the achievement or the credit due to the US Army cryptanalysts who were finally successful in breaking into the IJA mainline code commencing in June 1943. But it may illustrate to readers that the achievements of Eric Nave and his minor code section were far from minor. In his own words: 'Crews of medium bombers on a mission could handle only the most simple code, and this discovery showed that it was not only the high grade codes which provided valuable information.'

But the bureau was almost deprived of the Nave factor when, in mid-1943, the Admiralty tried again to get him back from the Australians. Eric was later told that General Blamey, Allied Land Force Commander and Australian Army Commander-in-Chief, had responded, 'It would be little short of disaster if Commander Nave was removed now'. And so he stayed.

In January 1943 Central Bureau was placed under the direct command of General Headquarters South West Pacific Area, and a decision was taken to raise an additional seven Australian Army field units and eight RAAF wireless units. Central Bureau field units were totally Australian until December 1942, when the US Army's 126th Signal Radio Intercept Company became operational. From January 1944, three additional US Army intercept units joined Central Bureau, but Australian teams made most of the intercepts worked on by Central Bureau throughout the war. In March 1943 a conference was convened in Washington DC to discuss the Central Bureau–FRUMEL impasse, but there were no substantive outcomes. Indeed the US Navy maintained that the Japanese Army and Navy codes were so different that there was little to be gained from joint action.[18] This claim will be refuted shortly. One change was that Fabian was replaced, resulting in a warming of relations between Central Bureau and FRUMEL.

Central Bureau was assisted markedly in breaking into IJA codes by captures of code material on the battlefield. The most dramatic was the discovery of the Japanese 20th Division's cryptographic material by Australian troops at Sio in late January 1944. It was in a steel trunk which had been dumped by the retreating Japanese in a water-filled pit, where Australian engineers sweeping the area for booby traps found it. Flown to Central Bureau, and still sopping wet, the precious codebook pages were hung on clotheslines to dry or baked gently in ovens.[19] The cryptanalysts now had an intact version of the latest IJA mainline code plus many others, and they were shortly overwhelmed by the quantity of intercepts for decryption. An emergency call to FRUMEL produced two naval experts, who helped to deal with the most important messages in the backlog. Central Bureau and Arlington Hall were saved a huge amount of hard cryptanalytical slogging with a code which, although partially broken, was proving extremely difficult.

While the polyglot community of Central Bureau worked well together, tensions between the Australian contingent of Central Bureau and the Americans at General Headquarters emerged in January 1944. At issue was the right of the Australians to continue to communicate with and pass information directly to British Empire authorities, and to participate in Empire conferences and meetings. General Akin had forbidden an Australian officer attached to Central Bureau to attend a British Empire conference in London, and had further directed that Central Bureau was to cease direct communications with British signals intelligence agencies in London and India. The Director of Military Intelligence and Mic Sandford, now promoted lieutenant colonel, took the matter up with General Blamey. Blamey did not beat around the bush. These were commitments which had been undertaken by the Australian Government, and it, not GHQ, would make decisions on their fulfilment. He said that 'the whole matter of Imperial liaison was one not open to question and outside the concern of SWPA'.[20]

The determination of General Blamey, no less than his subordinates in Intelligence and Central Bureau, to uphold Australian sovereign rights over the employment of Australian personnel and the use it made of signals intelligence product was in line with the stand taken by Eric Nave with FRUMEL. It was more than a matter of principle. As the Director of Military Intelligence pointed out to Blamey at the January meeting, 'if GHQ were in fact to have the control of Central Bureau, then they would be in a position to direct that all Australia Y Sections or Special Intelligence personnel should be put at the disposal of American forces if they so desired'. The Australians were not willing to concede this right, as they foresaw — correctly — that the day might well come when American and Australian interests diverged. There is no evidence of any kind to suggest that the Australian Army's position was influenced by the forthright views of Eric Nave, but it would be surprising if the issue was not discussed informally amongst the Australian officers at Central Bureau.

And they did meet socially. Eric had retrieved his family from Adelaide and moved them to Queensland. Elizabeth Nave, then four years old, has distinct recollections of life in Brisbane, and of a tall army officer who used to visit their home at Windemere Road, Ascot, not far from Central Bureau. It was typical of Queensland homes of the time, built on tall piles to allow the air to circulate under the house, with a large yard boasting many shrubs and a mature frangipani tree. This was big enough for a four-year-old to climb around in, and Mic Sandford found her engaged in this pursuit on arriving for one of his visits. She remembers him as her favourite visitor and still recalls him crooning to her: 'Don't go climbing that frangipani tree with any one else but me'. By this time Elizabeth had a sister as well, Helena Mary — known as Mary — born on 8 August 1944.

Eric was now one of two veteran cryptanalysts in his section, others having been posted to other units. He had been joined by others, however, including the Australian Robert 'Bob' Botterill whom Eric thought 'showed a real flair', and who was destined to become head of the Defence Signals Directorate from 1977 to 1982. Another was Army Captain Charles Jury, who spent most of his time working on the weather codes — on which much progress had been made by the other 'discard' from FRUMEL, Professor Room. In 1944, a few more British cryptanalysts were sent out to join Central Bureau. One of them, Hugh Melinsky, was put to work on the naval air desk and recalled:

What Captain Nave did not know about codebreaking was not worth knowing. He had a sixth sense which enabled him to sniff out a meaning in what looked to me to be a jumble of letters or numbers. He gave me a collection of messages with some words already translated and told me to do the rest. I learned the hard way, for six weeks.[21]

By this time information was flowing into Central Bureau from several of the field parties, either by teleprinter from sites in Australia or by coded messages from sites offshore. This diversity of interceptions covered the possibility of messages being missed, only partially received, or received and copied down incorrectly, thus frustrating or complicating the task of the cryptanalysts, and depriving the commanders of valuable operation intelligence.

Captain Nave received messages from several wireless units. This was useful because if one version of the message contained gaps or faults another version might put these right. The greater the quantity of material available the better was the chance of breaking the code.

There were two great helps in this process. The first was being familiar with the shape of the message. Many messages were routine and followed the same pattern. For example, weather reports gave the place and time of origin, the general weather, the temperature, the amount of cloud, the wind direction and speed and, perhaps, the further outlook. In addition the uncoded messages from or to the aircraft might very well give a clue to one or several groups in a coded message.[22]

Melinsky also provided a contemporary, twenty-year-old's description of Eric Nave as a 'short, slim man of forty-five, going grey and getting thin on top'.

But it wasn't only the British who sent linguist reinforcements to Central Bureau, as new US Army personnel also joined Nave's section. The twenty-two-year-old Claude Lancaster Jr. recalled his introduction to Central Bureau's work:

We received Japanese intercepts and one of my jobs was to work on the estimated times of arrival and departure of the aircraft and sometimes the naval traffic. I would keep Captain Nave's book of messages up to date as to the particular whereabouts of aircraft … This type of intelligence was

usually sent immediately to General MacArthur's HQ which was located
about five miles away in downtown Brisbane. Captain Nave was all business.
I sat about twenty feet from him for one and a half years but I didn't know
until after the war what a well-known cryptanalyst he was and his past
accomplishments.[23]

This picture of a stern, magisterial Nave was softened by his sense
of humour, often self-deprecating. A member of his team recalls one
anecdote Eric told against himself about his time at GCCS. He was
approached by a collector for a well-known charity, seeking discarded
clothing. When told the identity of the charity Eric replied, 'Gosh!
That's where I get most of my stuff from.'[24]

Meanwhile, the initiative in South West Pacific Area had swung
firmly in favour of the Allies. On the right flank, the Japanese had
been forced out of the southern Solomons and a series of landings
was moving South Pacific Command forces closer to Rabaul, step by
step. General Kenney's air power had enabled General MacArthur
to stage a series of successful landings along the north-east coast of
New Guinea and in the islands of the Bismarck Archipelago. The
strategy was to isolate Rabaul and not to attempt to storm this heavily
fortified and garrisoned Japanese bastion. Messages intercepted by
Central Bureau RAAF field units and decoded in Brisbane revealed
IJN plans to evacuate naval and air forces from Rabaul by February
1944, and Allied landings on New Britain in December 1943
followed.[25] A daring and risky assault on the Admiralty Islands, north
of New Guinea, succeeded only after the guns of the RAN/US Navy
Task Force 74 reduced the defences to rubble after a stiff fight, in
February–March 1944.

But what was to become, arguably, MacArthur's greatest military
feat was to follow, and its conception and execution owed an
enormous debt to signals intelligence produced by Central Bureau.
The cryptanalysts were now able to follow the build-up of Japanese
forces, to monitor their strength and battle readiness, and to break
messages revealing their operational plans. These indicated that
the IJA was prepared to defend fiercely its strong points on the
north coast of New Guinea, and that it expected the next Allied

amphibious assault at Hansa Bay, east of Wewak. Accordingly, it was building air and land forces to defend the position. MacArthur made the decision that he would simply bypass Hansa Bay and attack at Hollandia, some 300 miles behind the front line being developed by the Japanese. Decodes stating that Hollandia airfields were becoming overcrowded with IJA aircraft waiting to stage forward to Wewak led to pre-emptive strikes by Allied air forces and the destruction of more than 300 Japanese aircraft on the ground.[26] The amphibious landings on 22 April 1944 were a complete success and a deep shock to the Japanese high command. The Allies now had airfields only 800 miles from the Philippines.

It is impossible to tell what Eric Nave's personal contribution to this stunning success may have been, but it is interesting that on 21 July 1944 Mic Sanford wrote the following letter to the Director of Military Intelligence:

> 1. It will be remembered that Cdr. Nave is on loan NOT to the RAN but to the CGS [Chief of General Staff] from the Admiralty, for service with Central Bureau.
>
> 2. He joined this Unit on 22 December 1942 and has been in charge of a Department from that time.
>
> 3. Cdr. Nave's Department has been growing steadily more important, and some few weeks ago was reorganised by him on a 'shift' basis in order to minimise the delay in passing to Allied Naval HQ of operational information on which action can be taken. This arrangement is now working admirably, and the intelligence passed to Allied Naval HQ invaluable. The speed with which this intelligence can be obtained is due in very large measure to Cdr. Nave's long experience and exceptional technical skill.
>
> 4. He was promoted to the rank of Paymaster Commander in June 1937, and it is considered that the Admiralty might esteem it a compliment to themselves, as well as a suitable tribute to Nave, if the CGS were to suggest to their Lordships that he be promoted to the rank of Paymaster Captain.[27]

How ironic! Eric Nave, rejected as a 'security risk' by Fabian at FRUMEL and ejected from his command of the Special Intelligence Bureau in November 1942 by the US Navy, and now working for

the Australian Army at Central Bureau — also spurned by the US
Navy — had been instrumental in generating intelligence which
was deemed 'invaluable' by Allied Naval HQ. Moreover, the Army
thought so much of his contribution that it recommended he be
promoted, which he subsequently was — to acting captain — with
effect from 12 October 1944.

> A request came for me to see Captain Thomas, the Naval Officer in Charge
> Queensland, whose office was in premises requisitioned from a bank. His
> secretary explained that the air conditioning had broken down, and added;
> 'You must excuse Captain Thomas's dress'. He received me seated behind
> his desk presenting a bare chest; to the visitor he could have been completely
> naked. His information came as a pleasant surprise: I had been promoted.

The victory at Hollandia also led to the second of Central Bureau's
moves, of which there were five during its brief existence. The first was
from Melbourne to Brisbane in September 1942. In May 1944, an
advanced echelon was established at Hollandia; this moved to Leyte
in October 1944, and in May 1945 the majority of Central Bureau
functions were moved to San Miguel on Luzon. In September 1945,
Central Bureau transferred to Tokyo, leaving the Australians to clean
up and pack away in Brisbane. The war, and General MacArthur,
were both moving away from Australia, but the task of cryptanalysis
went on undisturbed. One significant change was that the younger
officers, including Mic Sandford, were deployed north with the
General Headquarters, leaving Sinkov, Booth and Nave as the senior
officers in Brisbane. After the move to San Miguel in May 1945, Eric
Nave was the only one left in Australia.

> Central Bureau had moved on to the Philippines in company with
> MacArthur's advance when he made good his promise 'I will return'. The
> doctors refused permission for me to go as I was declared unfit for tropical
> service, as much as I wished to go I knew it was hopeless. I was appointed
> in charge of the Rear Detachment and continued to handle the convoy
> signals.

As another illustration of the value of Eric's work and the way
in which he instructed personnel of the Central Bureau field units
in its use, when General MacArthur launched his assault on the

Philippines at Leyte in October 1944 his staff made sure that they took a specially formed RAAF wireless unit with them to intercept and warn of Japanese air attacks on the voyage.

> A couple of days later the group was ushered into a large room where top American 'Brass' were being briefed by G3 [Operations Section] and Navy Intelligence on the forthcoming operations. It was there that they officially learned that they were to be part of the Leyte invasion force. M/Gen Akin [Chief Signals Officer] introduced the assembled Australians and referred to them as the personnel who would be ensuring that no surprise air attacks would be made on the convoy during the journey north.[28]

This certainly indicates a high degree of customer satisfaction with the application of the work of the Air-Ground Section of Central Bureau and confidence it its abilities.

Although there was still much bitter fighting and dying ahead before the Japanese surrender in August 1945, the Allied invasion of Leyte in October 1944 and the associated naval battles effectively saw the end of the Japanese dream of empire. With fewer and fewer convoys sailing, there was less for Eric and his team to do and so he started on the task of compiling a record of the cryptanalytic activities of Central Bureau. Robert Brown recalls:

> When CB was being wound up, a multi-service group of 12 or so was assigned to complete the technical records. Eric Nave was in command of this team. I asked Eric's opinion on eliminating Americanisms; he gave me a free hand.
>
> My desk was a few metres from his, and one day I heard him asking on the phone that some recognition be given to the people working on the Technical Records. This seemed to indicate a generosity of spirit. A few months after demob [demobilisation], I received a personally signed letter from the DMI [Director of Military Intelligence] thanking me for my service with CB and especially in helping edit the records.[29]

In these final stages of the war against Japan it was not just Eric's skill as a cryptanalyst that counted; rather it was his ability to share his knowledge with a new generation of Australian and Allied codebreakers, who would form the backbone of the post-war signals intelligence organisations. His Central Bureau Technical

Records were so meticulous in giving guidance on how each code
was attacked and broken that, when these archives were eventually
'opened' to the public in 1986, the post-war authorities of the time
saw fit to extensively expunge most of what he wrote, leaving very
little available for public scrutiny. It was an odd — but entirely
appropriate — way for them to recognise the enduring value of his
achievements. Fortunately, the digital copies now available are not so
filtered, and the full range of Central Bureau activities can now be
understood and appreciated.

It is interesting, therefore, to observe that with the separation of
Central Bureau between the Philippines and Brisbane, Sandford's
opinion of Eric had changed. He made this point in a letter written
to Colonel Little from the Philippines on 20 August 1945:

> Sometime ago in conversation with DMI [Director of Military Intelligence]
> the matter of honours and awards of Central Bureau personnel was
> discussed. I told him at the time that I had recommended nobody since
> there were so many examples of outstanding work and devotion to duty that
> might be awarded. Now that the war is over, however, it seems appropriate
> to try to consider certain officers for special mention.
>
> I have recommended nothing in the case of Capt NAVE since I thought
> I should like to have your advice on this point. Technically, Capt NAVE is
> by far the most brilliant officer in the Unit, but he is so lacking in initiative
> and appreciation of changing operational requirements of war forces that
> his efforts must be consistently guided by Maj CLARKE [Head of Traffic
> Analysis] or myself. One cannot forget however that it was he who 'broke'
> the first Japanese cypher made by any of the military units during this war,
> and on that account alone he should perhaps be specially considered. Can
> you give me your advice on this.[30]

Was this the re-emergence of the Nave stubborn streak, which
had apparently exacerbated the tense relationships between the
Special Intelligence Bureau and CAST in Melbourne? Or was it
simply that Eric was not able to assimilate the demands of land
warfare as it was being fought in the Philippines? Whatever the
root of Sandford's complaint, the Army was moved to nominate
one Eric Nave for admission as an Officer to the Order of the
British Empire. The citation read:

Capt T.E. NAVE, RN, has been responsible for one of the finest contributions to our cryptographic work during the whole of the war in the Pacific. For Security reasons, details of his work and its results cannot be given in detail, but it can be said that from the time, some three years ago, when he first broke the Japanese Naval Code, the Allied Command in this theatre has, largely as a result of Capt NAVE's outstanding ability, always had access to a very considerable proportion of the enemy's signal traffic.

This award is recommended with an intimate knowledge of what Capt NAVE's work has contributed to the success of Allied operations in the Pacific.[31]

Sandford's letter also contained the first official expression by the men in the field of the Australian desire to sustain its signals intelligence capability, notwithstanding the end of hostilities in the Pacific:

You will have received my minute … by this time and will therefore understand why it is we do not desire to have the Unit disbanded. Further, the US Army is undertaking the monitoring of all Japanese signal links in and out of the Empire, and AUSTRALIA is to have a comparatively small commitment on behalf of SEAC [South-East Asia Command, under Lord Louis Mountbatten] … It should be possible within two months to disband the Unit except for such a nucleus as it is desired to maintain in peace time.

On the same day Sandford wrote a letter to Land Headquarters in Melbourne making vigorous recommendations about the need for Australians to understand the operation of the tabulating machines made by the American company International Business Machines (IBM) and from which Australians had been largely excluded:

Irrespective of whether or not IBM machines are obtained for use by CB [Central Bureau], it is considered absolutely essential to obtain all possible information about the development and application of these machines without delay.

Whatever may be the developments of Signal techniques in the post war period, it is certain that a modified type of IBM machine will be necessary to [word indecipherable] pass with them in the post war period.

Nave in Brisbane was marching to the same drummer. In a letter to Colonel Little dated 8 September 1945 he commented on the Central Bureau Technical Records:

As you know we are very busy writing our technical records. These will, I feel sure, be of the greatest importance to any organisation here in the future and I think that by the time we have finished they will be most satisfactory. Past experience is of the greatest value in this work and I am endeavouring to have everything recorded and illustrated as necessary.

However, these concrete expressions of a belief in the necessity of a Central Bureau in Australia after the war were not just 'home-grown'. In September 1944, Sandford accompanied the Director of Military Intelligence to the UK where they discussed with British authorities 'Post war plans and Australia's intelligence responsibilities in the Pacific islands and the islands to the North of Australia'. This was followed by a British paper to the Australian Government proposing that a 'Far East Joint Intelligence Bureau' be established in Australia after the war. The Department of Defence set up a special Intelligence Committee to study the proposal. In May 1945, Sir Edward Travis, the Director of GCCS, now renamed Government Communications Headquarters, arrived in Australia with a team of Intelligence experts and visited Central Bureau and the Army diplomatic intercept section in Melbourne. The British had brought their heavy artillery to bear in an effort to coax a response out of Australia. The outcome was the appointment of a brigadier to collate and make recommendations on the future shape of Australia's intelligence organisations and, when he delivered his report in November 1945, a 'Signals Intelligence Centre' was included in his proposed arrangements.[32]

On 29 November 1945 a conference of the senior Australian officers of Central Bureau under the chairmanship of Colonel Little was held in Brisbane to decide the disposal of Central Bureau records 'and other matters, pending determination of post-war policy'. Eric Nave was made responsible for the destruction of signals 'with the exception of some 50 messages to be selected by him for their value as examples of operational intelligence'. Other records and 'material already selected' was to be forwarded to Melbourne.[33] The Army had already made a decision on the manpower it was going to allocate to a Central Bureau, and the RAAF was asked to do likewise. To the veterans of Central Bureau, it was unthinkable that the government would let all their precious hard-earned experience dissipate just because the shooting had stopped. While the bureaucratic battle was being waged in Canberra and Melbourne, Australia's signals intelligence veterans were determined to keep alive the capability developed at such effort and expense.

Eric Nave had already made similar decisions. With the war winding down and Central Bureau in the Philippines, in mid-1945 he moved his family to a property near Dubbo in New South Wales to await developments.   Elizabeth Nave remembers this move distinctly because it meant that she could not start school until 1946, which was a great disappointment to her. With the war over and the logic for his loan to the Australian Army running out of steam, there was the possibility that the Admiralty might recall that there was a paymaster captain on the payroll who could well be demobilised or required to return to the UK for other duties. On 19 December, Eric was able to report to Colonel Little that the Technical Records had been despatched; his part in the war against Japan was complete. His had been a most significant contribution to the Japanese defeat.

As the noted writer on Australian military and political history, Professor David Horner, said in the conclusion of his 1978 article on Allied intelligence in Australia during the war:

> During the Second World War Australia advanced from a position of being almost totally dependent upon the British intelligence to the point where she had relatively large and effective intelligence organisations cooperating closely with similar American and British organisations. This was a substantial achievement which was to have important repercussions for the future.
>
> It may well be that present day Allied intelligence co-operation had proved to be the most lasting and important legacy of Australia's experience of coalition warfare in the Second World War. And the consequent development of the Australian intelligence services strengthened the nation's capacity for making independent judgments on foreign policy after the war.[34]

There are two postscripts to the tale of Eric Nave at Central Bureau, the first concerning an ally. The unit was under the direct command of General Headquarters and, regardless of what the British Empire thought of Captain Nave's services and any award it might want to make, the Americans no less wanted to recognise his contribution to the war against Japan with the award of a Medal of Freedom. Unfortunately, this was not to be since it contravened 'the principle of accepting US awards when a British award had been given for the same period of service'. In addition, the government had decided that it would only allow Australian servicemen and women to accept US decorations that were awarded for operational service, a category that excluded Central Bureau. [35]

The second concerns a former enemy, and was an incident recorded by an Australian Army sergeant interpreter who had been posted to the British Commonwealth Occupation Force in Japan.

> Nave must have been a very good linguist, too. I remember, a few days after we had landed in Kure in 1946, a Japanese sitting next to me in the train asked me if I had encountered a 'Lt. Nave'. He had met him when, as a cadet, he visited Australia with the Training Squadron in about 1924. He had been much impressed by Nave's mastery of the language.[36]

10 After the War

The end of the war did not bring with it the expected benefits of peace. While there had been one clear enemy to engage with in the struggle against the Japanese, the cessation of hostilities opened the door for a number of regional problems which had been dormant or had made their appearance because of the war. During the brief life of their overseas empire, the Japanese had tried to gain acceptance for their occupation by encouraging the population at large, and selected elites in particular, to see it as a step towards independence from the former European colonial powers. However, these powers had quite different ideas and moved to reassert their sovereignty as quickly as possible. This drive generated some bizarre results, with British troops engaged in running fights with Indonesian separatists in Surabaya and Lord Louis Mountbatten having no option but to deploy Japanese troops as policemen and security guards in French Indo-China. The defeat of Japan had bred not solutions but complex problems.

Australia emerged from the Pacific War a changed nation. Almost one-third of its population of a little over seven million people had been engaged in the war effort, either in the armed forces, in industries delivering war materiel, or engaged in production to meet the logistics demands of Allied and Australian forces. The involvement with the Americans had been instructive and profitable as their generous assistance in skills and infrastructure development had opened new opportunities for Australian industry. Esteem for the British had, however, suffered a severe blow over the Singapore debacle, and never again would Australian governments accept uncritically British assurances that impinged on the security of Australia.

World War II had bred a new certainty and confidence in Australians in dealing with the wider world. Her soldiers, sailors and airmen had won Australia the respect of other nations with which they had come in contact, and their military achievements were real enough. The disappointing aspect of the conduct of the war was that Australia had not had any means of influencing policy, even in decisions that affected her security directly, and Australian decision-makers were determined that this would not happen again. It was a newly assertive Australia that faced the post-war world with two key aims. The first was to create security arrangements which would keep any future enemy a long way from Australian shores. The second was to ensure that Japan could never again become a military threat.

A complicating factor was that the Alliance that had won the war began to disintegrate almost as soon as the peace was signed. American power became concentrated in Japan and Hawaii, with US legislators apparently showing little interest in the rest of the Pacific. Accordingly, successive Australian governments put emphasis on overhauling and strengthening British Commonwealth linkages, ensuring that the country could have an appropriate influence on policy for the South-East Asian region. As well, the Chifley Labor Government placed particular store in the United Nations as a collective security screen. Neither position attracted unqualified support from the British or the US. In their strategic planning, their major concern was with the Soviet Union and its satellites and the developing Cold War. But divisions also appeared between wartime partners as close as Britain and America. The Americans, conscious of their dominant part in winning the war and with a monopoly on nuclear weapons, chose to close down or to restrict the exchange of information through channels of military and technological access that had existed from the early 1940s.[1]

The British expected that their considerable generosity — albeit self-serving — in sharing their technological expertise in radar, anti-submarine warfare, intelligence and nuclear engineering with the US would guarantee them continued access to American councils. However, these hopes were frustrated.[2] The British responded by commencing their own nuclear weapons and missile development programs and other technological projects in which the Commonwealth, especially Canada and Australia, would be closely involved.[3] They were willing to grant Australia a bigger role in British Commonwealth defence planning as it offered a way of sharing the post-war Commonwealth defence burden, and it ensured Australian interest in British programs in which its participation was practically essential. The proposal was put to Commonwealth prime ministers in London in May 1946 at which Australia and New Zealand were described as one of five 'main support areas' for the defence of Western interests.[4] For Australia, access to British weapons and nuclear technology would boost its own defence capacity and enable it to play a larger physical and political role in the region to its north, through which the Japanese threat had materialised.[5] The Australian Government set up a New Weapons and Equipment Development Committee in 1946 to advise on and oversee the development of Australian atomic weapons — the 'Joint Project'. The first dramatic outcome of the project was the detonation of Britain's first atomic bomb in the Monte Bello Islands off the north-west of Western Australia on 3 October 1952.

The Australian Government's enchantment with the United Nations and involvement in the British weapons program were to have repercussions in the very near future, but in the immediate aftermath of the war there was a more pressing issue — that of intelligence support. Strategic decisions on issues as diverse as the civil war in China, Indonesian nationalism and the activities of the Viet Minh needed to be supported by intelligence. Before and during the war, either the British or the Americans had provided that intelligence. If Australia was to have an independent position, the intelligence to back that needed to come from sources that could be independently considered by Australian decision-makers.

Fortunately, the one element of Allied wartime cooperation that survived and prospered in the Cold War world was intelligence. Arrangements developed for collaboration and sharing of intelligence during the war were formalised in a series of agreements to which Australia became a partner. The Government, no less than the Chiefs of Staff, recognised the importance of an indigenous strategic intelligence capability to inform high-level decision-making, to support operational forces and to create a place for Australia at coalition intelligence councils. Australia's wartime intelligence organisation therefore needed to be reshaped to give effect to these requirements.

The priority in the reorganisation of Australian intelligence after the war went to signals intelligence. As seen in the last chapter, transformation of the Australian component of Central Bureau and the Wireless Intelligence residue of FRUMEL commenced as soon as Japan was defeated. While the development of a policy on the shape and functions of Australia's post-war intelligence was taking place at a Defence and government level, the remnants of Central Bureau headed south. Mic Sandford reported on his return from Manila in October 1945 that he was going to Melbourne to 'assist in the formation of the post war organisation'. Eric Nave also headed for Melbourne, where Jack Newman was already ensconced in the hutted camp close to Victoria Barracks into which FRUMEL had moved in 1944 when it became too large for Monterey. This was known as Albert Park Barracks.

These various movements assembled a formidable array of talent. Newman had supported the US Seventh Fleet throughout the war with direction-finding and traffic analysis services. His stations and their operators were well trained and experienced. Sandford had been one of the assistant directors of the Central Bureau since its inception in 1942 and had been intimately involved in its growth and development. He enjoyed the confidence of the British and MacArthur's General Headquarters, and had represented Australia in several wartime conferences on signals intelligence. Eric Nave was Australia's principal cryptanalyst with wide experience in military and diplomatic systems. He had created the first Australian signals intelligence organisation and had subsequently controlled the exploitation of all Central Bureau minor system codebreaking. He had also compiled the Central Bureau Technical Records. A Wing Commander Berry of Central Bureau was a fourth starter.

Remarkable though these Australians were they were unable to compete with the British. Sir Edward Travis paid a second visit to Australia in December 1945, and then played host to Australian Prime Minister Chifley during the May 1946 Commonwealth conference of prime ministers in London. Prior to the prime ministerial meeting, in February and March there had been a conference convened by the British to discuss the post-war arrangements for signals intelligence sharing between Commonwealth countries. Eric Nave led the Australian delegation to these talks — despite his being a serving officer of the Royal Navy. The outcomes were clear: Australia would be expected to shoulder the responsibility for monitoring communications in the greater part of East, South-East and South Asia.

Whatever else transpired at their meeting, Travis left Chifley in no doubt about two points. First, Australia had a duty to the Commonwealth to create and operate a signals intelligence organisation to discharge the responsibilities decided upon in March. Second, the British wanted to control it. Chifley took the message back to Australia and on 19 July 1946 submitted to Cabinet a proposal on Intelligence that included a 'Signals Intelligence Centre'.[6] There is circumstantial evidence that he waited until his Foreign Minister, Dr Evatt, was out of the country before making his proposal and, after it was accepted, he did exclude Evatt and his department from any involvement in Intelligence matters.

It does seem odd that Chifley acquiesced in having a UK Government Communications Headquarters man at the head of the Australian organisation, but Travis made his case very plainly. If the British were to have the necessary confidence in the new centre's product, then they could only do so if the director were someone in whom they could have 'complete confidence'.[7] That necessitated the appointment of one of Travis's own people. Wise heads in the

Department of Defence also observed that if having a British director guaranteed Australian access to British signals intelligence affecting South-East Asia and the Far East, then it was a small price to pay. Australians would have other opportunities to take the top job.

So here was the first of two factors which could have been seen as counting against the two obvious Australian candidates, Sandford and Nave — credibility. While they had each controlled component parts of their respective organisations, neither had the experience of running a fully integrated and modern signals intelligence bureau. They each might have learned to do so if given the position, but results were needed now and the first steps of the new bureau had to be confident to reassure suspicious allies of its value and the credibility of its product. The second consideration was that, with the exception of Sandford's time engaged with the Germans and French in 1941, they had become experts in assaulting and gaining intelligence from Japanese communications. These were no longer the signals intelligence target and the new bureau would need senior personnel who had something more relevant to offer.

The Australian Government accepted the British deal, and Commander Teddy Poulden RN, who had spent some of the war in Australia and had married an Australian, became the first head of the Australian Defence Signals Bureau on 1 April 1947. The new bureau was given primary responsibility for 'Ceylon [Sri Lanka], Malaya, Hong Kong, New Zealand, Australia and all areas within this perimeter'.[8] An additional twenty British officers were seconded to the bureau to oversee its foundation, but the Australians were integrated within its structure.

There is some lack of clarity on what Eric Nave himself was doing while all these preparatory moves were taking place. His RAN service record, covered with tightly penned annotations, verges on the chaotic and is little help in unravelling his activities immediately after his completion of duties at Central Bureau. The children remember that in 1946 the family was housed in Frankston, some forty kilometres south of Melbourne, and they seem to recall that Eric may have spent some months at Bletchley Park during this period. David has a memory of travelling regularly with his father in a Navy car to the large RAN training depot at Flinders about an hour's drive south of Frankston. There he would be whisked away for an hour or so while his father transacted some business. On the return journey they would stop at the farming hamlets along the route and buy fresh produce.

On the last of these trips, David remembers that he was retrieved from the whaleboat being rowed by cadet midshipmen from the Naval College, and returned to shore in a dinghy. There he found his father furious following an argument with the Commodore Superintendent; the visits to the training depot ceased after that. What the business being transacted and the cause of the argument might have been can only be conjectured. However, Flinders Naval Depot was the site of the RAN Communication School and before the war it had operated as a training intercept site for Japanese traffic.[9] Eric may well have been visiting to lecture telegraphist classes on signals intelligence and coding.

A colleague remembers being told by Eric that he was attached to the office of the Chief of Naval Staff during this period, his attachment to the Army being a front to cover his signals intelligence work. This seems to corroborate the Flinders Naval Depot recollections of David Nave, and the Navy Office posting is supported by an anecdote, again told by Nave. It seems that the admiral was as keen on playing the stock market as Eric and they would meet each morning to compare notes and make investment decisions. These were conveyed to the stockbrokers by a chief petty officer on the admiral's staff. Noting that the two senior officers appeared to be making some money at this, the chief decided to make some investments of his own acting on the officers' decisions. According to Eric, the chief was extremely successful in the stock market and was able to leave the Navy and invest his money well, shortly becoming a millionaire. This apparent 'insider trading' aggrieved Eric, and he lamented that the chief petty officer had made a fortune while he still had to earn a living.[10]

Further confirmation that Eric was in all probability seconded to the Chief of Naval Staff's office comes from the extensive exchange of correspondence on the signals intelligence organisation between the Secretary of the Department of Defence, Sir Frederick Shedden, and Travis at Government Communications Headquarters throughout 1946.[11] The channel of communications on this highly secret and sensitive subject was via the admiral's office, where Eric would have been one of the only officers in Australia with the security clearance to handle the material.

As well, at the end of 1946 the family moved to Brighton, a pleasantly upmarket bayside suburb of Melbourne within easy commuting distance of both Navy Headquarters and Albert Park Barracks. Cochrane Street was to be Eric's home for the remainder of his life. Here, when time permitted, he could indulge his interest in gardening, but there was little enough time for that in the immediate future, as he slipped into familiar harness and surroundings. His service record shows that he was still on loan from the RN to the Australian Army: one suspects that some bargain had been transacted between the Australian and British governments to leave him in Australia. The only change apparent was the target of his codebreaking and the fact that he had shed the paymaster prefix to his rank. He was now a member of the Supply '(S)' Branch. And his family was growing too; on 22 June 1947, new arrival Margaret was welcomed into the family.

In the organisation of the new centre, Eric Nave was given the key task of Head of Cryptography.[12] If his failure to be appointed director was a disappointment to Eric, he did not record it as such in his memoirs. His sole written reference to it came in a letter in 1974 when he said: 'Sometime I must set down the facts of the establishment of D.M.B. [Australian Signals Intelligence Centre] and how Poulden came to be Director'. Unfortunately, however, there is no trace of that story in his memoirs or correspondence.

At the end of 1946, a Signals Intelligence delegation headed by Nave went to London to participate in an Imperial Sigint Conference called by Government Communications Headquarters. The conference laid the basis for the Commonwealth Sigint Organisation, headed by Government Communications Headquarters, and agreed in outline the spheres of responsibility of each of the members. This formed the basis of the British bargaining position in the discussions with the US in 1947, which culminated in the UKUSA agreement of 1948. Britain and the US were the 'first parties' to this agreement, with Australia, Canada and New Zealand termed 'second parties'.[13] Under the agreement, the Defence Signals Bureau — as the Signals Intelligence Centre was renamed from 12 November 1947 — shared with the British the running of a Sigint station in Hong Kong and targeted at China. In 1948 the US established a liaison office with the bureau.

Integration of the bureau into the UKUSA arrangements was closely held within government, being overseen by a committee comprising only Prime Minister Chifley and Defence Minister Dedman. Defence contrived to exclude the Minister for External Affairs, Dr Evatt, and his Secretary Dr John Burton. Burton was scornful of signals intelligence, dismissing the bureau as the 'gnomes of Melbourne' and refusing to undertake the indoctrination necessary to be given access to signals intelligence product.[14] These attitudes were to cause Australia much pain in the immediate future.

The new global targets for the Allied signals intelligence community were diverse, but the cryptographic systems of the Soviet Union, its satellites and Communist China were the highest priorities. In 1943, GCCS and the Americans reached a working arrangement on the interception and decryption of the traffic of their Soviet ally and by war's end they had made some progress. Australia was also associated with the task, with Mornington commencing intercept operations against targets in the Soviet Far East in December 1945, and Darwin following in mid-1946. At the same time the Director of Military Intelligence reached agreement with the Australian cable company Amalgamated Wireless (Australasia) to receive copies of all Soviet cables passed through the Sydney General Post Office.[15]

There is a supreme irony in this because the Australian Signals Intelligence Centre and the later Defence Signals Bureau were unwittingly involved in collecting intelligence that would shortly be used against Australia by the US. What the British and Americans had discovered under a cryptanalytic project codenamed Venona was that the Soviet Union had established a spy ring in Australia involving senior members of the Australian Public Service. The key evidence was found in cables sent between 1943 and 1948 to Moscow from the Committee for State Security [KGB] representative — the *rezident* — in the Soviet Legation and, from 1947, Embassy in Canberra.[16]

The break into this system came at an unfortunate time in Australian–American relations. The enthusiastic espousal of the principles of the UN Charter regarding the use of force to resolve disputes and the right to independence of colonial peoples by Dr Evatt in the United Nations General Assembly induced some suspicions in American minds about the ideological 'soundness' of the Government. At the same time the Americans were not supportive of British efforts to create its own nuclear deterrent and the means of delivering it, a program in which Australia was deeply involved. The Venona revelations showed that Australia's security apparatus had failed to detect and deal with serious leaks at senior governmental levels. The end result was a US reluctance to share classified information directly with Australia, and even to deny this to the British if there was the chance it could be handed on to Australians. An embargo was imposed from 23 October 1947 on the transfer of US classified material to Australia.[17]

The Americans had legitimate concerns, although suspicion of the ideological line being pursued by the Australian Government may have exaggerated the scope of the problem. For nearly thirty years, responsibility for security intelligence in Australia had been a running sore between the Commonwealth Investigation Service under the Attorney General's Department and the security and intelligence agencies of the Australian armed forces. Coordination, if it happened at all, was reluctant and spasmodic and there was no national strategy for detecting and weeding out subversive elements from government departments. Wartime efforts by the British to insinuate their own operatives into the system only created new tensions. The situation was overdue for major change.

It seems that the Australians were not made party to the Venona information until 1949.[18] It does not appear that any bureau personnel were working on Soviet systems, and there was more than enough to do in attempting to honour the commitments Australia had already made in South-East Asia and Hong Kong. Eric Nave was almost certainly unaware of the impact that Venona was to have on his future. In the Defence Signals Bureau, shortage of personnel was, again, the critical issue. There were too few trained people and the intelligence world was not getting what it regarded as the required degree of priority in accessing Commonwealth Government employees.[19] The intelligence function of the bureau was not to be revealed by the Australian Government until 1977, so all transactions with the Commonwealth Public Service were necessarily closely held.

In early 1948, there was a change in Eric's employment status. His service record bears the bureaucratic inscription 'Accepted as C'wealth liability (Dept. of Defence) as from 1 Jan 48 & while attached to Defence Signals Bureau as a serving officer'. The Admiralty had clearly become impatient with paying an officer who wasn't doing any Admiralty work, and had prevailed upon the Australian Government to accept the responsibility for Eric. Australia had had an excellent free ride for nearly eight years at the expense of the British. But there had been no change in the quality of Eric's contribution, as may be judged from a report rendered on him in October 1948:

> During his service with the Australian Military Forces, Acting Captain (S) NAVE has carried out his duties in the most highly commendable manner. His ability in his specialist work upon which he has been engaged has been outstanding. In addition he has proved himself a most loyal and zealous officer, both in his dealings with his senior officers and with his own subordinates.

The occasion for the report was a half-yearly recommendation for promotion. The Vice-Chief of the General Staff added his comments, saying; 'I concur in the above report and strongly recommend the promotion of this officer'. But at this juncture, almost for the first time since his Supply Course in Portsmouth in 1931, Eric now tangled with Supply Branch bureaucracy. His promotion to rear admiral was a possibility, especially with the kind of reports he was receiving, but for this to occur Nave would have to serve a term in a seagoing posting. Setting aside his codebreaking service and experience since 1932, he would have to re-learn how to be a supply officer in an RN ship. It was a very tough call and came on top of a family tragedy.

Helena and Eric's third child Mary had never been a lively one, and Helena with her nursing background sensed that there was something seriously wrong with her daughter. Visits to pediatricians in Brisbane and in Melbourne had not provided any satisfactory answers as to why Mary was not thriving. Now the diagnosis came — an inoperable brain tumour. It was shocking and distressing news. The diagnostic and surgical techniques we enjoy today might have saved Mary, but in 1948 there was little to be done except for a series of periodic operations to relieve the pressure on Mary's brain and to make the child as comfortable as possible. Helena must have been devastated at the prognosis, and more than ever she needed Eric's support. This was not the time that he could even contemplate leaving his family to take up a seagoing posting in the RN.

Meanwhile, the stand-off between Australia and the US over security was a serious issue, and the Australians seem to have had some difficulty in devising a strategy to redress the situation. In the end, it was the British who initiated the corrective action. Concerned at the US perception of laxness in Australia security, which not only jeopardised their own access to classified US information but also threatened the security of the Joint Project, the British Government sent an expert team from their own counter-intelligence agency, MI-5, to Australia to investigate and report. The team then made a number of recommendations to the Australian Government on sorting out the security intelligence mess in a report that pulled no punches.

> It is known that there is in existence in Australia a Soviet spy network which has, or had, means of obtaining information from Australian Government Departments. Two of the agents of the network have been identified. One worked in the Department of External Affairs and is known to have passed information to the Soviet intelligence machine which was available to him as a result of his work. The other worked in Dr Evatt's private office and, though not engaged on secret work, may have had access to official material.[20]

There seems to have been some bewilderment at senior Australian ministerial levels about all this talk about 'security intelligence'. A minute from the Secretary to the Minister for Defence in late 1948 had to state that:

> There is a distinction between Intelligence Organisations and counter-Intelligence Organisations. The primary function of the latter is to prevent potentially hostile powers obtaining Intelligence relating to our activities. This will involve a study and close check on subversive organisations and activities within the civil community, and measures to prevent the leakage of classified information. The proposed new National Security Organisation in Australia will be responsible for these matters.[21]

The end result was the establishment of the Australian Security Intelligence Organisation (ASIO) on 16 March 1949 under the control of the Attorney General. The title originally selected — Australian Security Service — was discarded when it was realised that the resulting three-letter acronym of the agency would present its detractors with a ready weapon of ridicule. ASIO's first director general was a South Australian judge, Justice Geoffrey Reed.

It is unfortunate (for researchers at least) that the ASIO Act mandates that the names of ASIO officers and their correspondents be deleted from files made accessible to the public. So we will never know which member of the Melbourne Club it was who forwarded Eric's application for a position with the organisation on 13 May 1949. The member believed Nave to be 'of ability, experience and integrity', but noted that he did not know him well. He had written the covering letter at the request of the Attorney General of Victoria, 'who I gather is a personal friend' (of Nave's, presumably).

The associated Personal Particulars form illustrates the longevity of Eric's social contacts both in Australia and the United Kingdom. In the section headed 'Give the names and addresses of two responsible British subjects, not your relatives, to whom reference can be made', Eric listed Rear Admiral Sir Eldon Mainsty, a fellow paymaster who rose to be the secretary of several First Sea Lords of the Royal Navy, the chief manager of the National Bank of Australasia and the chairman of the Commonwealth Public Service Board. In the

'Acquaintance Dating from Year' spaces he recorded 1929, 1925 and 1930 respectively. One can surmise that Eric was not only showing off, but also demonstrating the reach and nature of his personal network of contacts in Australia and abroad.

His stratagem worked and he got the job. In a letter to Navy Office on 15 December 1949, Justice Reed said:

> I attach the greatest importance to the closest liaison and co-operation between A.S.I.O and your Department, particularly in the field of preventative security, and I propose to appoint Captain (S) T.E. Nave, R.N. Retired, of the Melbourne Directorate as Defence and Services Liaison Officer[22]

The proposal was enthusiastically endorsed the following day by Navy Office as 'entirely suitable to this Department', so the deal had already been done, but it must be asked why Eric decided to take up this very different role in a very new organisation. Again, there is almost no material that might cast some light on his decision, but a number of factors can be surmised. In the first place, the Nave naval career was over. His service record shows 'Loan appointment terminated to date 17:3:49'. One suspects that Eric himself initiated the action, because the file bears another notation stating, 'Benefits under Post War Reconstruction to UK personnel cease on 30 June 1949, if disposal has not been effected request you execute before 30 June 49'. The Admiralty agreed to the termination of Eric's service with a signal on 4 March, so he did gain access to his entitlements. He was also owed an extensive period of leave — 160 days in all. Finally his pension of £825 Sterling per annum, which commenced on 22 August 1949, made a welcome addition to his ASIO salary of £1281 Australian.

Eric probably needed a rest. With only short breaks he had been leading the assault on Japanese diplomatic and naval codes for twenty years, and had completed another three years in charge of the Defence Signals Bureau's efforts to break into those of its new target countries. He was fifty years old and may well have felt that it was time to leave the cryptanalytic effort to younger men. He may have known that the search for an eventual replacement for Poulden as director had begun, and perhaps he had been advised that his name was not on the list of possibilities. And finally, in the special situation in which the family found itself, he may have thought that a less demanding position at ASIO would be more appropriate than continuing on at the bureau.

On 10 November 1949 Eric wrote to Justice Reed expressing the wish that his services would be of value to ASIO and giving 'my personal assurance that I will at all times do my utmost to help in every way'. The letter raised another issue — that of superannuation. At first glance this seems an odd association of ideas but Eric, amongst other ASIO officers, was concerned that his service might not be as secure as that of other Commonwealth employees, a matter that was resolved by the ASIO Act of 1956. As well, his RN pension would terminate on his death without residual benefits to Helena and his growing family. It was a prudent step to draw this to the director general's attention.

The headquarters of ASIO until the 1970s were at Queens Road, Melbourne, not far from Defence Headquarters at Victoria Barracks or the Defence Signals Bureau at Albert Park. An organisational chart of the time shows that Eric was attached to the Melbourne Directorate — termed C2 — as Senior Officer C. C Branch was responsible for 'protective security' which meant, in brief, the checking of Australian government and commercial personnel who might have access to classified information. Eric's task was to assist the Department of Defence and the Departments of Supply, Army, Air and Navy with the development of the processes by which service personnel and Defence civilians would be selected for background security checks, known as vetting, and with the vetting procedures. It was a responsible job but hardly an onerous one. As well, Justice Reed had attempted to interest Eric in the post of Officer-in-Charge Adelaide but, as he had not been prepared to move at that time, the offer lapsed.

This pleasant life came to an abrupt end in 1950 when Justice Reed was replaced. There were suggestions that this was because of perceptions that he lacked the ruthless streak that his office required.

In fact, Reed had insisted that his appointment be for one year. This had already been extended following the election of a new Liberal Government in 1949 and the search for a new director general in 1950. Reed's successor was Colonel (later Brigadier) Charles Spry, an infantry officer with a long involvement in intelligence, who before his selection to head ASIO had been the Director of Military Intelligence. The colonel made a number of sweeping changes in the manning and structure of the organisation. He preferred his senior staff to have had Service experience and in October 1950 he elevated Eric from Staff Officer C to Assistant Director C Branch — Investigation and Research. By August 1952 Eric had become Director C Branch.

Spry's motivation for these moves was the advice of an MI-5 officer who he had invited to review the ASIO organisation and to recommend changes. He was determined to make ASIO 'respectable' as quickly as possible. Although the US embargo had been partially lifted in December 1949, Australia was still being denied access to material at higher security classifications. He therefore needed men in key positions in ASIO who had the kind of established background and record that would attract the respect of the government departments and the domestic and international intelligence agencies with which ASIO had to work. They also had to be people of some standing in the wider community. [23]

Eric certainly filled the bill on the first criterion. His name and achievements were well known in senior intelligence circles in the UK, the US and Australia, although the achievements could not be divulged to people outside this select community. The Nave name had also become well known in South Australia through Eric's father Thomas and his involvement in the field of the performing arts. This had culminated in his appointment as a Member of the Order of the British Empire in the Queen's Birthday honours of 1948 for services to the cultural life of Adelaide. In 1946, Eric had been accepted as a member of the Melbourne Club, at that time a bastion of privilege and power in the state of Victoria and beyond. His two brothers held important positions in the Australian banking community. With those credentials, his community service (of which more later), and the support of personalities such as former DNI Cocky Long, Eric was a man of eminent social respectability with access to personages of real community standing. In short, Nave fitted admirably into Spry's concept.

> I've never known a man that had a network like his — he knew everyone in town! How he did this in the beginning I don't quite know, but at the time he joined ASIO and then came to the Victorian office he went almost every day to the Melbourne Club and did the rounds, met everyone and, of course, anyone who was anyone in Melbourne was in the Melbourne Club. So he had that type of network; he could pick up the phone and talk to anyone. I think Spry appreciated that and it was a great strength of the organisation because, as you know, in Intelligence work that's extremely important.[24]

Not that those were the only characteristics that Eric brought to his work in C Branch. He understood quite clearly the vital link between personal trust and the sharing of classified information. Writing later of his time at GCCS in the 1930s, he said: 'In this situation [Imperial defence planning] personal relationships are all-important and information was only passed when there was a vital need, that is if Australian cooperation was required'.[25]

Information exchange could only take place satisfactorily when the party supplying the information trusted the recipient to afford it the required degree of protection. To that end, the British and the Americans needed to be convinced that Australia had in place a program that was at least as good as their own to ensure that Australian recipients could be trusted not to leak their information.

By the time Eric became its director, C Branch had three sections — Vetting, Key Points and Travel Control. Its principal functions were the planning and direction of Australian protective security, developing policy for and advising government departments and other organisations on protective security measures and practices, and vetting applications for immigration and visits to Australia by foreign subjects. It had officers attached to most Australian posts through which these matters were processed. The branch represented ASIO in departmental meetings on protective security issues and was authorised to liaise with 'friendly Security Services overseas'.[26]

In his 1994 book *Australian Spies and their Secrets*, Australian left-wing journalist and author David McKnight took ASIO to task for its excess of zeal in denying security clearances to people who had an association with communism and the Communist Party of Australia. While some criticism is justified, one feels some sympathy for the task that confronted Eric Nave and C Branch in the early 1950s. The major threat to Western security had been identified as communism and international communism had already bared some of its fangs — in the Berlin blockade, in the overthrow of the Nationalists in China, in the Korean War. The first Soviet detonation of an atomic bomb had occurred in August 1949.

On the espionage front, British atom spy Alan Nunn May had been uncovered in 1946, and another, Klaus Fuchs, had been arrested in January 1950. Bruno Pontecorvo had defected in July 1950, and Burgess and McLean were to flee to the Soviet Union in 1951. The Venona decrypts showed that the members of the Soviet spy ring in Australia all had links with the Communist Party. That must have seemed the logical place to start looking for potential or active spies in the Australian public service. It was not against the law to profess an attachment to communism, but such an admission (or revelation) was not going to improve one's chances of getting access to classified information so far as Eric Nave was concerned. In a 1992 interview with David McKnight, he responded to questions on the vetting and clearance process for communist fellow travellers with:

> We wouldn't have a bar of them. They had to be detected and kept out of access of any kind. The only real disagreement I had with Spry was over a couple of those — CSIRO [Commonwealth Scientific and Industrial Research Organisation] scientists. I wouldn't give them a clearance: you had to be a cleanskin to get one. Spry said, 'Oh no, you've got to clear those two'. I don't know why Spry wanted to clear them. It might have been because it would have created a storm because they were senior men. It didn't make any difference to me how senior they were; if they had a record they were out.[27]

Looked at with the benefit of hindsight, this might seem a draconian attitude for Eric to have taken, but is seems clear that Spry was — generally — very supportive of his actions, as was the Prime

Minister. In addition, it has to be remembered that during his first
years at ASIO, C Branch was literally flying by the seat of its pants.

> In relation to C Branch work, security vetting was very important in those
> days and he was totally responsible for the policy. It was at the formative
> stage and it was a pretty grey area. The organisation, technically, was under
> the control of the Attorney General's Department and the Attorney General.
> Spry largely ignored those; he talked with the Prime Minister and that was
> that. The policy formulation within the organisation was the responsibility
> of two people: Spry at a very high level such as the Prime Minister, and
> the other work was done by Nave, who was working out what were the
> appropriate areas which required access.[28]

Eric's responsibilities were not limited to government employees.
The Joint Project was constructing a complex of facilities for the
weapons test range at Woomera in South Australia. This was work
of international importance, and much of it carried a high security
caveat. How far down through the organisation and the construction
teams did vetting have to go? The Chief Scientist wanted all personnel
working on the site security cleared — a huge, expensive and time-
consuming task. Eric Nave declined to take that on, excluding
the construction teams from vetting provided they were properly
supervised. This prevented sizable delays in this expensive and time-
critical project. [29]

Similar considerations had to be applied to other major projects,
such as the Snowy Mountains Hydroelectric and Irrigation Scheme,
and to installations and facilities identified as 'key points' in the
Commonwealth War Book. This had been compiled to identify those
items of national infrastructure vital to Australia's war effort in any
future conflict, including private industries that would be involved in
supporting the armed forces. The number of government and private
employees who potentially needed a security clearance was enormous,
but pragmatism considerably reduced the workload.

> The thing was just growing like Topsy. It was an area in which everyone was
> concerned that they'd end up with a few Communists in their organisation
> and that could be the end of the organisation and even the head of the
> Department himself. This, of course, was not the case; nevertheless it

showed the level of emotion that surrounded the situation. So they took a 'fail-safe' approach — 'We want everyone vetted!' That was a contentious point.[30]

As Nave gradually got on top of his quite daunting responsibilities he faced a devastating situation at home, as Mary's health steadily worsened. The eight-year-old died on 18 December 1952. The children still remember this as a traumatic time for their parents, and Eric must have felt some despair as his vaunted network of contacts proved helpless in the face of the progress of the disease. Eric and Helena had even discussed a plan for Eric to take Mary to Sweden, where there was the possibility of an operation that might save their daughter's life. The child's poor health in the face of the long sea voyage to the other side of the world, the possibility of a lengthy recuperation period in Sweden before she could be returned to Australia, and the difficulties involved with this absence from work and family separation eventually saw the plan, reluctantly, shelved.

ASIO was also battling against a lack of appreciation by Australians generally of the need for security-conscious practices. The discovery and exploitation of Australia's reserves of uranium ores created another call on C Branch. The Premier of South Australia was particularly keen on developing his state's reserves of uranium, which was (and is) a strategic mineral, particularly with regard to the development of nuclear weapons. The director general, with Eric, called on the Premier to discuss his plans.

> We explained to him we understood that he intended to mine a uranium deposit, and that all the information regarding such treatment was classified, and we felt he needed a Security Officer who was fully aware of the conditions. He agreed that he would abide by all the security requirements and conditions. ... Brigadier Spry was returning to Melbourne and I was to remain temporarily to ensure that the correct proceedings were followed. I discovered that they had no filing system as we understood it; instead all the papers on any subject were enclosed in one envelope called a docket, and this would be circulated to the various Departments.

An ASIO officer seconded to the South Australian Government for that purpose swiftly put proper procedures for the handling of classified material in place. It was as well, because the US sent a delegation to Australia to ensure that the South Australian development was being correctly managed from a security viewpoint and Eric was able to send them home 'very satisfied with our treatment of the uranium'. In the same vein, Eric's branch had to develop and implement procedures for the despatch, receipt and storage of classified material within the Commonwealth Government, including mandating the appropriate construction of safes used for storing it. Matters which might now be regarded as routine were strange and new to many affected by them in the 1950s.

Perhaps the most important legacy of Eric Nave's time in ASIO was the Protective Security Handbook. This was written by C Branch to codify the rules for personnel and physical security that had to be implemented in all Australian government departments and agencies. As different departments had quite different views and practices at the time, development of the handbook required a massive amount of work.

> When they decided to have that manual he started it off as I remember and then he got one of his staff officers to do all the detailed work. It was he who took it round and I think there were individual consultations with departments to determine how they felt about it, because it imposed quite substantial burdens on them, as well as financial requirements. They then had the inter-departmental committee which gave the imprimatur to it — that was the process.[31]

It was logical that Nave represented ASIO in inter-departmental committees in Canberra, and in dealings with government authorities and commercial organisations generally. At that time, much about ASIO and its activities was closely held, including the identities of ASIO officers other than the director general. Eric became the public face of ASIO, and he was good at it. Nobody attending a meeting at which Eric Nave was present would believe they were in the presence of a 'gnome'. His staff referred to him as a 'crafty old fox'.

> I don't know whether it was his naval experience or just his innate intelligence but he was an excellent representative of the organisation in Canberra. And in those days C Branch Director represented us on all those bodies in Canberra; the other two [branch heads] didn't.[32]

Eric's time with ASIO covered three of the biggest security operations undertaken by the agency in its early days — the first visit to Australia by Queen Elizabeth in February 1954, the Petrov Affair commencing in April 1954, and the Melbourne Olympic Games in November–December 1956. A reigning monarch had never visited Australia, although several members of the Royal Family had done so. In March 1868, while on a visit to Sydney, Prince Alfred, a son of Queen Victoria, had been shot and wounded by an Irish zealot. This precedent cannot have been far from the minds of ASIO, Commonwealth and state police in planning security for the visit of Queen Elizabeth II in 1954. In modern terms the two-month tour was a potential security nightmare, with the Royal couple riding in an open vehicle through the streets of Australia's major cities, which were collectively thronged with six million hopefully loyal subjects. C Branch's role was to advise Commonwealth and state authorities on security planning and procedures, an exercise which must have required extensive use of the Nave Network.

Contemporary records of the security aspects of the Royal Visit, however, show that very modern dimensions of VIP security were in place for the tour. One report records that installations to be visited by the Queen had been inspected and checked and that security arrangements were put in place to prevent tampering with apparatus like lifts. Advice and information on any possible 'attempt to cause any form of embarrassment for the Royal Party' had been obtained from the British Special Branch in New Scotland Yard in London. Nor was ASIO inactive.

> A booklet with photographs and descriptions of some 200 persons who might be a potential source of embarrassment has been prepared and 400 copies circulated to all protective forces. A.S.I.O. have issued periodical confidential bulletins to me supplying information on Communist Party activity in regard to the Royal Visit, and these have been circulated and are in the possession of state police ... Details of the Commonwealth Security precautions have been discussed with senior officers of A.S.I.O. ... All persons nominated for Commonwealth [Press] accreditation have been checked.[33]

In the end the visit went off without a hitch and, as those who were privileged to witness the royal progress will recall, in an aura of public euphoria. C Branch had played its part in the protective security cordon well. But it must have been a tough time personally for Eric. On 18 April his beloved father, Thomas, died in Adelaide.

The defection of Vladimir Petrov, the KGB *rezident* in the Soviet Embassy in Canberra, was nominally a matter for the counter-espionage element of ASIO —B2 Branch. The involvement of Eric Nave seems to have been a personal decision by Brigadier Spry, who 'was after a defector, I'm sure because MI5 had lost people to the other side and he wanted to do the reverse and show that he was a bloody side better than MI5'.[34]

> One afternoon, Margaret Tucker the Secretary to the Director General Security [Spry], came to my office saying 'Captain Nave, the D.G. would like to see you'. Going to his office he said 'Eric sit down, what do you think of these Russians. I don't think they're all that good.' I replied that 'It's not so much them as the Public Service officers that they have sucked into their orbit; they are our worry'. 'Yes, I agree, well we will do something about it, we will cover their Embassy for 24 hours a day for a month to see what we find out'.

The huge volume of documents that Petrov brought with him created a need for staff to be co-opted from the other branches to assist in its examination and processing, and C Branch assisted in this. Eric had a more direct involvement.

> Eric's role in that, as I understood it, was this liaison role of getting out and talking to people. Everybody, of course, wanted to know 'Does this affect us?' Michael Thwaites [Director B2 Branch] at that time was fully occupied with all of this so Eric, therefore, did the liaison work, which was a bit out of organisational line but he was the one who had all the contacts and the one who could have done it.[35]

Spry's plan, to use a defection to demonstrate that ASIO had 'come of age', was successful. ASIO shared the debriefing with the British and provided summaries to the Americans. In 1955, Spry was invited to visit the US and formed a particularly close relationship with J. Edgar Hoover of the Federal Bureau of Investigation. The Central Intelligence

Agency was also impressed with ASIO's handling of the case, and the relationship between the organisations never looked back. But Eric had another involvement with Petrov, again employing his network.

> Now that Petrov had defected and was living in Australia it became necessary for him to have a new identity for which many arrangements had to be made. I went to see the Commonwealth Electoral Officer and explained the situation to him. He then rang the Commonwealth Officer at Bentleigh, a suburb of Melbourne, and instructed him to have Mr 'Sven Allyson' placed on the electoral roll.

The 1956 Melbourne Olympic Games — another first for Australia — involved a number of security problems mercifully absent from the Royal Visit. Whereas the security authorities had to protect Queen Elizabeth only from deranged people and those with a grudge against Britain, the Games brought teams from sixty-seven countries, some of whom bore others a great deal of ill-will. Complicating the problem was the presence in Australia of a considerable number of refugees and migrants, many with deeply held animus against the governments of countries whose teams would compete. The potential for incidents was high. Eric was given the responsibility for the security arrangements.

> Unfortunately international politics raised its ugly head resulting in Egypt, Iran and Lebanon withdrawing in protest against the Israeli-led take over of the Suez Canal. Then we learned of three countries, Holland, Spain and Switzerland deciding to boycott the games in protest at the Soviet-led invasion of Hungary ... On the opening day we had to wait till the actual start to see which flag the Hungarians would hoist in the village.

One seemingly impossible issue — that of completing the necessary immigration formalities for the anticipated large numbers of athletes and visitors from countries for whose citizens the Australian Government would normally require visas — was resolved in an interesting manner. Rather than requiring all to have background security checks, as normally was the case, the Government decided to accept the Olympic Identity Card issued by the International Olympic Committee as sufficient documentation for athletes. An Immigration Aid document was attached to this, one half recording arrival details and the other for departure. Visitors required passports but the same Immigration Aid was used instead of the normal visa documentation. This innovative solution bears the hallmark of Eric Nave, and it was entirely successful. However, ASIO was not unaware of the opportunity this created for clandestine activities. An ASIO report of the Games states:

> Thus it will be seen how greatly simplified entry into Australia was made for all official representatives of Iron Curtain countries. It would have been surprising indeed if this facility were [sic] not taken advantage of by the Soviet Intelligence Service, who had been denied official 'cover' for their cadre workers since the PETROV defection three years before.
>
> That this opportunity was not overlooked is demonstrated later in this paper. Never before has the R.I.S. [Russian Intelligence Service] congregated so many Intelligence workers in this country at one time as during the Olympic Games.[36]

ASIO identified forty-six confirmed intelligence officers and thirty suspects among the 206 officials who accompanied the team from the USSR. Another ten confirmed and twenty-two suspects were detected in other Soviet Bloc teams competing in the Games However, Eric's arrangements obviously worked well as incidents at the Games were few. In the pool, there was a boil-over in the water polo match between Hungary and the Soviet Union in which eyes were blackened, but that was a minor clash compared with what might have been expected. ASIO became involved after the defection of a Russian stewardess from the liner on which the Soviet Union team travelled, but only to back up the local police when the embassy challenged the story of her disappearance. Just as the Games themselves were a huge success for Australia, so the capacity of ASIO to act in support of such a significant event was effectively demonstrated.

Eric's travelling days were not yet over, either. Presumably in pursuit of liaison with 'friendly Security Services overseas', in April 1955 he visited 'Siam [Thailand], Djakarta and Singapore on official business'. The ASIO file does not indicate how long the trip lasted or its results, but it was organised at short notice, involving a scramble to have Eric's passport arranged and his course of inoculations completed in time.

Then in mid-1957, as Eric was undoubtedly buoyed by the outcomes of the challenges he had surmounted, he was told by Spry to that he was to take up the position of head of ASIO's Victorian regional office, also located in Melbourne — an ostensible demotion in status. This move was confirmed in writing on 15 August, directing Eric to take up his new post on 1 October. Regional offices were largely responsible for ASIO's operational activities and were normally headed by officers from that background. Eric was not and he struggled. His skills were in policy; he was very good at paperwork but he had no experience of counter-intelligence. Speaking of the change of positions, a former senior officer said:

> I thought it was very inappropriate, as the person who replaced him was inadequate and was removed after two years and that had quite a dramatic effect on C Branch, something that I think was most unfortunate. There were all types of rumours going around. The suggestion was that he was getting a bit too big for his boots as far as Spry was concerned, so he moved him out. I don't know if that was the case or not. However, that was the common feeling amongst the staff. But there had to be a reason for it.[37]

Once again, Eric left no material to give his side of the story and, although he seemed unhappy and not at home in his work in the Victorian office, he apparently made no complaint. Perhaps he had outlived his usefulness to the organisation: now that ASIO was firmly established and had some operational successes to its credit, and the protective security message had been accepted by the government agencies and contractors, Spry had to turn his attention to operational matters and staff development. He apparently had no succession plan, but he did want to improve the quality of his staff by introducing graduates into the organisation, and he may have felt that it was time to put old war horses like Eric out to pasture. Eric had only eighteen months before his mandatory retiring age of sixty.

The Nave Network was still intact, however, and Eric used it to his benefit.

Just as a sideline, when he came into the Victorian Office he used to play the stock exchange — that was a huge interest that he had. He would come into the office at 9 and between 9 and 9.30 the door would be shut and no one could go in. He'd go up to the Melbourne Club at half past 12, come back at 2 shut the door and at 2.30 the door would be opened. Of course, during those two half hours he was dealing with his stockbrokers. [38]

In March 1959, Eric Nave bade government service farewell. He had served his country in peace and war, as a naval officer and as a public servant, for a total of forty-two years. His wide range of experience covered employment as a supply officer in two navies, working with and then transferring to the Royal Navy, codebreaking in British cruisers, in GCCS in London, in shore headquarters in Hong Kong and Singapore, and in setting up his own codebreaking bureau in Melbourne. He had been poorly treated by the US Navy but welcomed by the Australian Army and its fellow services in Central Bureau in Brisbane. Although nominally still a British naval officer, he had led the Australian delegation to discussions on the Commonwealth Signals Intelligence Organisation and had been a key player in the development of the Defence Signals Bureau. Finally, he had been instrumental in establishing the reputation, policies and practices of ASIO and he had been its public face in Australian government and industry circles for seven crucial years.

There had been disappointments along the way. He might have expected to head FRUMEL rather than Fabian, and his ambition to be the director of the Australian Signals Intelligence Centre had been dashed. He might also have hoped that his retirement from ASIO would have been from his C Branch position. But he must have drawn a deep sense of satisfaction from his achievements in intelligence and security, and from the fact that he was now a figure of some standing in Australia. The teenage clerk from the South Australian Railways had come a very long way.

11 In Retirement

For someone as active and vigorous as Eric Nave, retirement might have come as something of shock. But the term 'retirement' is misleading, for he had already accepted a number of appointments which would ensure that his time and his mind would be pleasantly and gainfully occupied and exercised.

In 1950, he had been appointed to the board of the Victorian Mission to Seamen, and joined its finance committee the following year. Also in 1950, he became deputy director of the White Ensign Club, an organisation dedicated to providing cheap temporary accommodation in Melbourne for naval personnel on leave, especially young sailors from Flinders Naval Depot up to catch the bright lights on weekend leave. Located in the city's Exhibition Building, the club had sleeping accommodation and a cafeteria. In a curriculum vitae I found in Eric's correspondence he noted that, 'The young recruits greatly appreciated a clean bed and good meals. This was all provided by voluntary labour and special fund raising activities, a great improvement to sleeping in the park or in undesirable beds on offer.' The club later became the Melbourne Naval Centre, and Eric was to serve as its president for twenty years from 1971.

He also received at least one employment offer. On leaving ASIO, Eric's knowledge of the stock market and prowess in investing recommended him to his brokers — Potter Partners — as a potential partner. Eric was flattered by the offer but declined, deciding apparently that for him investing was an interesting hobby but not a full-time job. It continued to give him pleasure and an income throughout his life.

An interest in the welfare of his former naval colleagues caused Eric to become a member of the Ex-Naval Men's Association. The association had its origins in Melbourne in 1920 and had been formed to promote the interests of naval personnel by making representations on their behalf to government. It also provided a social security umbrella for ex-naval people who needed the support of their former shipmates in making ends meet in civilian life. In 1957 Eric was elected Victorian state president. It was a period of change in the organisation, as older veterans passed away and the interests of the World War II cohort of ex-naval personnel became dominant. A change of structure, organisation and name was decided upon in discussions among the state branches, and the Naval Association of Australia came into being in February 1960, with Eric as its first national president.

This was to be a busy job for Eric, with a heavy round of representational work, national executive meetings held every two months and three national conferences to be organised in different capital cities during his successive terms. But his access to Australia's decision-makers through his network of contacts made him a formidable asset to the association and its members. He was a tireless worker in the interests of ex-naval personnel and in raising the profile of naval service in the eyes of his fellow Australians. The records of the Association show that much of Eric's first two terms was spent in having a series of administrative and organisational reforms debated and accepted by the fractious and often antagonistic component elements of the association. But accepted they were, and it is clear that Eric used his considerable powers of friendly persuasion to achieve that result and to unite the association. At the 1972 conference one finds a resolution:'That in view of the sterling work performed by the Federal President and members of the Federal Executive during the past nine years, this State Conference [WA] submits the nomination of Captain T.E. Nave as Federal President ... for re-election at this 1972 Conference'.

Much of the work of the federal executive of the association was concentrated on gaining access by veterans and serving personnel to a range of government benefits. To an extent this was motivated by the self-interest of the members, but other proposals were directed at the present and future navy and showed considerable foresight. These included insurance benefits to cover death or injury whether due to combat or the normal course of naval duties, extension of government responsibility for the health problems of serving personnel beyond their separation from the service, and the introduction of bonuses to encourage re-engagement of sailors. In these three areas the Naval Association under Eric Nave's leadership was well in advance of contemporary defence thinking, and it was not until the 1990s that they were finally accepted by government.

Benefits were not the only area in which the association was active. The inauguration in 1966 of Navy Week as a fixture in Australia's calendar of commemorations came as a result of representations made by Eric on behalf of the association. At its meeting on 5 June 1964 the Naval Board discussed the proposal with Eric — a considerable honour — and the minutes record that:

> Captain Nave stated that the Naval Association favoured 4th October because of the naval historical interest [arrival of the first Australian Fleet in 1913] and because existing Trafalgar Day [21 October] functions could possibly absorbed, but he felt that the selection of the day was a matter for the Naval Board and whatever day was chosen would have the support of the Naval Association. The Naval Board agreed that 4th October would be the best suitable date to select for an annual Australian Naval Day.[1]

This was an achievement of which Eric and the Association can be justifiably proud.

A second departure from the Naval Association's normal fields of interest under Nave's leadership was its advocacy for greater spending on the Navy and on the strategic realignment of RAN basing policy. From the late 1960s Eric wrote a number of media articles on the first issue in his capacity as federal president. Then in 1974 he was successful in engaging the support of the recently retired Chief of Naval Staff, Sir Richard Peek, in lobbying the Whitlam Labor

Government to pay more heed to naval defence. Letters exchanged between the two men show awareness of political realities and the importance of the media in influencing and responding to government policy decisions.

At its conference in 1966, at the height of Indonesia's Confrontation with Malaysia, the association passed resolutions calling on the Naval Board to 'establish a naval base on Australia's Western Seaboard' and recommending that 'An approach be made to the Federal Government to have a number of HMA Ships and a larger number of Air Force planes stationed in the West'.[2] Whether because of this call from the association or through other influences, it was in 1966 that the RAN dusted off the proposals made by Admiral Henderson in 1911 for a naval base at Cockburn Sound south of Fremantle and three years later a start was made on its construction. Again, Eric used the media to back up the association's push and to urge government action.

The association's members continued to elect Eric their national president until he stepped down in March 1975. Throughout his presidency he had shown his leadership abilities and political and diplomatic nous. He had united the association behind its executive and ensured that all levels of government were aware of the Naval Association and its members. His lobbying went as high as Queen Elizabeth II, to whom the 1972 conference sent its 'loyal assurances', which were 'received with pleasure' by Her Majesty.[3] When Eric stepped down the federal executive received a letter from Lord Louis Mountbatten expressing regrets at Eric's retirement but also adding that the work of Captain Nave was well known. Lord Louis felt sure that Eric 'was owed the gratitude and appreciation of all naval personnel throughout the Commonwealth'. More prosaically, Eric was made a Life Member of the Naval Association in 1978.

Throughout this period, Nave family issues also assumed greater importance for Eric. Daughter Elizabeth turned eighteen in 1958 and, despite Eric's quiet advocacy for her to select a career in law, she elected to take up teaching. In turn, David chose medicine as a career. Eric was concerned about this ultimate choice of David's with its long years of training, which followed several false starts down career paths including electrical engineering and field work for the Department of Civil Aviation. David's subsequent success in his chosen field proved his father's concern to be unfounded. When it came time for Margaret to choose a career she opted for nursing, like her mother. But it was not only career choices that exercised Eric's mind. According to his daughters and their husbands, he was a doughty defender of propriety in affairs of the heart. A curfew was a curfew and woe betide the boyfriend who returned Elizabeth or Margaret to their father late! One is even reputed to have leapt the front fence at Cochrane Street when he realised that Eric was hovering impatiently in the doorway waiting to give him a piece of his mind.

When it came to proposals, Eric was a stickler for the correct form. He grilled prospective bridegrooms on the traditional issues of prospects and intentions, and required them to justify why Eric should be prepared to give him a daughter's hand in marriage. One of his ASIO colleagues described him as 'forthright' and Eric was undoubtedly prepared to be so if the prospective swain did not show promise of matching his criteria. Hearing these stories, one cannot help but be reminded of Thomas's stern advice in his 1930s letters to Eric about choosing the proper mate. Despite these barriers which had to be overcome, Elizabeth was married to Trevor Neal in March 1966 and in January 1968 Eric, now nearly sixty-nine, became a grandfather with the arrival of Timothy John.

Health concerns reappeared for Eric in 1962. He had accepted the position of executive officer for the Victorian Council of the Freedom From Hunger Campaign. It was a stressful position, made the more so because of serious divisions and disagreements within the board, and the result was that Eric suffered a severe heart attack in September that year. He was in a serious condition and, at one stage, family members were advised to prepare themselves for the worst. Fortunately, Eric pulled through but he was not able to resume his involvement with Freedom From Hunger.

However, this happy period in the family's life was overshadowed by tragedy a second time when, in 1968, Helena was diagnosed with cancer. Her condition did not respond to treatment and she died on 22 March 1969. At seventy, Eric was a widower. In the friends who rallied around to his support, he was supremely fortunate to find Margaret Richardson, and the couple was married in December 1970. The wedding took place just a week after the marriage of Eric's youngest daughter Margaret to Ian Forbes.

In January 1972 Eric was awarded a second Order of the British Empire, this time in the Civil Division, for his service to the ex-service community. My research has not been able to establish whether an award in both the military and civil divisions of the order is unique, but it is certainly an extremely rare honour. Eric was a foundation member of the Victorian Association of the Most Excellent Order of the British Empire in 1974, remaining a member of the committee until his retirement from the association in May 1986.[4]

One characteristic of Eric's much remarked upon by his children was his gregariousness. He loved to talk and to tell stories, but was not above embellishing them when he deemed it necessary for the benefit of the audience. He enjoyed the company of his many friends but, if they were not to be found, he would simply make more. Complete strangers could rarely resist Eric's engaging manner as he charmed them with his tales. He was equally at home with all strata of society and had the ability to win the confidence of all. But, if he decided that someone was not worthwhile spending time with, he would simply ignore them.

There is one rider to this portrait of Eric, offered by a personal friend of long standing. He did enjoy his opportunities for exposure to the public in a position of authority, such as the presidency of the Brighton Branch of the Liberal Party of Australia and of the Brighton Horticultural Society, a position he held for many years. It was almost as if he was making up for the strict confines of security his previous life had placed upon him. His circle of friends was not particularly extensive, and he tended to stick with those that he knew who moved in circles familiar to him. Hence his devotion to the Melbourne Club and his work with ex-servicemen and women. The stress induced from his brief time working in the Freedom From Hunger executive suggests that he was not comfortable out of his circle. Those who knew him use phrases such as 'quiet and cultured' and all agree that he had an acute mind and was capable of absorbing and marshalling facts readily.

Eric's duties towards ex-service personnel did not end with his stepping down as Naval Association National President in 1975. In 1976 he was appointed a trustee of the Services Canteen Trust Fund, an authority charged with the administration and eventual winding up of funds generated by the operations of service canteens from World War II and beyond. The fund's assets were dispersed as benefits to ex-servicemen and women who could meet the criteria for loans and grants and to their families in the form of funeral benefits. In 1982, four years before the trust's funds were to be totally depleted, Eric wrote in his characteristic way to the federal secretary of the Naval Association:

> I am quite concerned that there is room for great improvement in the dissemination of information regarding benefits available to eligible persons. The vast majority of applications we receive are from former members of Army, *very few come from the Navy* ... I suggest this *Report should be read at all Sub-Section meetings*. [emphasis in the original] [5]

With son David's marriage to Catherine O'Toole in November 1977, Eric was now the head of a growing clan. His children were to present him with nine grandchildren all told and a photograph taken on his eightieth birthday shows him surrounded by young people. He did not, however, seem to enjoy his grandchildren a great deal. He had married late and the charm of growing children might not have been so appealing to an octogenarian as it is to one twenty years younger. He took more interest in them as they grew older. In September 1992 he wrote an affectionate letter to his granddaughter Anne, who had decided to study law — the fulfillment of Eric's early hopes for himself. He confessed himself 'so interested in your Law course', and told Anne that he had even approached Melbourne and Monash Universities seeking ways to study law by 'correspondence course'. There is no evidence that Eric did make these inquiries, but perhaps he wished he had done so.

From the end of World War II, the many tens of thousands of

Allied personnel, both military and civilian, who had worked in the
signals intelligence network against the Axis had remained faithful to
their undertaking not to reveal anything about their wartime service.
As a former Central Bureau codebreaker recalled, this responsibility
was made very clear to him by Eric Nave when he joined the bureau.

> He was the first person to explain to me and the others that we were to be
> inducted into a secret organisation, trained in cryptanalysis and breaking
> enemy codes; that we would be sworn to secrecy under the Commonwealth
> [Crimes] Act, which would include a period 30 years after the war, nothing
> ever to be revealed.[6]

For his part, Eric was extremely cautious about discussing his
work in codebreaking, but he was always pursued by his reputation
as 'the man who broke the Japanese codes'. It was not unexpected then
that, when the 'thirty year rule' on release of records in the National
Archives of Australia made files and correspondence from the pre-
war period available to researchers, Eric began to field approaches for
his comments and recollections.

The first approach documented in his correspondence was by a
graduate student at the Australian National University in Canberra,
B.N. Primrose, who was researching a PhD on the subject of
'Australian Naval Policy, 1919–1941'. In July 1973, Primrose sought
Eric's assistance in the following area:

> It seems to me that one of the most telling indicators of the British–
> Australian relationship is in the field of exchange of intelligence … What
> I want to show is the growth of the intelligence sharing arrangement
> throughout the period and the extent to which the R.A.N. was accepted
> into the system by 1941.[7]

Eric agreed to assist but he was careful, asking that Primrose
send him questions to which he would respond, if he could. Eric's
responses are only partially available in his correspondence, but
Primrose remembers that he discussed some of his work in the 1930s
and provided valuable background to the thesis. 'He was helpful and
forthcoming and displayed a real professionalism, but he was very
careful to protect information.' He was also very cautious about

Primrose, using his security contacts to have the student's *bona fides* checked.[8]

The veil of the wartime signals intelligence temple was rent asunder by the publication in 1974 of a book titled *The Ultra Secret* by a Group Captain F.W. Winterbotham, who had been involved in providing security for signals intelligence material during the war. This ushered in a torrent of works on signals intelligence and prompted the British to commission an official history of British wartime intelligence, the first volume of which appeared in 1979. However, the official historians shirked their job when it came to describing Britain's attack on Japanese codes and cyphers, declaring:

> Even at this last level [reconstruction of the influence of intelligence on the general conduct of the war] there are unavoidable omissions. The most important of these is that we have not attempted to cover the war in the Far East; when this was so much the concern of the United States, it is not possible to provide an adequate account on the basis of British Archives alone.[9]

The result was a large gap in the coverage given to the assault on Japanese codes by the British. Eric noted in his correspondence with Primrose that while the Americans were publishing their side of the story, they made scant mention of the British contribution.

> The Americans have published a book 'Cryptographers' [Eric was probably referring to David Kahn's *The Codebreakers*] but mention of British cryptographic efforts was not made, although we gave them the original information which led to Midway and Yamamoto [the shooting down of the Admiral's plane in 1943].[10]

By the early 1980s, Eric was moved to try to redress this omission as far as his own experiences were concerned and the stimulus came in 1985. Responding to a newspaper advertisement by the Australian War Memorial offering grants to former servicemen and women for their memoirs, Eric started compiling his recollections of his service career, a task that continued for nearly two years. It was as well that he had made that start because he was about to become the centre of considerable international attention on the subject of the breaking of Japanese codes. In 1986, he responded to one researcher's appeal for assistance with the remark: 'I am engaged in writing a book on my naval life which will contain the story of my part in Japanese cryptography commencing in 1925 when I started it for the British'. [11]

The researcher in question, David Sissons, then at the Australian National University, was puzzled about why so little reference was made in official histories to Japanese diplomatic decodes emanating from Australia during World War II. He had teased some of the story out of archival and other sources, but needed Eric's help to clarify his understanding. Sissons had done a lot of digging and had pieced together most of the story of the Army's 'cipher-breaking' group, the Special Intelligence Bureau and the later Special Intelligence Section, Diplomatic, but he did need confirmation of this. Eric was happy to oblige, although with the caveat that 'I have seven people from around the world pressing for information'. Two interesting facts emerged from the exchange with Sissons. The first was that even in 1941 the Department of External Affairs was not being supplied with decodes of Japanese diplomatic traffic. '[T]he Dept. at the time was very small and not equipped to handle such traffic,' noted Eric.

The second revelation was that Eric was relying on his memory rather than finding and consulting archival records to confirm his recollections. This was undoubtedly one of the contributing factors to the errors of fact that I have unearthed in his memoirs. It is true that the security authorities have steadily — with some prompting — revised the former blanket refusal to release material on signals intelligence activities, and so today's researcher is more likely to find what he or she is looking for; it would not have been as easy in 1986. However, this researcher envies the ready access that Eric could have had to the National Archives of Australia which, at the time, were located in his suburb. One must also bear in mind that he was now eighty-seven and had problems with his eyes, a condition not rectified until an operation in late 1988.

The big influence on the last few years of Eric's life was, however, James Rusbridger, an inveterate fantasiser. Rusbridger's career as a businessman had ended in 1977, when he pleaded guilty to four counts of theft from his employer. He was sentenced to two years probation and ordered to undergo psychiatric counselling. He then turned to journalism, specializing in Intelligence matters.[12] In 1985 he was collecting information on the breaking of JN-25 for his next book, which was to discuss how it was the Americans could have been surprised at Pearl Harbor if they and others had broken the code. His interest was fired by Eric's statements that FECB had broken Code D/JN-25A in 1939. From the initiation of contact by letter in September 1985, Rusbridger pursued Eric for more and more information, and eventually made the trip to Australia in February 1988 for an interview. To speed communications, they faxed letters to one another.

The two men apparently hit it off well. Rusbridger was interested in the Nave memoirs and found a publishing house in London — The Bodley Head — willing to publish them in a book incorporating his own research under the working title *Codebreaker Extraordinary*. They entered a co-authorship contract and an advance of money was made. All seemed to be proceeding well until the British Government, alarmed by pre-publicity circulated to some London newspapers by Rusbridger, expressed an interest in seeing the work before publication. This was a reasonable request — the British Official Secrets Act, to which Eric was subject because of his RN service, makes provision for the procedure. Having read several chapters of the Bodley Head version of *Codebreaker Extraordinary*, I have not encountered any information which might have caused the British Government to request changes. But it was too much for the publisher and the contract with Nave and Rusbridger was abruptly terminated in February 1989.

The story was seized upon by the Australian media. The Melbourne *Age* of 9 March carried headlines thundering: 'Britain suppresses war secrets book' and 'WWII code-breaker's memoirs banned'. Eric was going to have more than fifteen minutes of fame. In the prime time television interviews with all the Australian TV networks that ensued Eric played his hand with a great deal of canniness. As the tapes of an interview of 9 March 1989 demonstrate, he was not at all flummoxed by the sudden celebrity, and seemed to be enjoying himself immensely. The interviewers were all seized by the audacity of the claims – attributed to Eric — that he personally had known of Japanese plans to attack Pearl Harbor in 1939, that Churchill had been informed of this and must, therefore, have failed to alert the Americans for deeply Machiavellian reasons of state. In fact, this was Rusbridger's theory, based on Eric's statement that before he left FECB the Imperial Japanese Navy main naval code had been read with ease. That he had left in February 1940, had not worked on JN-25 until around April 1942 and that the IJN had not even considered attacking Pearl Harbor until the first months of 1941 was not allowed to spoil this sensational claim. Nevertheless, probably with a view to sales of the book in mind, Eric defended this implausibility with great skill. Typical is his exchange on 9 March with George Negus from Channel 9:

> **Negus:** Is it the case, as your book is suggesting, that Pearl Harbor should never have happened, that there was enough information available to people like Winston Churchill to have warned the Americans in advance and therefore could have prevented the attack from occurring or at least being prepared for it?
>
> **Nave:** I think you could say that, yes.
>
> **Negus:** So have the British been lying for all these years?
>
> **Nave:** I wouldn't say that at all.
>
> **Negus:** What would you say, then?
>
> **Nave:** Well, what you tell other people is a matter of national diplomacy, isn't it.

It may well be that the attention that these interviews focused on Nave's co-authorship responsibilities caused some rethinking on his part. Having only seen the part of his manuscript that Bodley Head had prepared, he was having to defend the part he hadn't yet seen against criticisms from interviewers who only had Rusbridger's central theme in their sights. The straight bat defence offered in the TV interviews of 9 March had been replaced with a more considered strategy when Eric was interviewed by the *Australian* newspaper, the account being published on 13 March. In the interview he deprecated Rusbridger's misuse of the information Nave had provided, stated that the substance of the claims made by Rusbridger about foreknowledge of the Pearl Harbor attack were untrue, and indicated that he could not lend his name to a book with so many errors in it until major revision was undertaken.[13]

Back in London, a second publisher initially showed interest in the Nave/Rusbridger manuscript but then backed away. However, a third publisher was soon found and, again, advances of money were proposed. By this time, Eric had embarked on a series of pre-publicity television interviews with the Australian and British Broadcasting Corporations. After these were aired Eric told Rusbridger in a letter of 6 April:

> Margaret has been very tired lately, in fact we both are, she has had a lot of strain with the many telephone calls, T.V broadcasts etc. In fact we found it necessary to take the telephone off the hook for some hours each day for quite a period, this gave us a little peace.

Once again, however, the publication deal fell through. The sensational slant to Rusbridger's pre-publicity campaign had clearly made British publishing houses somewhat wary of the manuscript. Whether the British Government had exerted pressure on them to decline the manuscript is not clear.

Not surprisingly, in view of Eric's comments in the *Australian* interview, at this stage a disagreement between Nave and Rusbridger over the direction and format of *Codebreaker Extraordinary* became apparent in their correspondence, with Rusbridger urging a more 'dynamic' start to the book. On 28 April he faxed Eric telling of his meeting with representatives of the American publishing house, Simon & Schuster, and that the idea of two books had emerged. Besides Eric's memoirs, there was to be another, because the publishers thought that there was a 'bigger story to be told'.

> The first would be the story of Pearl Harbor re-told from a new British viewpoint incorporating Eric's work at GCCS and FECB and the new material we have from the archives and the National Security Agency,

thus effectively a re-worked *Codebreaker Extraordinary* with a title change to make it appeal to American readers where it is estimated 75 percent of copies would be sold.

The Americans offered a huge advance to the co-authors — $US 33,000 each according to Rusbridger — but Eric's justifiable suspicions were evident in a penscript comment he made on Rusbridger's letter: 'My autobiography is entirely my business and I have not decided on a title, and it cannot be part of an offer with another book'.

From that point onwards the relationship went downhill. The first book, now titled *Winds of Warning*, was originally to be published in early 1990 but Eric, the co-author, did not receive a copy of the draft. There began to be disagreements over expenses and money. Rusbridger paid a second, apparently cordial, visit to Melbourne in February 1990, but the bickering continued. Eric may have been in pain and more than usually prickly at the time, as he entered hospital for a hip replacement operation the following month. The operation was a success, but in July he had a fall and had to be re-admitted. In November, Margaret wrote on a letter from Eric, in which he apologised for his recent peevishness, 'I must admit that Eric has had more pain this year than he can bear and at times it gets too much for him and he does lash out'.

Rusbridger continually promised a copy of the draft book but it was always 'held up' by one problem or another. Then, in July 1990, he advised that the publisher wanted to make drastic revisions to the draft to accentuate the 'conspiracy theory' angle of Churchill denying intelligence on Pearl Harbor to Roosevelt. In October, he said that he was still struggling with the changes wanted by the publisher, but in the following month his tenth draft was rejected by a new editor who wanted 'major alterations'. One could feel some sympathy for Rusbridger, but he was apparently not interested in notes that Eric continued to send regarding the subject material.

Eric made a plaintive request for a copy of *Winds of Warning* in February 1991:

Could I please see a copy of our book for examination? I don't know whether the various people involved in your discussions are aware that you have a co-author. They should be told I have to approve the final draft, to tell them may help you.[14]

In response, on 20 February Rusbridger advised that the draft was still with the publisher being converted to American spelling and style. He also revealed that there had been some minor changes to *Codebreaker Extraordinary* in the revision process:

> All I have done is to remove the parts in the beginning, dealing with your early family life, service with the RAN during World War 1, your career after December 1941 with the Central Bureau, and post-war at ASIO. These will now go in the second book. What [the American editors] have been doing is restructuring the book so that it appeals more to an American readership since that is where our largest sales would be.

The letter also revealed there had also been a title change: the book would now be called *Betrayal at Pearl Harbor*. The file of correspondence thereafter contains a number of very bitter draft responses by Eric, but his response of 20 March is less vituperative, although still direct:

> I find your letter of 20th February quite difficult to appreciate, in paragraph four you describe some massacre of my manuscript which is a large part of book two of our contract with Summit Books [a Simon & Schuster subsidiary], and you have no right to interfere with my story at all, neither has anybody else … So far I have no evidence of anything you have written and I still await a promised draft. The dust jacket you sent looks appalling, my name just makes the line as it is short.

Eric got his long-awaited draft in April 1991, just before he retired to his winter retreat at Mooloolaba in southern Queensland until September. Unfortunately, there is nothing further on the file to show what he thought of Rusbridger's work, but his family confirms that he was very disappointed with it, and disputed several of the key claims made by Rusbridger. He had already expressed his views in a 1989 interview with the Melbourne *Age*: 'I wrote a manuscript which had a lot of things about personal matters, about sport, my cricket and tennis and all kinds of things. Now he [Rusbridger] has got the story and cut it all out. He's after the kill, the big story.'[15]

Betrayal at Pearl Harbor was published in November 1991 and received serious reviews by a number of noted historians of the period it covered. Not all were flattering. One described it as 'yet another conspiracy theory'.[16] One of the more reasoned reviews said:

> If nothing else, these authors have served as useful irritants, stirring the historical community, accelerating the pace of discussion and illustrating the need for more complex formulation of the key questions. Had the authors of this book been less extravagant in their claims, advancing them as possibilities rather than absolute certainties, readers might have been more inclined to accept their answers.[17]

The noted writer on cryptanalysis, and author of *The Codebreakers* — David Kahn — made the following reference to *Betrayal at Pearl Harbor* in an October 1991 article defending the work of the codebreakers in the lead-up to the Japanese attack:

> Aside from the fact that Churchill wanted the United States to fight Germany, not Japan, the claim [that Churchill concealed foreknowledge of the attack from Roosevelt] is not only not substantiated by any documents (it is based chiefly on hypothesis and 'must have beens') but is vitiated by technical errors … It is improbable that the British … would have limited exchanging code group recoveries with the Americans, when they would have benefited as much if not more than the Americans from learning as much as they could about the Japanese.[18]

These are, in my view, perfectly fair criticisms of the book but, as the reader will now realise, the hypotheses and 'must have beens' were not the work of Eric Nave. Its publication damaged his reputation and portrayed him as something of a crank, both unfortunate and unforeseen consequences of a desire to set straight the part of history in which he had been actively involved. It would have been better had his name been left off the title page.

Eric was more forthright in defending his reputation against the opprobrium stemming from his co-authorship of *Betrayal* in an interview with the Japanese television station NTV, which screened a documentary titled 'Unravelling the Puzzle of the Century: Had Roosevelt Foreknowledge of the Pearl Harbor Attack?' on 7 December 1991, the fiftieth anniversary of the event. Although the program was in Japanese, Eric responded in English to questions about a passage from the book which claimed that Far East Command Bureau had intercepted and decoded a message from Yamamoto ordering his Task Force to sail on 26 November 1941. The interviewer pointed out that there was no record in Japanese archives of such a message ever having been sent.

> **Nave:** Yes. This is James, without a doubt. This is what the other man, Rusbridger, has written. Because he was writing the book he asked me to become joint author. And this is what he has written. The book is based on my records and what I told him. In my opinion 80 per cent of what he has written is based on accurate research and records. The remaining 20 per cent is speculation that he has added so that it will be taken up by the newspapers and radio.
>
> **Interviewer:** Rusbridger's speculation?
>
> **Nave:** Yes, to make the book sell.[19]

Notwithstanding his personal feelings about *Betrayal at Pearl Harbor*, Eric did very well financially out of its publication, which must have been some compensation for his troubles. As well, he placed an order for twelve copies of the book after it had been published, presumably to distribute to friends. Elizabeth also recalls that Michael Smith's *The Emperor's Codes*, in which Eric's role in the unravelling of IJN codes was partially described, made the best-seller list in bookstores for several weeks because the family kept buying out their stock. *Codebreaker Extraordinary* never did find a publisher, but after his treatment at the hands of James Rusbridger and at ninety-two years of age, Eric had probably given up trying.

As for Rusbridger, his journalistic sensation-making with *Betrayal at Pearl Harbor* brought him more notoriety than fame, and precious little fortune. He died by his own hand on 16 February 1994, in allegedly bizarre circumstances, apparently unable to meet the demands of his creditors.[20]

Eric Nave died at his holiday home in Mooloolaba on 23 June 1993. He had packed an interesting, varied and even exciting life into his ninety-four years, and had achieved great things. His knack of being in the right place at the right time had served him well, and he had his fair share of luck. We must not forget that his success had been tempered by tragedy in the loss to illness of his first wife Helena and daughter Mary, and that a number of professional disappointments marked his course. The inglorious end of his publishing enterprise at the hands of his co-author was one such disappointment, but it also brought him and some of his codebreaking exploits to international attention — which had after all been his intention in compiling his autobiography. There is nothing to suggest that he did not enjoy his temporary status as a celebrity, because while the interviewers concentrated on the Pearl Harbor conspiracy aspect of *Betrayal*, their questions also demonstrated that Eric had been active in breaking Japanese codes long before that. The interviews did not, however, fully illuminate his remarkable career, which had been Eric's motive for offering the autobiography *Codebreaker Extraordinary* for publication. I hope, that in revealing in this biography the full details of his work, the true value of Eric Nave's contributions to Australia and to the Allied cause in World War II can for the first time be considered and appreciated on their merits.

And, just as Rusbridger and *Betrayal at Pearl Harbor* had dominated the final years of Nave's life, this was reflected in his obituaries. In Melbourne, the *Age* led with 'Code king warned of Jap bomb plan', re-tagging Eric with a claim he never made, but one that Rusbridger had made on his behalf. The first sentence of the obituary got closer the mark: 'He was the stuff of all great intelligence operators — but much more. James Bond would have been put to shame.'[21]

Epilogue

Before he died in 1993, Eric Nave could look back upon a full and interesting life. He had certainly endured his share of tragedies in his family life and setbacks in his professional life, but he could also reflect with pride and satisfaction upon his achievements in three distinct areas — codebreaking, security intelligence and community service.

His combination of Japanese language skills and cryptanalytical flair, together with his significant codebreaking achievements, puts Eric Nave in select company indeed. Nevertheless, his contribution to the effort which eventually involved the signals intelligence community of five Allied nations in the attack on Japanese diplomatic and military communications has never been fully acknowledged.

If history is written by the victors, the editorial prerogative usually rests with those who own the biggest battalions. In US official accounts of the signals intelligence war with Japan, Nave is mentioned only briefly and then only in connection with his time working alongside Fleet Radio Unit Melbourne. One might have expected more from the British, but their official intelligence history confined itself to the attack on German and other European codes and cyphers. Reference to Nave's work does appear, in varying degrees, in non-official accounts of this extraordinary intelligence saga. He is mentioned in several Australian books on the signals war with Japan and receives honourable mention in perhaps the best unofficial account — *The Emperor's Codes* by the British author Michael Smith.

The slow and painful development of cooperative arrangements in signals intelligence and codebreaking between Australia and the UK, the Allies, and no less between the US armed forces, is reflected in Nave's experiences. There remains disagreement still about the relative success of the British, Americans and Dutch in breaking Japanese naval operational codes prior to the Japanese attacks of December 1941. This book was not intended to resolve that issue, but Eric Nave was closely caught up in the drama — as James Rusbridger discovered and exploited.

Readers will also have learned that, contrary to received wisdom, Australia and Australians — Eric Nave and many others — performed crucial roles in the development of both an indigenous intelligence intercept and codebreaking capability, and the Allied signals intelligence apparatus. They continued to provide key elements of the attack on Japanese communications until the war's end. Largely unrecognised and unrecorded, and some of it still wrapped tightly in coils of security 'in the national interest', it was the development of these capabilities that earned this country a seat at the table when the division of responsibility for post-war signals intelligence was decided. It also laid the solid foundations upon which the whole modern edifice of cooperation in signals intelligence has been constructed. In setting up this post-war organisation, Eric Nave played a significant role.

The book does not purport to show readers how to make or break codes or cyphers: there are already a number of excellent publications listed in the Bibliography for those so inclined. But I hope it has explained in layperson's terms how Eric Nave and his colleagues made their breaks into Japanese codes. More importantly, it has related those breaks to the intelligence that could be derived from Japanese communications. Readers will be entitled to wonder why the British in particular — but not exclusively — did not heed the warning signs of Japanese preparations for attack in the Far East that their signals intelligence organisations were delivering to them. To say that signals intelligence had a 'credibility gap' at the time is an understatement.

Nave's work also tracked the development of the art and science of modern cryptography — the making of codes and cyphers — and signals intelligence — the means of deriving intelligence from them. Cryptanalysis — the breaking of codes — is only one aspect of signals intelligence, but it was for a considerable period the only one to which the British had access in the Far East. As World War drew nearer, there were other tools to support cryptanalysis but never to supplant it as the jewel in the Allied crown.

Nave's career of public service did not end with his departure from codebreaking in 1949. In his role in establishing the structure, procedures and credibility of ASIO, both nationally and abroad, he continued to apply those characteristics and skills that marked everything he did. The abrupt termination of his term as Director Section C ended his involvement in the development of the organisation, but the policies and processes he developed served ASIO and the nation well.

In retirement, he continued to serve his former comrades and the wider Victorian community in several ways, attracting a second appointment as an officer of the Order of the British Empire for his services to the ex-service community in 1972. Altogether, his was a most interesting life, which this book has been written to celebrate. Australia was very lucky to have had the skills and services of Theodore Eric Nave.

Finally, in writing this book I have attempted to place Eric Nave's activities in the context of their day. The world he lived and worked in has long passed and the strategic realities that directed his efforts are now matters of history. It is difficult for Westerners now, as it was then, to imagine the depth of feeling engendered in the Japanese national psyche by the twin blows of the abrogation by Britain of the Anglo-Japanese Treaty and the rejection of her claim to naval parity at the Washington Naval Conference in 1922. These setbacks strengthened Japanese determination to achieve recognition as a great power, and guaranteed Eric Nave's employment in breaking Japan's codes until this imperial ambition was ruthlessly crushed by Japan's defeat in 1945.

We know that immense technological sophistication is now applied to the collection of intelligence, but this had its origins in the steady development of technical means that were employed in providing Eric Nave and his colleagues with the material they needed to work on. We also know that enormous quantities of computer power and expertise are now routinely devoted to cryptanalysis by most countries, but we need to be reminded that the successful codebreaking assault on Japanese military ambitions started with individuals wielding pencils and using intuition and innate good sense.

The official view of Eric Nave's contribution to the secret world was encapsulated in the words provided by the director of the Defence Signals Directorate and delivered in his eulogy by Naval Association president Ron Clarke:

> Much of what he did in support of Australia's national interests during World War Two, in helping to establish the Central Bureau in Melbourne (the precursor of today's Defence Signals Directorate, which is represented here today) and assisting General Douglas MacArthur, cannot be made public, even today. Suffice it to say that he played a vital role in breaking Japanese naval and diplomatic codes in the time leading up to the outbreak of hostilities in the Pacific with the attack on Pearl Harbor. After the war, Nave continued his distinguished career in Australian intelligence.[22]

But it would be difficult to find more appropriate words to sum up the life and career of Theodore Eric Nave that those used by his son David in farewelling his father:

> Well, the ancient mariner has gone, and those of us who knew and loved him will miss him terribly. My sisters and I have lost our father; many of you have lost a cherished friend. We all have lost a little piece of living history.

Bibliography

Unpublished Records

National Archives of Australia

A458   Department of External Affairs, Central Office.
A461   Department of External Affairs Correspondence Files, 1901–1950.
A816   Department of Defence Correspondence Files, 1935–1958.
A981   Department of External Affairs Correspondence Files, 1927–1970.
A1067   Department of External Affairs Correspondence Files, 1942–1953.
A1217   Correspondence Files, Honours and Awards: Foreign Awards to Australians.
A1608   Prime Minister's Department Correspondence Files, 1914–1950.
A1813   Department of the Navy/Department of Defence Correspondence Files,
          1959–1974.
A1838   Department of External Affairs Correspondence Files, 1914–1993.
A1945   Department of Defence Correspondence Files, 1946–1985.
A2031   Defence Committee Minutes, 1926–1989.
A2585   Naval Board Minutes Book, 1905–1948.
A2670   Reference Set of War Cabinet Agenda, 1939–1946.
A2671   War Cabinet Agenda Files, 1939–1946.
A2676   War Cabinet Minutes, 1939–1946.
A2680   Advisory War Council Agenda Files, 1940–1945.
A2684   Advisory War Council Minutes Files, 1940–1945.
A2880   Governor-General's Correspondence, 1912–1957.
A2937   Department of External Affairs, London Correspondence, 1924–1947.
A3978   Confidential Reports — Naval Officers.
A5799   Defence Committee Agenda, 1932–
A5954   Department of Defence, 'The Shedden Collection', 1937–1971.
A6059   Department of Army Correspondence Files, 1925–1966.
A6119   Australian Security Intelligence Organisation, Personal Files.
A6122   Australian Security Intelligence Organisation Files.
A6661   Governor-General's Correspondence, 1898–1936.
A6768   Department of External Affairs Correspondence Files (East Asia Top Secret),
          1941–1952.
A6923   Directorate of Military Intelligence.
A7942   Defence Committee Papers, 1936–1985.
A9787   Council of Defence Minutes and Agenda Papers, 1905–1950.
A10908   Central Bureau Correspondence Files, 1940–1945.

A10909   Fleet Radio Unit Melbourne Correspondence and Photographs, 1943–1944.
A11066   RAAF Headquarters Eastern Area, Penrith NSW Correspondence Files, 1943–
         1948.
A11803   Governor General's Correspondence relating to War of 1914–1918.
A11804   General Correspondence of Governor-General (excluding war files), 1887–1937.
B197   Department of Defence Correspondence Files.
B5436   Central Bureau Technical Records.
B5553   Fleet Radio Unit Melbourne Periodic Summaries, 1943–1945.
B5554   Fleet Radio Unit Melbourne, Volume of Technical Records relating to
         Naval Codes and Cyphers, 1940–1946.
B5555   Fleet Radio Unit Melbourne, Translations of Cypher Messages, 1945–1946.
B5832   RAAF School of Languages.
B6121   Naval Historical Files.
C443   Security Branch NSW, Consular Investigation Files.
MP151   Department of the Navy General Correspondence Files, 1923–1950.
MP472   Department of the Navy Personnel Files.
MP508   Department of Defence General Correspondence Files, 1898–1972.
MP742   Department of Army, General and Civil Correspondence Files, 1920–1956.
MP729   Department of Army, Secret Correspondence Files, 1939–1960.
MP981   Navy Office General Correspondence Files, 1923–1950.
MP1049   Department of the Navy Correspondence Files.
MP1074   ACNB Inward and Outward Messages, 1939–1945.
MP1185   Department of the Navy Correspondence Files, Secret and
         Confidential.
MT1214   Department of the Navy Personnel Files.
SP339   Commodore-in-Charge Sydney General Correspondence Files.

Australian War Memorial
35   HMA Ships Logs, 1905–1954.
54   Written Records 1939-1945 War.
59   History of the G-2 (Intelligence) Section HQ SWPA and Affiliated Units, 1942–1945.
79   Records of HMAS *Rushcutter*.
119 Office of the Military Secretary, Honours and Awards, Confidential
     Working Files, 1939–1980.
121 Directorate of Military Operations and Plans Files.
123 Special Collection II, Defence Committee Records, 1923–1960.
124 Naval Historical Collection, 1943–1974.
252 Records 1814-1918 War, 1914–1937.
MSS 1183   Nave Manuscript.
3DRL/6643 Blamey Papers.
3DRL/6906 Papers of Commander R.B.M. Long.

UK National Archives
ADM 1   Admiralty and Secretariat Papers.
ADM 116 Admiralty and Secretariat Cases.
ADM 178 Admiralty and Secretariat Papers and Cases, Supplementary Series.
ADM 223 Naval Intelligence Papers, 1921–1961.
ADM 233 Wireless News, 1918–1921.
CAB 21   Cabinet Office: Registered Files.
CAB 79   War Cabinet, Chiefs of Staff Committee, Minutes of Meetings.

CAB 131 Cabinet Defence Committee Minutes and Papers, 1946–1963.
CAB 158 Ministry of Defence and Cabinet Office, Central Intelligence Machinery: Joint Intelligence Committee.
CO 968 Defence: Original Correspondence, 1941–1963.
CO1022 South East Asia Department: Original Correspondence, 1950–1956.
DEFE 7 Ministry of Defence Registered Files, 1942–1979.
DO 35 Dominions Office and Commonwealth Relations Office Original Correspondence, 1915–1971.
FO1091 Commissioner General for the UK in SE Asia and UK Commissioner for Singapore and SE Asia Registered Files, 1950–62.
HS 1 Special Operations Executive: Far East: Registered Files.
HW 8 Government Code and Cypher School: Naval Section: Memoranda of Daily Activities.
HW 41 Government Code and Cypher School: Services Field Signals Intelligence Units: Reports of Intercepted Signals and Histories of Field Signals Intelligence Units.
WO106 Directorate of Military Operations and Intelligence, 1837–1961.
WO193 Directorate of Military Operations: Collation Files, 1917–1956.
WO 208 Directorate of Military Intelligence.
WO305 Army Unit Historical Records and Reports.

US National Archives and Records Administration
RG38 Records of the Chief of Naval Operations.
RG313 COMSUBSOUWESPAC Restricted-Secret General Administrative Files, 1942–1945.
RG457 Records of the National Security Agency.

Theses
Gobert, Wayne, 'The Origins of Australian Diplomatic Intelligence Reporting in Asia, 1933–1941' (MA sub-thesis, Australian Defence Force Academy, 1985).
Pfennigwerth, Ian, 'Reducing the Margin of Ignorance: The Contribution of Intelligence to Royal Australian Navy Operations, 1939–1972' (PhD Thesis, University of Newcastle, 2005).

Books

Agawa, Hiroyuki, *The Reluctant Admiral: Yamamoto and the Imperial Navy*, Tokyo: Kodansha International, 1979.
Alderman, Geoffrey, *Modern Britain, 1700–1983: A Domestic History*, London: Croom Helm, 1986.
Aldrich, Richard J., and Michael F. Hopkins, eds, *Intelligence, Defence and Diplomacy: British Policy in the Post-War World*, London: Frank Cass, 1998.
Andrew, Christopher, and Jeremy Noakes, eds, *Intelligence and International Relations, 1900–1945*, Exeter: University of Exeter, 1987.
Asakawa, Michio, 'Anglo-Japanese Military Relations, 1800–1900', in *The History of Anglo-Japanese Relations, 1600–2000, Volume III: The Military Dimension*, ed. Ian Gow and Yoichi Hirama, pp. 13–34. Basingstoke, Hants: Palgrave, 2003.
Babij, Orest, 'The Royal Navy and the Defence of the British Empire, 1928–1934', in *Far-Flung*

Lines: Studies in Imperial Defence in Honour of Donald Mackenzie Schurman*, ed. Keith Nielson and Greg Kennedy, pp. 171-89. London: Frank Cass, 1997.

Ball, Desmond, and David Horner, *Breaking the Codes: Australia's KGB Network, 1944–1950*, Sydney: Allen & Unwin, 1998.

Ballard, Geoffrey, *On Ultra Active Service: The Story of Australia's Signals Intelligence Operations During WWII*, Richmond, Victoria: Spectrum Publications, 1991.

Barnett, Corelli, *Engage the Enemy More Closely: The Royal Navy in the Second World War*, London: Hodder & Stoughton, 1991.

Benson, Robert Louis, *A History of US Communications Intelligence During World War II: Policy and Administration*, Fort Meade, Md: National Security Agency, 1997.

Best, Antony, *British Intelligence and the Japanese Challenge in Asia, 1914–1941*, London: Palgrave Macmillan, 2002.

Blair, Clay, *Silent Victory: The US Submarine War Against Japan*, Philadelphia: Lippincott, 1975.

Bleakley, Jack, *The Eavesdroppers*, Canberra: Australian Government Publishing Service, 1992.

Bosscher, M., *De Koninklijke Marine in de Tweede Wereldoorlog, Part 2*, The Hague: T. Wever, 1986.

Brown, Anthony Cave, *Bodyguard of Lies*, London: W.H. Allen, 1957.

Budiansky, Stephen, *Battle of Wits: The Complete Story of Codebreaking in World War II*, London: Viking, 2000.

Chapman, J.W.M., 'Japanese Intelligence, 1918–1945: A Suitable Case for Treatment', in *Intelligence and International Relations, 1900–1945*, ed. Christopher Andrew and Jeremy Noakes, pp. 145–89. Exeter: Exeter University Publications, 1987.

Chapman, J.W.M., 'Britain, Japan and the "Higher Realms of Intelligence", 1900–1918', in *The History of Anglo-Japanese Relations, 1600–2000, Volume III: The Military Dimension*, ed. Ian Gow and Hirama Yoichi, pp. 151–72. Basingstoke, Hants: Palgrave, 2003.

Deacon, Richard, *The Silent War: A History of Western Naval Intelligence*, London: Grafton Books, 1988.

Denham, Hugh, 'Bedford-Bletchley-Kilindili-Colombo', in *Code Breakers: The Inside Story of Bletchley Park*, ed. F.H. Hinsley and Alan Stripp, pp. 264–81. London: Oxford University Press, 1993.

Drea, Edward J., *MacArthur's ULTRA: Codebreaking and the War Against Japan, 1942–1945*, Lawrence, Ka: University of Kansas Press, 1992.

Elphick, Peter, *Far Eastern File: The Intelligence War in the Far East, 1930–1945*, London: Hodder & Stoughton, 1997.

Ferris, John, 'The Last Decade of British Maritime Supremacy, 1919–1929', in *Far-Flung Lines: Studies in Imperial Defence in Honour of Donald Mackenzie Schurman*, ed. Keith Nielson and Greg Kennedy, pp. 171–89. London: Frank Cass, 1997.

Funch, Colin, *Linguists in Uniform: The Japanese Experience*, Melbourne: Japanese Studies Centre, Monash University, 2003.

Gill, G. Hermon, *Royal Australian Navy, 1939–1942*, Canberra: Collins in association with the Australian War Memorial, 1985.

Gill, G. Hermon, *Royal Australian Navy, 1942-1945*, Canberra: Collins in association with the Australian War Memorial, 1968.

Gobert, Wayne, *The Origins of Australian Diplomatic Intelligence in Asia, 1933–1941*, Canberra: Strategic and Defence Studies Centre, Australian National University, 1992.

Gow, Ian, and Hirama Yoichi, eds, *The History of Anglo-Japanese Relations, 1600–2000, Volume III: The Military Dimension*, Basingstoke, Hants: Palgrave, 2003.

Gow, Ian, 'The Royal Navy and Japan, 1900–1920: Strategic Re-Evaluation of the IJN', in *The History of Anglo-Japanese Relations, 1600–2000, Volume III: The Military Dimension*, ed.

Ian Gow and Hirama Yoichi, pp. 35–50. Basingstoke, Hants: Palgrave, 2003.

Hagihara, Nobutoshi, 'Postscript to Chapter 4: Anglo-Japanese Attitudes, 1940–41', in *Anglo-Japanese Alienation, 1919–1952: Papers of the Anglo-Japanese Conference on the History of the Second World War*, ed. Ian Nish, pp. 97–102. Cambridge: Cambridge University Press, 1982.

Hinsley, F.H., with E.E. Thomas, C.F.G. Ransom and R.C. Knight, *British Intelligence in the Second World War: Its Influence on Strategy and Operations* (3 volumes), London: Her Majesty's Stationery Office, 1979–84.

Hinsley, F.H., and Alan Stripp, eds, *Code Breakers: The Inside Story of Bletchley Park*, London: Oxford University Press, 1993.

Holmes, W.J, *Double-Edged Secrets: US Naval Intelligence Operations in the Pacific During World War II*, Annapolis, Md: Naval Institute Press, 1979.

Holmes, W.J, 'Naval Intelligence in the War Against Japan, 1941–1945: The View From Pearl Harbor', in *New Aspects of Naval History: Selected Papers Presented at the Fourth Naval History Symposium, United States Naval Academy, 25–26 October 1979*, ed. Craig L. Symonds, pp. 351–9. Annapolis, Md: Naval Institute Press, 1981.

Holtwick, Jack S., *Naval Security Group History to World War II*, Washington, DC: Department of the Navy, 1971.

Horner, David, *Australia and Allied Intelligence in the Pacific in the Second World War*, Canberra: Strategic and Defence Studies Centre, Australian National University, 1980.

Hosoya, Chihiro, 'Britain and the United States in Japan's View of the International System, 1919–1937', in *Anglo-Japanese Alienation, 1919–1952: Papers of the Anglo-Japanese Conference on the History of the Second World War*, ed. Ian Nish, pp. 3–26. London: Cambridge University Press, 1982.

Howell, P.A., *South Australia and Federation*, Adelaide: Wakefield Press, 2002.

Huie, Shirley, *Ships' Belles: The Story of the Women's RAN Service in War and Peace, 1941–1985*, Sydney: Watermark Press, 2000.

Ishimaru, Tota, *Japan Must Fight Britain*, London: The Paternoster Library, 1938.

Jenkins, David, *Battle Surface! Japan's Submarine War Against Australia 1942–44*, Sydney: Random House, 1992.

Jose, Arthur W., *The Royal Australian Navy, 1914–1918*, Sydney: Angus & Robertson, 1943.

Kahn, David, *The Codebreakers: The Story of Secret Writing*, New York: Scribner, 1996.

Komatsu, Keiichiro, *Origins of the Pacific War and the Importance of 'Magic'*, New York: St Martin's Press, 1999.

Laffin, John, *Special and Secret*, Sydney: Time-Life Books (Australia), 1990.

Layton, Edwin T., 'And I Was There': Pearl Harbor and Midway – Breaking the Secrets, New York: William Morrow, 1985.

Lewin, Ronald, *Ultra Goes to War: The Secret Story*, London: Hutchinson, 1978.

Lewin, Ronald, *The Other Ultra: Codes, Ciphers and the Defeat of Japan*, London: Hutchinson, 1982.

Loewe, Michael, 'Japanese Naval Codes', in *Code Breakers: The Inside Story of Bletchley Park*, ed. F.H. Hinsley and Alan Stripp, pp. 257–63. London: Oxford University Press, 1993.

McKnight, David, *Australia's Spies and Their Secrets*, Sydney: Allen & Unwin, 1994.

McLachlan, Donald, *Room 39: Naval Intelligence in Action, 1939–1945*, London Weidenfeld & Nicolson, 1968.

Maneki, Sharon, *The Quiet Heroes of the Southwest Pacific Theater: An Oral History of the Men and Women of CBB and FRUMEL*, Fort Meade, Md: National Security Agency, 1996.

Marder, Arthur J., *Old Friends New Enemies: The Royal Navy and the Imperial Japanese Navy, Vol 1: Strategic Illusions, 1936–1941*, Oxford: Clarendon Press, 1981.

Marder, Arthur J., Mark Jacobsen, and John Horsfield, *Old Friends New Enemies: The Royal Navy and the Imperial Japanese Navy, Vol. 2: The Pacific War, 1942–1945*, Oxford: Clarendon Press, 1990.

Melinsky, Hugh, *A Code-Breaker's Tale*, Derham, Norfolk: Larks Press, 1998.

Morton, Peter, *Fire Across the Desert: Woomera and the Anglo–Australian Joint Project, 1946–1980*, Canberra: Australian Government Publishing Service, 1989.

Mountbatten, Louis, *Eighty Years in Pictures*, London: Macmillan, 1979.

Neale, R.G., P.G. Edwards, H. Keneway, and H.L.J. Stokes, eds, *Documents in Australian Foreign Policy, 1937–1949, Volume II: 1939*, Canberra: Australian Government Publishing Service, 1976.

Nielson, K., and Greg Kennedy, eds, *Far-Flung Lines: Studies in Imperial Defence in Honour of Donald Mackenzie Schurman*, London: Frank Cass, 1997.

Nish, Ian, ed., *Anglo-Japanese Alienation, 1919-1952: Papers of the Anglo-Japanese Conference on the History of the Second World War*, Cambridge: Cambridge University Press, 1982.

Nish, Ian, and Yoichi Kibata, eds, *The History of Anglo-Japanese Relations, Volume 1: The Political-Diplomatic Dimension, 1600–1930*, Basingstoke, Hants: Palgrave, 2000.

Norman, Bruce, *Secret Warfare: The Battle of Codes and Ciphers*, New York: Dorset Press, 1973.

Odgers, George, *The Royal Australian Navy: An Illustrated History*, Sydney: Child & Kent, 1982.

Ong Chit Chung, *Operation Matador: Britain's War Plans Against the Japanese, 1918–1941*, Singapore: Times Academic Press, 1997.

Packard, W.H., *A Century in US Naval Intelligence*, Washington, DC: Naval Historical Center, 1996.

Parker, Frederick D., *The Priceless Advantage: US Navy Communications Intelligence and the Battles of Coral Sea, Midway and the Aleutians*, Fort Meade, Md: National Security Agency, 1993.

Prados, John, *Combined Fleet Decoded: The Secret History of American Intelligence and the Japanese Navy in World War II*, New York: Random House, 1995.

Richelson, Jeffrey T., and Desmond Ball, *The Ties That Bind*, Sydney: Allen & Unwin, 1990.

Rusbridger, James, and Eric Nave, *Betrayal at Pearl Harbor: How Churchill Lured Roosevelt Into World War II*, New York: Simon & Schuster, 1992.

Smith, Michael, *The Emperor's Codes: Bletchley Park and the Breaking of Japan's Secret Ciphers*, London: Bantam, 2001.

Spector, R.H., ed., *Listening to the Enemy: Key Documents on the Role of Communications Intelligence in the War With Japan*, Wilmington, De: Scholarly Resources, 1988.

Stevens, David M., ed., *The Royal Australian Navy in World War II*, Sydney: Allen & Unwin, 1996.

Stevens, David M., ed., *The Australian Centenary History of Defence, Volume III: The Royal Australian Navy*, Melbourne: Oxford University Press, 2001.

Stripp, Alan, *Codebreakers in the Far East*, London: Frank Cass, 1989.

Thomson, Judy, *Winning with Intelligence: A Biography of Brigadier John David Rogers, CBE, MC 1985–1978*, Sydney: Australian Military History Publications, 2000.

Van Der Rhoer, Edward, *Deadly Magic: An Account of Communications Intelligence in World War II in the Pacific*, London: Robert Hale, 1979.

West, Nigel, *SIGINT Secrets: The Signals Intelligence War, 1900 to Today*, New York: William Morrow, 1986; also published as *GCHQ: The Wireless War, 1900–86*, London: Weidenfeld & Nicolson, 1986.

Winton, John, *ULTRA in the Pacific: How Breaking Japanese Codes and Ciphers Affected Naval Operations Against Japan, 1941–45*, London: Leo Cooper 1993.

Wilkins, John M., *A Short History of Naval Intelligence and the Royal Australian Navy Intelligence Department*, self-published, 2001.

Winter, Barbara, *The Intrigue Master: Commander Long and Naval Intelligence in Australia, 1913–1945*, Brisbane: Collaring Press, 1995.

Winterbotham, F.W., *The Ultra Secret*, London: Weidenfeld & Nicolson, 1974.

Wohlstetter, Roberta, *Pearl Harbor: Warning and Decision*, Stanford, Ca: Stanford University Press, 1962.

Journal Articles

Aldrich, Richard J., 'Conspiracy or Confusion? Churchill, Roosevelt and Pearl Harbor', *Intelligence and National Security*, 7 (1992): pp. 335–46.

Andrew, Christopher, 'The Growth of the Australian Intelligence Community and the Anglo-American Connection', *Intelligence and National Security*, 4 (1989): pp. 218–29.

Ball, Desmond, 'Allied Intelligence Cooperation Involving Australia During WW2', *Australian Outlook*, 32 (1978): pp. 299–309.

Ball, Desmond, 'Over and Out: Signals Intelligence (Sigint) in Hong Kong', *Intelligence and National Security*, 11 (1996): pp. 474–96.

Barnes, Ken, 'The Defence Signals Directorate — Its Roles and Functions', *Australian Defence Force Journal*, 108 (1994): pp. 3–7.

Best, Antony, 'Constructing an Image: British Intelligence and Whitehall's Perception of Japan, 1931–1939', *Intelligence and National Security*, 11 (1996), pp. 403–23.

Best, Antony, 'Intelligence, Diplomacy and the Japanese Threat to British Interests, 1914–1941', *Intelligence and National Security*, 17 (2002): pp. 87–102.

Best, Antony, '"This Probably Over-Valued Military Power": British Intelligence and Whitehall's Perception of Japan, 1939–41', *Intelligence and National Security*, 12 (1997): pp. 67–94.

Cain, Frank, 'Missiles and Mistrust: US Intelligence Responses to British and Australian Missile Research', *Intelligence and National Security*, 3 (1988): pp. 6–22.

De Graff, Bob, 'Hot Intelligence in the Tropics: Dutch Intelligence Operations in the Netherlands East Indies During the Second World War', *Journal of Contemporary History*, 22 (1987): pp. 536–84.

Denniston, A.G., 'The Government Code and Cypher School Between the Wars', *Intelligence and National Security*, 1 (1986): pp. 49–70.

Donovan, Peter, 'The Flaw in the JN25 Series of Ciphers', *Cryptologia*, 28 (2004): pp. 325–40.

Erskine, Ralph, 'The Holden Agreement on Naval Sigint: The First BRUSA?', *Intelligence and National Security*, 14 (1999), pp.187–97.

Gobert, Wayne, 'The Evolution of Service Strategic Intelligence, 1901–1941', *Australian Defence Force Journal*, 92 (1992): pp. 56–62.

Gobert, Wayne, 'The Evolution of the RAN Intelligence Service, Part One: 1907–1918', *Journal of the Australian Naval Institute*, 15 (1989): pp. 39–43.

Horner, David, 'Special Intelligence in the Southwest Pacific Area in WW2', *Australian Outlook*, 32 (1978): pp. 310–27.

Kaiser, David, 'Conspiracy or Cock-Up? Pearl Harbor Revisited', *Intelligence and National Security*, 9 (1994): pp. 354–72.

Layton, Edwin T., 'America Deciphered Our Code', *US Naval Institute Proceedings*, 105 (1979): pp. 302–3.

Mellen, Greg, 'Rhapsody in Purple: A New History of Pearl Harbor, 1 — by Dundas P. Tucker', *Cryptologia*, 6 (1992): pp. 193–228.

Reynolds, Wayne, 'Atomic Weapons and the Issue of Australian Security, 1946–1957', *War and Society*, 17 (1999): pp. 57–79.

Richard, Joseph E., 'Memories of CB', *Central Bureau Intelligence Corps Association Newsletter*, December 2004, pp. 3–5.

Sims, John Cary, 'The BRUSA Agreement of May 17, 1943', *Cryptologia*, 21 (1997): pp. 30–8.

Sissons, D.C.S., 'More on Pearl Harbor', *Intelligence and National Security*, 9 (1994): pp. 373–9.

Verney, G.S., 'Oriental Studies, University of Sydney', *United Service*, 34 (1981): p. 1.

Wark, Wesley, 'In Search of a Suitable Japan: British Naval Intelligence in the Pacific Before the Second World War', *Intelligence and National Security*, 1 (1986): pp. 189–211.

Internet Material

'About ASIO', on http://www.asio.gov.au/About/comp.htm, read 25 November 2004.

'AF is Short of Water', in NSA pamphlet on Midway on http://www.nsa.gov/publications/publi00023, read 25 March 2003.

'DSD – Past & Present', on http://www.dsd.gov.au/evolution2.html, read 7 June 2001.

Manera, Brad, 'Anniversary talks: Battle of the Bismarck Sea, 2-4 March 1943', on http://www.awm.gov.au/atwar/remembering1942/bismarck, read 21 November 2005.

'Sydney University, T.G. Room and Codebreaking in WWII', on http://www.maths.usyd.edu.au:800/ww2codes/gazette.html., read 18 August 2004.

'The Naval Association of Australia', on http://www.navalassoc.org.au, read 22 March 2005.

'Tropical Sprue', on http:// health.allrefer.com, read 6 June 2005.

Newspapers

Adelaide *Advertiser*.

Melbourne *Age*.

Brisbane *Courier-Mail*.

Notes

AWM Australian War Memorial
NAA National Archives of Australia
NACP US National Archives, College Park, Md.
UKNA UK National Archives

1 — Early Days
1 Adelaide *Advertiser*, 6 October 1913 — 'Australia's Navy: Vessels Arrive At Sydney'.
2 Adelaide *Advertiser*, 11 November 1914 — 'In German New Guinea: South Australian in the Fight'.
3 Stevens, *Royal Australian Navy*, pp. 47–8.
4 The correspondence on Nave's Japanese language training can be found in NAA MP472/1, Item 5/18/8562 – Training in Foreign Languages in the RAN.
5 Ibid. The RAN decided that 'consideration will be given, on termination of hostilities, to providing facilities for Junior Account Officers to be sent to Japan to study Japanese'.
6 Funch, *Linguists in Uniform*, pp.12–14.
7 NAA A 816/1, Item 44/301/9 — Study of Japanese Language in the Services.
8 NAA B6121, Item 311J — Report on Penang Conference 1921. Ironically, Penang had been the scene of the last successful raid by the German cruiser Emden in October 1915, and in World War II it became a base for German submarines assisting the IJN in attacking Allied convoys in the Indian Ocean.
9 NAA A981, Item Jap 113 – Japan & Australia: Study of Japanese Language in Australia. In a memo of 13 April 1922 Major Piesse, formerly head of Military Intelligence and then of the Pacific and External Affairs Branch of the Prime Minister's Department, in his report on the Washington Conference made the observation that 'the whole position of Australia vis à vis Japan had changed' and 'that … Australia would be in a position to rely closely on British sources of information'. He then recommended that the training of one language officer already in Japan should cease and 'that the future study of Japanese affairs should be drastically curtailed'.
10 Best, *British Intelligence*, pp. 93–5 and 108–9.

11 Agawa, *The Reluctant Admiral*, pp. 121–4, 141–4, and 183–86. Yonai was anti-war and very much opposed to Japan's entry into the Tripartite Pact with Germany and Italy.

12 NAA MP1049, Item 1997/5/196 — HMA Squadron: Wireless Telegraphy Procedure Y, Japanese Wireless Telegraphy Interception, Nave letter to CCAS of 14 October 1924.

13 Ibid., Navy Office letter S.C. 1997/7/75/3317 of 19 November 1924.

14 NAA A3978, Item NAVE T. E. — Personal Records — Nave, Theodore Eric.

15 Ishimaru, *Japan Must Fight Britain*. The reason given by Ishimaru was that Britain was actively conspiring to frustrate Japan's rightful imperial ambitions and that Singapore was the cornerstone of the strategy.

2 — First Breaks

1 Asakawa, 'Anglo–Japanese Military Relations', pp. 26–7.

2 Gow, 'The Royal Navy and Japan', pp. 38–42.

3 Ibid., pp. 43–8.

4 Best, *British Intelligence*, pp. 24–6.

5 Major General F.S.G. Piggott quoted in Elphick, *Far Eastern File*, p. 21.

6 Chapman, 'The Higher Realms of Intelligence', p. 154.

7 This doesn't quite tie in with Nave's 1924 letter to his superiors about his codebreaking ambitions in HMAS *Sydney*. In writing his memoirs, Eric may simply have forgotten; however, a more likely explanation is that he did not want to reveal his earlier highly classified activities. Most of those who have written on codebreaking have still concealed some areas of their work.

8 NAA MP1049/9, Item 1997/5/196 — HMA Squadron W/T Procedure Y: Japanese W/T Interception, Navy Office minute S.C. 1997/5/85 undated 'Interception of W/T Messages'.

9 Ibid., Admiralty letter M. 0749/26.

10 As suggested by the name, a slice of bread covered with cheese surmounted by a layer of ham and topped by a fried egg — an early example of 'fusion' cuisine.

11 NAA MP1049/9, Item 1997/5/196, Admiralty letter M.00408 of 13 January 1926 to Commander in Chief China.

12 NAA A3978, Item NAVE T.E.

13 NAA MP1049/9, Item 1997/5/196, Admiralty letter M.00408 of 16 June 1926.

14 Ibid., Admiralty letter M. 02753/27 of 9 November 1927.

15 NAA MT1214/1, Item 559/215/1135 — Extract from ANR Report No. 49, N.C. 276, N.R. 17817 of 26 October 1925.

3 — Government Code and Cypher School

1 Gill, *Royal Australian Navy, 1939–1942*, pp. 7–12.

2 Barnett, *Engage the Enemy More Closely*, pp. 24–5.

3 NAA MP1049, Item 1997/5/196 — HMA Squadron W/T Procedure Y: Japanese W/T Interception, Secretary's minute S.C. 1997/5/132 of 6 August 1927.

4 NAA MT1214/1, Item 559/215/1135 — Admiralty letter C.W. 3609/27 of 16 August 1927.

5 Kahn, *The Codebreakers*, pp. 282–97.
6 Hinsley, *British Intelligence*, pp. 19–20.
7 Smith, *The Emperor's Codes*, p. 78.
8 Denniston, 'GCCS Between the Wars', p. 54.
9 Best, *British Intelligence*, pp. 93–6.
10 Smith, *The Emperor's Codes*, p. 45.
11 Ibid., pp. 46–7.
12 Ibid., p. 31–33.
13 Best, 'Constructing an Image', p. 404.

4 — China Station
1 Barnett, *Engage the Enemy*, pp. 20–4.
2 Ibid., pp. 23–4.
3 Ibid., p. 27.
4 The Japanese had an extensive network of agents, both overt and covert, throughout Asia. These not only engaged in espionage but also subversion, particularly amongst colonial nations like India. See Best, 'This Probably Over-Valued Military Power', pp. 71–4.
5 The full process is explained in Kahn, *The Codebreakers*, pp. 440–4.
6 Windeyer later resigned from the RN and settled in Canada. During the Pacific War he was recalled and served in the Royal Canadian Navy's signals intelligence organisation. His family also had links with The University of Sydney, where his uncle was vice-chancellor. The university was to become an important part of Australian codebreaking, although any association of Guy Windeyer with this is tenuous.
7 Smith, *The Emperor's Codes*, pp. 44, 47.
8 Prados, *Combined Fleet Decoded*, p. 40.
9 Best, *British Intelligence*, pp. 100–1.
10 Babij, 'Royal Navy and Defence of Empire', p. 180.
11 Best, *British Intelligence*, pp. 109–10.

5 — The Drift to War
1 Best, *British Intelligence*, p. 110.
2 Quoted in Best, 'Constructing an Image', pp. 407–8.
3 Quoted in Smith, *The Emperor's Codes*, p. 51.
4 National Maritime Museum, TAI/8 — Tait Papers, Digest of the Report on Intelligence by Captain W.E.C. Tait.
5 Budiansky, *Battle of Wits*, pp. 4–5.
6 Kahn, *The Codebreakers*, pp. 358–61.
7 Quoted in Lewin, *The Other Ultra*, pp. 28–9.
8 Layton, 'And I Was There', pp. 34–35.
9 Mountbatten, *Eighty Years in Pictures*, pp. 114–17.
10 Agawa, *The Reluctant Admiral*, pp. 99–103.
11 Hosoya, 'Britain and the United States in Japan's View', p. 58.
12 Elphick, *Far Eastern File*, p. 46.
13 Alderman, *Modern Britain*, pp. 223–8.

6 — Far East Combined Bureau

1 Elphick, *Far Eastern File*, pp. 73–5.
2 Smith, *The Emperor's Codes*, pp. 48–49.
3 Best, 'Constructing and Image', pp. 417–18.
4 Rusbridger and Nave, *Betrayal at Pearl Harbor: How Churchill Lured Roosevelt into World War II*, p. 73. Copyright 1991 by Eric Nave and James Rusbridger. Reprinted by permission of Simon and Schuster Adult Publishing Group.
5 Ibid., p. 77.
6 Elphick, *Far Eastern File*, pp. 82–3.
7 NAA MP 1185/8, Item 2037/3/29 — List of D/F Stations Home and Abroad, Admiralty letter M01003/40 of 1 February 1940.
8 Quoted in Smith, *The Emperor's Codes*, pp. 79–80.
9 NARA RG457, NSA Oral Histories OH-1982-11, Wright, W.A. 'Ham', Capt., p.10.
10 Layton, 'America Deciphered Our Code', pp. 98–9.
11 Elphick, *Far Eastern File*, pp. 75–6.
12 Denniston, 'GCCS Between the Wars', p. 61.
13 Benson, *A History*, pp. 20–21.
14 Best, *British Intelligence*, p. 190.
15 Website http//: health.allrefer.com, read 6 June 2005.

7 — Australia Revisited

1 NAA MT1214/1, Item 559/215/1452 — DNMS Minute 559/215/1349 of 2 May 1940.
2 NAA MP1185/8, Item 1997/5/343 — Strategic DF, minute DSC to ACNS 20 July1939.
3 Winter, *The Intrigue Master*, p. 13.
4 NAA A816, Item 43/302/18 — Cryptographic Organisation, CNS Minute of 28/11/39.
5 NAA A6923/3, Item 37/401/425 — CGS Branch, Military Intelligence: SI Section, Eastern Command Report 'Cryptography' of 18/10/40.
6 NAA A6923/3, Item 37/401/425   CGS Branch, Military Intelligence: SI Section, DNI minute of 26 November 1939.
7 NAA A816/1, Item 44/301/9 — Study of Japanese Language in the Services.
8 NAA C443/1, Item J421 — Japanese Language in Australia — Re teaching of.
9 Letter Nave to Sissons, 11 November 1986.
10 NAA MT 1214/1, Item 559/215/1452 — ACNB message DTG 040718Z July 1940.
11 NAA MP1185/8, Item 2021/5/523 — Intelligence Problems discussed with Captain Wylie, COIS Letter No. 648/054 of 17 January 1941, Appendix 2, p. 5.
12 NAA MP1185/8, Item 1937/2/415 — Cryptographic Organisation in Australia, Comments by Paymaster-Commander Nave R.A.N. [*sic*], Folio 5.
13 NAA MP1185/8, Item 2021/5/523 — Intelligence Problems discussed with Captain Wylie.
14 NAA B5554, Item Whole Series — Technical Records relating to Naval Codes

and Cyphers (The Red Book), Folio 375.
15 Holmes, *Double-Edged Secrets*, pp. 37–8.
16 NAA B5554, Item Whole Series — Technical Records relating to Naval Codes
and Cyphers (The Red Book), Folios 374–2, 327–5.
17 Ibid., Folios 364–3.
18 Ibid., Folio 373.
19 Ballard, *On ULTRA Active Service*, pp. 43–6.
20 Wohlstetter, *Pearl Harbor*, pp. 171, 175.
21 NAA A5954, Item 558 — Far Eastern Crisis — November December 1941:
Instructions from Japanese Foreign Office to Posts Overseas, Second Naval Member
letter of 4 December 1941.
22 Wohlstetter, *Pearl Harbor*, p. 173.
23 NAA A5954, Item 558 — Far Eastern Crisis — November December 1941:
Instructions from Japanese Foreign Office to Posts Overseas, Second Naval Member
letter of 4 December 1941.

8 — Pearl Harbor and the Arrival of the Americans
1 Quoted in Wohlstetter, *Pearl Harbor*, p. 45
2 Nave interview with George Negus, Channel 9, 9 March 1989.
3 The percentage to which the code had been penetrated differs between accounts.
In his recollection Captain Wright thought it might have been as low as 10 percent.
NARA RG457, NSA Oral Histories, NSA-OH-11-82, Wright, W.A. 'Ham', Capt.,
p. 39.
4 Smith, *The Emperor's Codes*, p. 124.
5 Komatsu, *Origins of the Pacific War*, p. 258.
6 NAA B5554, Item Whole Series — Technical Records relating to Naval Codes and
Cyphers (The Red Book), Folio 375.
7 NACP RG457, SRMN-006 — Royal Australian Navy Support to United States
Navy through Australian Commonwealth Naval Board: Summaries/Translations of
Japanese Messages February to December 1942. The title is a misnomer: there were
several originators of the messages recorded.
8 NAA A816, Item 43/302/18 — Cryptographic Organisation in Australia, Tropic
No. 178.
9 Fabian interview by Rusbridger, December 1989, quoted in Rusbridger and Nave,
Betrayal, p. 93.
10 Benson, A History, p. 20.
11 Fabian's biographical details have been assembled from a variety of sources,
including Smith, Layton, the NSA oral histories and the later 'Cryptologic Histories',
all of which are listed in the Bibliography. He seems to have evoked very different
responses in most of those he came in contact with, regardless of nationality.
12 Chamberlin in Maneki, *The Quiet Heroes*, p. 74.
13 NARA RG457, NSA Oral Histories, NSA-OH-11-82, Wright, W.A. 'Ham',
Capt., p. 27. When asked his opinion of Fabian, Wright replied, 'I never really
knew him. He didn't impress me as a youngster … I don't think he was particularly
interested in decryption — I didn't get that impression.'

14 NAA MP1185/8, Item 2021/5/689 — Loan of Additional Japanese Interpreters.
15 Huie, *Ships' Belles*, pp. 177–8.
16 NAA A6923, Item SI/2 — Australian Military Forces — Y Organisation in Australia, Minutes of Conference Coordinating 'Y' Intelligence in Australia.
17 Ballard, *On ULTRA Active Service*, p. 164.
18 UKNA ADM223/297, NID Vol. 42, 'Far East and Pacific', III, Special, undated and unsigned report of Summer 1942.
19 UKNA, HW8/102, Early Signals (Naval) Between GCCS–Washington–Melbourne and Singapore, 1939–1942.
20 NARA RG457, NSA Oral History 09-83, Interview with CAPT Rudolph T. Fabian (USN Retired) 4 May 1983, p. 43.
21 Huie, *Ships' Belles*, p. 183.
22 Richard, 'Memories of CB', p. 5.
23 Neale, *Documents in Australian Foreign Policy*, Vol. IV, Paper 510, pp. 818–20.
24 Winter, *The Intrigue Master*, p. 146.
25 NAA A6923, Item 37/401/425 — CGS Branch: Military Intelligence, SI Section.
26 Benson, *A History*, p. 88. The correct date is 1 October 1942.
27 Jenkins, *Battle Surface*, p.159.
28 Quoted in Winter, *The Intrigue Master*, p. 146.
29 Erskine, 'The Holden Agreement', p.193.
30 NAA MP1074/8, Item 1/11/42 to 16/11/42 — Flag Signals (Top Secret) 1–16 November 1942.
31 NAA A6923, Item 37/401/425 — CGS Branch, Military Intelligence: SI Section.
32 'Sydney University, T.G. Room, and Codebreaking in WWII', p. 12.

9 — Central Bureau Brisbane
1 MacArthur to Washington, 1 April 1942, quoted in Lewin, *The Other ULTRA*, p. 149.
2 NAA A6923, Item SI/2 — Australian Military Forces — Y Organisation in Australia, Minutes of Committee Meeting 2 May 1942, shows Fabian as present, but he appears on no other minutes in the series.
3 Fabian quoted in Benson, *A History*, p. 87.
4 Drea, *MacArthur's Ultra*, pp. 20–21.
5 General Willoughby affidavit filed 8 May 1945 with Pearl Harbor inquiry quoted in Wohlstetter, *Pearl Harbor*, p. 181n.
6 Fabian, for his sins, spent most of the rest of the war as a liaison officer with a British codebreaking unit in India. As one who had frequently expressed his disdain for the British, this must have been particularly galling for him.
7 Girhard interview in Maneki, *The Quiet Heroes*, p. 30.
8 Sinkov interview in Maneki, *The Quiet Heroes*, p. 39.
9 Bleakley, *The Eavesdroppers*, pp. 82–3.
10 NAA B5436, Item Part A — Central Bureau Technical Records — Organisation, p. 9. 364

11 NAA A6923, Item 16/6/289 — Australian Military Forces — Central Bureau.
12 Manera, 'Anniversary talks: Battle of the Bismarck Sea, 2–4 March 1943', on
Website http://www.awm.gov.au/atwar/remembering1942/bismarck.
13 Drea, *MacArthur's ULTRA*, pp. 77–8.
14 Bleakley, *The Eavesdroppers*, p. 197.
15 Drea, *MacArthur's ULTRA*, pp. 74–5.
16 Ibid., pp. 75–6.
17 Ibid., p. 38.
18 Benson, *A History*, pp. 87–8.
19 Joe Richards quoted in Smith, *Emperor's Codes*, p. 307.
20 NAA A6923, Item 16/6/289 — Australian Military Forces — Central Bureau,
Precis of an Interview Held on 21 Jan '44 with DMI and C-in-C.
21 Melinsky, *Code-Breaker's Tale*, p. 22.
22 Ibid., p. 23.
23 Quoted in Smith, *The Emperor's Codes*, p. 314.
24 Robert Brown, correspondence with author, 14 March 2005.
25 Bleakley, *The Eavesdroppers*, pp, 116–17.
26 Smith, *The Emperor's Codes*, p. 310.
27 NAA A6923, Item 16/6/289 — Australian Military Forces: Central Bureau.
28 Bleakley, *The Eavesdroppers*, p. 176.
29 Brown, correspondence with author, 15 March 2005.
30 NAA A6923, Item 16/6/289 — Australian Military Forces: Central Bureau.
31 AWM 119, Item 248/18 — End of War Awards: Submissions by Directorates of
'G.' Branch, Land Headquarters.
32 Ball and Horner, *Breaking the Codes*, pp. 160–1.
33 NAA A6923, Item SI/7 — Australian Military Forces — Signal Intelligence to be
returned to ADMI, notes of conference 29 November 1945.
34 Horner, 'Allied Intelligence', pp. 43–4.
35 NAA A816/1, Item 66/301/233 — Proposed Award of US decoration to
Brigadier J.D. Rogers, AMF.
36 Letter Sissons to author, 26 January 2005.

10 — After the War
1 Cain, 'Missiles and Mistrust', pp. 6–7.
2 UKNA DEFE 7/291 — Exchange of Military Information: Working of the
Burns/Templer Agreement, DTS (Air) minute of 17 December 1951.
3 Reynolds, 'Atomic Weapons', pp. 58–64.
4 UKNA CAB131/2, Report by UK Chiefs of Staff 2 April 1946: 'Strategic Position
of the British Commonwealth'.
5 Reynolds, 'Atomic Weapons', p. 62.
6 NAA A5954, Item 2363/2 — Establishment of a Joint Intelligence Organisation,
Cabinet Agendum 1213.
7 Ball and Horner, *Breaking the Codes*, p. 167.
8 Andrew, 'The Growth of the Australian Intelligence Community', p. 224.
9 NAA MP1049, Item NAA MP1049/ 9, Item 1997/5/196 — HMA Squadron:

Quarterly reports on Procedure 'Y', Minute by DSC 27 May 1933.
10 Unattributable source interview with author, 16 December 2004.
11 Ball and Horner, *Breaking the Codes*, p. 167.
12 Andrew, 'The Growth of the Australian Intelligence Community', p. 222.
13 Richelson and Ball, *The Ties that Bind*, pp. 142–3.
14 Andrew, 'The Growth of the Australian Intelligence Community', p. 224.
15 Ball and Horner, *Breaking the Codes*, p. 185.
16 Ibid., p. 177.
17 Reynolds, 'Atomic Weapons', p. 64.
18 Ball and Horner, *Breaking the Codes*, pp. 296–7.
19 Ibid., p. 167.
20 Ibid., p. 297
21 NAA A5954, Item 849/5 — Joint Intelligence Organisation: Functions, minute of 20 December 1948.
22 NAA MP1185/8, Item 2021/5/858 — ASIO Liaison with Defence and Service Departments.
23 Nave interview with David McKnight, 22 March 1992.
24 Unattributable source interview.
25 Letter Nave to B.N. Primrose, undated, of late 1973.
26 NAA A6122, Item 1414 — Selected Appendices of Unpublished History of ASIO (Security Intelligence).
27 Nave interview with David McKnight, 22 March 1992.
28 Unattributable source interview.
29 McKnight, *Spies*, pp. 128–9.
30 Unattributable source interview.
31 Ibid.
32 Ibid.
33 NAA A1533, Item 1957/758C — Security Arrangements for Royal Visit 1954.
34 Nave interview with David McKnight.
35 Unattributable source interview.
36 NAA A6122, Item 1414 — Selected Appendices of Unpublished History of ASIO (Security Intelligence), Olympic Games 1956, pp. 2–3.
37 Unattributable source interview.
38 Ibid.

11 — In Retirement
1 NAA A2585, Item 1961–1964.
2 Naval Association of Australia, National Conference 1966, Items 83, 84 and 85.
3 Letter HM Queen Elizabeth to Captain T.E. Nave, 17 March 1972.
4 *Victorian Association Newsletter* Number 25, April 1989.
5 Letter T.E. Nave to Naval Association of Australia, 21 June 1982.
6 Frank Hughes quoted in the Brisbane *Courier-Mail*, 31 August 2005.
7 Letter Primrose to Nave, 10 July 1973.
8 Author's discussion with Dr Primrose, 18 January 2005.
9 Hinsley et al., *British Intelligence*, pp. ix–x.

10 Letter Nave to Primrose, April (?) 1974.

11 Letter Nave to Sissons, 8 April 1986.

12 Adams, 'Sidelined by history, the fantasy is over for the spy who never was', London *Sunday Times*, 20 February 1994.

13 *Australian*, 13 March 1989.

14 Letter Nave to Rusbridger, 16 February 1991.

15 Melbourne Age, 9 March 1989.

16 Sissons, 'More on Pearl Harbor', pp. 373–9.

17 Aldrich, 'Conspiracy or Confusion?', pp. 343–4.

18 Kahn, 'Pearl Harbor and the Inadequacy of Cryptanalysis', *Cryptologia*, 15 (1991): p. 287, fn 56.

19 Translation by David Sissons, 28 October 2005.

20 Rusbridger's obituaries appeared in the London *Times* on 18 February, the London *Sunday Times* on 20 February, and the *Weekly Telegraph* on 1 March 1994.

21 Melbourne *Age*, 26 June 1993.

Epilogue
1 DSD letter to author, 10 February 2005.

Index

Prince George, Duke of Kent, 59, 80, 92
Procedure 'Y', 53

Room, Professor T.G., 168, 195-6, 205, 210, 220
Royal Australian Air Force, 159, 206
Royal Australian Navy
– origins, 15-16
– service in WWI, 17
– interception of Japanese wireless, 62
– role in FECB, 130
– WWI experience in codebreaking, 155
– Coastwatcher Service, 155-6
– working relationship with China Fleet, 156
– direction-finding facilities, 156
– ambition to have own signals intelligence organisation, 158-9
Royal Visit, 1954, 252-4
Rusbridger, James, co-author of *Betrayal at Pearl Harbor*
– inaccuracies, 37, 62
– misuse of Nave information, 137-8
– on foreknowledge of Pearl Harbor, 178-80
– previous life, 267
– initiation of contact with Nave, 267
– demands change in manuscript, 270
– delays provision of draft to Nave, 272
– *Betrayal at Pearl Harbor*, 272
– critical reviews, 273
– death, 274
Rutland, Major Frederick, 117-18

Saito, Vice Admiral Shichigoro, IJN, 35
Sandford, Lieutenant Colonel A.W. 'Mic', 172, 191, 203, 208, 210, 214, 215, 219, 220, 223, 224, 226, 227, 228, 234, 236
Shanghai, 58-9, 98, 103-5, 107, 116.
Shaw, Harry , Captain RN, 29, 99, 111, 131, 133, 183, 142, 145, 148, 195
Shedden, Sir Frederick, 175, 176, 238.
Sinclair (C), Admiral Sir Hugh 'Quex', 71, 82, 114, 117-8, 122, 126
Singapore Naval Base
– first mooted, 38
– delays in construction, 96-7
– preparations for FECB, 139
– unreadiness for FECB, 145
– surrendered to Japanese, 184
Sinkov, Abraham, Lieutenant Colonel USA, 208, 210, 211-12, 213, 224
Sissons, D.C.S., 267
Special Intelligence Bureau
– concept supported by FECB, 165
– inauguration, 167-8
– attacks on IJN codes, 169-70
– shortages of skilled personnel, 170
– access to diplomatic cables, 171
– intimations of Japanese intentions, 172
– interception of 'winds' message, 175
– value of to Australia, 177
– South American cables decoded, 185
– collocation with FRUMEL, 186
– philosophical differences with FRUMEL 188
– relegation to and progress on 'minor' codes, 189